Communications in Computer and Information Science   691

Commenced Publication in 2007
Founding and Former Series Editors:
Alfredo Cuzzocrea, Dominik Ślęzak, and Xiaokang Yang

Editorial Board

More information about this series at http://www.springer.com/series/7899

Olivier Camp · Steven Furnell
Paolo Mori (Eds.)

Information Systems Security and Privacy

Second International Conference, ICISSP 2016
Rome, Italy, February 19–21, 2016
Revised Selected Papers

 Springer

Editors
Olivier Camp
MODESTE/ESEO
Angers
France

Paolo Mori
Consiglio Nazionale delle Ricerche
Pisa
Italy

Steven Furnell
Plymouth University
Plymouth
UK

ISSN 1865-0929   ISSN 1865-0937   (electronic)
Communications in Computer and Information Science
ISBN 978-3-319-54432-8   ISBN 978-3-319-54433-5   (eBook)
DOI 10.1007/978-3-319-54433-5

Library of Congress Control Number: 2017932790

Printed on acid-free paper

This Springer imprint is published by Springer Nature
The registered company is Springer International Publishing AG
The registered company address is: Gewerbestrasse 11, 6330 Cham, Switzerland

Preface

This book includes extended and revised versions of selected best papers from the Second International Conference on Information Systems Security and Privacy (ICISSP), which was held in Rome, Italy, during February 19–21, 2016. This conference reflects a continuing effort to increase the dissemination of recent research results among professionals who work in the areas of information systems security and privacy. The conference topic areas define a broad spectrum in the key areas of information systems security and privacy. This wide-view reporting made ICISSP appealing to a global audience of engineers, scientists, business practitioners, ICT managers, and policy experts. The papers accepted and presented at the conference demonstrated a number of new and innovative solutions for information systems security and privacy, showing that the technical problems in these closely related fields are challenging and worth approaching in an interdisciplinary perspective such as that promoted by ICISSP. ICISSP 2016 received 91 papers in total, with contributions from 27 different countries, in all continents, which demonstrates its success and global dimension. To evaluate each submission, a double-blind paper evaluation method was used: Each paper was blindly reviewed by at least two experts from the international Program Committee. In fact, most papers had three reviews or more. The selection process followed strict criteria in all tracks. As a result, only 17 papers were accepted and orally presented as full papers (18% of submissions), with a further 27 as short papers (29% of submissions). Additionally, 19 papers were accepted for poster presentation. This strict acceptance ratio shows the intention to preserve the high quality of this event, which we expect to improve even further in the years to come. The papers included in this book were selected from the set of full papers, which were submitted to a double-blinded reviewing process, where they received at least three reviews. The result scores of this reviewing process, as well as the quality and clarity of the oral presentation at the conference, were the criteria applied for this selection. We hope that you will find this collection of the best ICISSP 2016 papers an excellent source of inspiration as well as a helpful reference for research in the aforementioned areas.

February 2016

Olivier Camp
Steven Furnell
Paolo Mori

Organization

Conference Chair

Olivier Camp   MODESTE/ESEO, France

Program Co-chairs

Steven Furnell   Plymouth University, UK
Paolo Mori   Istituto di Informatica e Telematica, Consiglio
       Nazionale delle Ricerche, Italy

Program Committee

Carlisle Adams	University of Ottawa, Canada
Magnus Almgren	Chalmers University of Technology, Sweden
Mario Alvim	Federal University of Minas Gerais (UFMG), Brazil
David Aspinall	University of Edinburgh, UK
Elias Athanasopoulos	VU University, Amsterdam, The Netherlands
Benjamin Aziz	University of Portsmouth, UK
Kensuke Baba	Fujitsu Laboratories Ltd., Japan
Yan Bai	University of Washington Tacom, USA
Alessandro Barenghi	Polytecnic University of Milan, Italy
Catalin V. Birjoveanu	Al.I.Cuza University of Iasi, Romania
Carlo Blundo	Università di Salerno, Italy
Reinhardt A. Botha	Nelson Mandela Metropolitan University, South Africa
Alessio Botta	University of Naples Federico II, Italy
Oscar Cánovas	University of Murcia, Spain
Jaime S. Cardoso	Universidade do Porto, Portugal
Hervé Chabanne	Morpho and Télécom ParisTech, France
Xiaofeng Chen	Xidian University, China
Feng Cheng	Hasso Plattner Institute at University of Potsdam, Germany
Yannick Chevalier	Université Paul Sabatier Toulouse 3, France
Hung-Yu Chien	National Chi Nan University, Taiwan
Stelvio Cimato	Università degli studi di Milano, Crema, Italy
Mathieu Cunche	INSA-Lyon/Inria, France
Mingcong Deng	Tokyo University of Agriculture and Technology, Japan
Josée Desharnais	Université Laval, Canada
Andreas Dewald	Friedrich-Alexander-Universität Erlangen-Nürnberg, Germany
Josep Domingo-Ferrer	Universitat Rovira i Virgili, Spain

Naranker Dulay	Imperial College London, UK
Isao Echizen	National Institute of Informatics, Japan
Alekander Essex	Western University, Canada
David Eyers	University of Otago, New Zealand
Steven Furnell	Plymouth University, UK
Alban Gabillon	Université de la Polynésie Française, French Polynesia
Clemente Galdi	Università di Napoli Federico II, Italy
Debin Gao	Singapore Management University, Singapore
Christos Georgiadis	University of Macedonia, Greece
Bok-Min Goi	Universiti Tunku Abdul Rahman, Malaysia
Ana I. González-Tablas	University Carlos III of Madrid, Spain
Gilles Guette	University of Rennes, France
Sara Hajian	Eurecat Technology Center, Spain
Mark Harris	University of South Carolina, USA
Martin Hell	Lund University, Sweden
Fu-Hau Hsu	National Central University, Taiwan
Lei Hu	Institute of Information Engineering, Chinese Academy of Sciences, China
Dong Huang	Chinese Academy of Sciences, China
Dieter Hutter	German Research Centre for Artificial Intelligence, Germany
Ludovic Jacquin	Hewlett Packard Laboratories, Bristol, UK
Mariusz Jakubowski	Microsoft Research, USA
Rasool Jalili	Sharif University of Technology, Iran
Jens Jensen	STFC Rutherford Appleton Laboratory, UK
Rafael Timoteo de Sousa Junior	University of Brasilia, Brazil
Ghassan Karame	NEC Laboratories, Germany
Anne Kayem	University of Cape Town, South Africa
Hiroaki Kikuchi	Meiji University, Japan
Elisavet Konstantinou	University of the Aegean, Greece
Hristo Koshutanski	University of Malaga, Spain
Nadira Lammari	Conservatoire National des Arts et Métiers, France
Gabriele Lenzini	University of Luxembourg, Luxembourg
Yair Levy	Nova Southeastern University (NSU), USA
Zhiqiang Lin	University of Texas at Dallas, USA
Flamina Luccio	Università Ca' Foscari Venezia, Italy
Ilaria Matteucci	Istituto di Informatica e Telematica, CNR, Italy
Ali Al Mazari	Alfaisal University, Saudi Arabia
Patrick McDaniel	Penn State University, USA
Catherine Meadows	US Naval Research Laboratory, USA
Florian Mendel	TU Graz, Austria
Nele Mentens	Katholieke Universiteit Leuven, Belgium
Ali Miri	Ryerson University, Canada
Mattia Monga	Università degli Studi di Milano, Italy

Paolo Mori	Istituto di Informatica e Telematica, Consiglio Nazionale delle Ricerche, Italy
Charles Morisset	Newcastle University, UK
Kirill Morozov	Tokyo Institute of Technology, Japan
Tim Muller	Nanyang Technological University, Singapore
Mehrdad Nojoumian	Florida Atlantic University, USA
Gabriele Oligeri	Università di Roma Tre, Italy
Donal O'Mahony	Trinity College Dublin, Ireland
Carles Padro	Universitat Politecnica de Catalunya, Spain
Yin Pan	Rochester Institute of Technology, USA
Günther Pernul	University of Regensburg, Germany
Andreas Peter	University of Twente, The Netherlands
Makan Pourzandi	Ericsson Research, Canada
Vassilis Prevelakis	Technische Universität Braunschweig, Germany
Kenneth Radke	Information Security Institute, Queensland University of Technology, Australia
Michelle Ramim	Georgia State System, USA
Wolfgang Reif	University of Augsburg, Germany
Jean-Marc Robert	ETS Montreal, Canada
Neil Rowe	Naval Postgraduate School, USA
Hossein Saiedian	University of Kansas, USA
David Sanchez	Universitat Rovira i Virgili, Spain
Andrea Saracino	Consiglio Nazionale delle Ricerche, Istituto di Informatica e Telematica, Italy
Michael Scott	Certivox Ltd., Ireland
Kent Seamons	Brigham Young University, USA
Qi Shi	Liverpool John Moores University, UK
Abdulhadi Shoufan	Khalifa University of Science, United Arab Emirates
Jordan Shropshire	University of South Alabama, USA
Nicolas Sklavos	University of Patras, Greece
Angelo Spognardi	Technical University of Denmark, Denmark
Paul Stankovski	Lund University, Sweden
Rainer Steinwandt	Florida Atlantic University, USA
Hung-Min Sun	National Tsing Hua University, Taiwan
Nadia Tawbi	Université Laval, Canada
Cihangir Tezcan	Middle East Technical University, Turkey
Raylin Tso	National Chengchi University, Taiwan
Yasuyuki Tsukada	Nippon Telegraph and Telephone Corporation, Japan
Udaya Tupakula	Macquarie University, Australia
Shambhu J. Upadhyaya	University at Buffalo, USA
Adriano Valenzano	Consiglio Nazionale delle Ricerche, Italy
Rakesh M. Verma	University of Houston, USA
Ching-Nung Yang	National Dong Hwa University, Taiwan
Alec Yasinsac	University of South Alabama, USA

| Amr Youssef | Concordia University, Canada |
| Huafei Zhu | Institute for Infocomm Research (I2R), A-Star, Singapore |

Additional Reviewers

Sebastien Chabrier	French Polynesia University, French Polynesia
Christoph Dobraunig	TU Graz, Austria
David Froelicher	NEC, Germany
Wenting Li	NEC Europe Ltd., Germany
Dongxia Wang	School of Computer Engineering, Singapore
Junyuan Zeng	FireEye, USA

Invited Speakers

Jason Hong	Carnegie Mellon University, USA
Hans-J. Lenz	Freie Universitat Berlin, Germany
Edgar Weippl	SBA Research, Austria

Contents

Invited Papers

Tax Fraud and Investigation: A Framework for a Knowledge Based Methodology

Hans-J. Lenz[✉]

Institute of Statistics and Econometrics, Freie Universität Berlin,
Boltzmannstr. 20 K30, 14195 Berlin, Germany
hans-j.lenz@fu-berlin.de

Abstract. Tax Fraud is a criminal activity done by a manager of a firm or a tax payer who intentionally manipulates tax data to deprive the tax authorities or the government of money for his own benefit. Tax fraud is a kind of data fraud and fraudsters in business manipulate balance sheets, revenues and expenses data. Such fraud happens every time and everywhere. Fraudsters may be individuals, households, firms, foundations or political parties. Even religious communities are not free of betraying. Tax fraud betrayers manipulate bookkeeping figures and tax declarations either by increasing expenses or decreasing revenues. There is no, and never will be not a clear boundary between fraud and the balance sheet policy of firms, especially if we consider enterprises where accounting and valuation latitude is utilized. Tax fraud investigation performed by a tax fraud authority can be embedded into approaches called "Knowledge-based systems". There exists a great lack of data due to the singularity of a single fraud event. Therefore missing data must be substituted by assumptions, experience and ideas. In this paper we focus on the Bayesian Learning Theory. In this theory hints, belief, investigation, evidence, integration of partial information, subjective probabilities, and belief updates are the main elements of the methodology.

1 Introduction

Tax Fraud is a criminal activity done by a firm or a tax payer who intentionally manipulates tax data to deprive the tax authorities or the government of money for his own benefit. The borderline between tax fraud and tax avoidance is a gray shaded area, is time and society dependent, and needs some specific attention in each single case. It is a matter of fact that whenever financial chances show-up the risk of tax betrayers becoming active will arise. In Germany, during the past ten years, say, the tax fraud caused by Deutsche Bank and the former president of the football club Bayern München, Ulli Hoeness, for instance, is striking with respect to its size and evident loss of ethics of the defrauders. Unfortunately, tax fraud goes far beyond companies or individual taxpayers. Today, the tax fraud scandal concerns many kind of trusts and foundations like those in Panama City, and even the Vatican. The following Fig. 1 shows the variety of some few current tax fraudsters.

© Springer International Publishing AG 2017
O. Camp et al. (Eds.): ICISSP 2016, CCIS 691, pp. 3–13, 2017.
DOI: 10.1007/978-3-319-54433-5_1

Fig. 1. Some prominent actors involved in recent tax fraud.

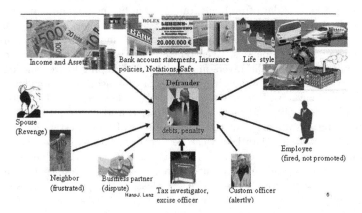

Fig. 2. Actor roles (below) and investment alternatives of evaded taxes.

It is worth while looking at the different roles of actors involved in tax fraud, First of all, there must exist a defrauder who became guilty. Furthermore, any tax fraud prosecution starts with a "kick-off" by a hint delivered to the tax authorities. Such sources are quite different as can be seen from the lower part of Fig. 2.

The saying goes that in about 40% of all cases the spouse is engaged. Business partners and employees follow as next frequent group. As can be seen from the figure above they all have a different motive. Besides a denouncing neighbour the administration becomes active if a local excise officer becomes suspicious while checking a given income tax declaration, or at the state border custom officers detect an illegal transport of money or jewelry, and send an alert to the tax authority.

Figure 2 illustrates a further aspect of tax fraud in its upper part. Tax fraud-sters have various strategies to cover and hide the black money they collected. One alternative is to keep it cash in a safe at home or at a bank. Until some few years it was quite simple to transfer such money from Germany into countries (so-called tax havens) like Switzerland or Luxembourg because the (German) banks supported the tricksters. Alternatively, cash can be changed into gold or invested into life assurance policies or real estates, luxurious sailing boats, aircrafts, premium class automobiles or any other premium assets. Finally, the black money can be used to improve the life style beyond a level which could not be explained by the declared income. The gangster Al Capone is said to have invested his black money into washing saloons thus originating the term "Laundry Washing".

2   Some Specific Aspects of Tax Fraud

Tax fraud investigation has a quite remarkable feature besides its role to guarantee justice. Opposite to *Big Data Analytics* tax fraud belongs to a class of problems with nearly no or very small data at hand in the start of an investigation. We call this class "Sparse Data". Aircraft or train crashes, averages or explosions of nuclear power plants, call backs in the automotive industry, or murder and terrorist attempts are further examples. They represent singular events in most cases. In the beginning of an investigation or trouble shooting only evidence (hint) of an accident or a singular case is at hand, and the main point is to collect pieces of evidence in a step-by-step way similar to build a mosaic or the way Sherlock Holmes was hunting murders. Evidently, "Big Data Analytics", "Data Mining", "Explorative Data Analysis" or even "Machine Learning" play a secondary role here. More formally speaking, there is only a prior belief at hand in the beginning, a lot of missing data exists, and only partial information is available. For example, assume the location where cash (black money) is hidden in a villa is on the investigator's target. Even the income tax file of the suspect is of limited information because it includes historical records only. Information elicitation combined with case dependent brain storming and further investigations is essential. Due to the lack of data missing information is substituted by assumptions, approximate reasoning and belief updates. Consequently, we will look in more detail into the cycle "Prior Belief (and Targeting) - Taking Evidence - Action - Likelihood and Belief Update - Posterior Belief" in the following. Especially, we present a framework for tax fraud investigation with a learning mechanism which is called in the statistical literature *Bayesian Learning*, cf. [3]. This way of reasoning truly goes far beyond tax fraud investigations.

3   Plausibility of Data, Fermi Assessment and Subjective Probability Reasoning

The main target of *tax fraud investigation* is classifying a suspect as "guilty", "not guilty" or "negligent" given all unscrambled facts and background information. In so far the well-established theory of decision making under imprecision and uncertainty can be used here as an effective methodology. Due to the inherent uncertainty of those cases subjective probabilities are applied as measures of expectation to have become "guilty" etc.

Let have a short look of how "tax fraud" can be defined. If we exclude the wealth tax which does not exist in Germany today we can formally define (income) delinquent tax as $\theta_1 = max\{0$, excisable income - declared income$\}$. Note, that θ_1 does not include neither a penalty nor legal or debit interest charge. Therefore we define as a state space of tax fraud $\Theta = \mathbf{R}^4 \times \mathbf{N}_0 \times \{0,1\}$. The components have the following semantics:

- θ_1: Delinquent tax (EUR)
- θ_2: Penalty (EUR)
- θ_3: Debit interest charge (EUR)
- θ_4: Legal Charges (EUR)
- θ_5: Imprisonment (m)
- θ_2: Indicator "Prison on Probation" (1/0) - (yes/no)

Later on when reporting some cases we shall consider mainly $\theta = \theta_1$ because the remaining variables are positively correlated with this attribute.

Let us consider cases where firms are tax fraudsters, and some numerical data is at hand. The plausibility of data of both type stocks or flows can be examined by the methodology *Model Conformity of Data*, [1]. For instance, we can use the inventory equation to check stocks:

$$I_t = I_{t-1} + x_t - r_t \tag{1}$$

I_t represents the inventory at end of period $(t-1, t]$, and x_t and r_t refer to the production and demand rate in t. Assume that a restaurant evades the value-added tax by illegal non-booking of services delivered to guests. Such behavior implies a reduced recorded demand rate r_t. If the output x_t or the stock at hand, I_t, is not adapted the balance equation will not be fulfilled. A similar reasoning can be applied to check flows like profit, revenues and expenditures. In the eighties a Taxi driver in Cologne declared a down-sized number of transportation orders, n, and paid only a fraction of the real total VAT tax to the local tax authorities. He was convicted by the Higher Financial Court (OFD) in Cologne, and had to pay the embezzled difference and a penalty. In this case simple approximate reasoning can be applied as follows: Let us assume that the mileage (km) recorded by the speedometer of his taxi, FL, was not manipulated. Dividing this variable by a proxy of the average distance (d) per passenger "normally" traveled in the city, i.e. $FL/d = \hat{n}$ gives an estimate of the number of transportation orders. By the way, the newspaper *Tagesspiegel* reported in Berlin this year that about 2/3 of the checked data captured from Berliner taxi firms were manipulated, [6].

We remember that the assessment of a difference between declared income and reported income of a tax suspect is on target at the tax authority and investigator site. The slogan *Better to be approximate right than exactly wrong* coined by the economist J.M. Keynes, leads to embed the approach into what we call *Fermi assessment* in honor of the famous Italian physicist and Nobel Price winner: Take facts and (numerical) data as far as possible, and substitute missing data by reasonable, context-dependent assumptions within a simple but smart model (system of equations). Taschner in [4] reported that Fermi once asked his students at the Univ. of Chicago about the no of piano tuners (NT) in their city. Due to a lack of real data at hand he used instead six rough assumptions for modeling and estimation in the following way:

- A1: $PS = 4$ Mio population size
- A2: $h = 4$ mean household size
- A3: $k = 1/5$ piano density.

It follows $NP = PS \times k/h = 200.000$ as the number of pianos in Chicago. Furthermore we have

- A4: $f = 1/4$ annual tuning frequency.

Consequently, it follows $TL = f \times NP = 50.000$ tunings per year. Finally,

- A5: $p = 4$ daily tuning productivity
- A6: $ND = 250$ annual no of working days.

Fermi derives $NT = TL/(p \times ND) = 50$ as a *smart estimate* of the number of tuners in Chicago. The example highlights the potential of the Fermi assessment of numerical data like revenues and expenditures and of checking discrepancies between a seemingly propagated and the real life style of a tax suspect. Such quantitative reasoning or assessment can be extended to checking longitudinal and cross-sectional data by applying linear regression models with errors in the variables, [1]. Köppen (2008) made a careful comparative study of model consistency of data with errors in the variables using Probability Theory, Fuzzy Logic and Monte-Carlo-Markov-Chain (MCMC) simulation, cf. [5].

4   Tax Investigation Workflow

As we have seen above tax fraud investigations start with an initial suspicion as the target of investigation and follow the stereotyped schema "Belief - Action - Evidence - Belief Update". In Figs. 3 and 4 we look at the first steps of this workflow in more detail.

The tax fraud investigation generally starts with an initial suspicion supplied by a custom or excise officer or a third party as illustrated in Fig. 2 above. The tax investigators react on such hints by opening a new case and creating an investigation file. They insert insider information or some other background information if available. In the next step the investigator sends a request to the local tax authority to pass over the tax file of the suspect. It contains the whole history of his tax declarations. The file is carefully checked and the size of the delinquent tax, θ_1, and its probability, $p(\theta_1)$, assessed as prior belief. For instance, $(100.000, 75\%)$ means that the fraud may sum-up to 100.000 EUR and is "likely" - a linguistic term corresponding to the probability $0, 75$.

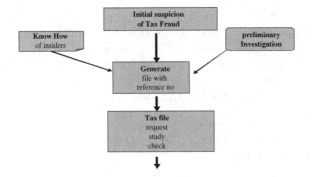

Fig. 3. Part I of workflow "Tax Investigation".

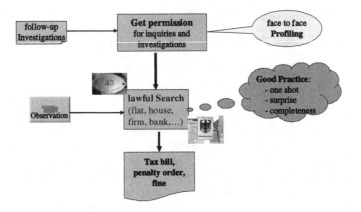

Fig. 4. Part II of workflow "Tax Investigation".

Let us turn to the phase II of the workflow, see Fig. 4. The next phase is started by getting a search warrant issued by the local court. Then the investigators can execute the search warrant, and perform a lawful search of the flat, the firm or the summer house of the suspect. However, note that generally the needed information on the fraud must be elicited, and is neither supplied by opening a file nor by querying a delinquent database. The same lack of information happens with respect to the location of assets like money, bank safes, jewelry, boats etc. While the bank accounts of the suspect can be identified in most cases in his neighborhood - if not located in a tax haven, and the same is true for cars and luxurious (domestically registered) boats, things are more complicated if cash is to be tracked down. For example, the safe of a suspect may not be hidden behind pictures hanging at a wall but be below the floor somewhere in the house. If black money is found the prior belief is updated from "likely" to "confident" (95%). In 2016 fraud cases related to taxi drivers in Berlin, cf. [6], show that the manipulation of the taximeter for decreasing the number of transports per day is still a problem in the city and elsewhere. In such cases

Fermi assessments can help to convict criminal drivers. If facts and evidence is not sufficient for a prosecution of a suspect observations applying multi media technique becomes mandatory. For instance, restaurants with evident inconsistent VAT tax declarations can be convicted of manipulations when carefully checking their real input data with the declared output (dishes served) using the production function approach. Sometimes the wine and beer consumption rates deliver contradictions between real and declared figures. In the worst case, the tax authority can start real-time video observations of a suspicious company for a well designed sample of business days.

5   Bayesian Learning and Tax Fraud Investigation

As we have seen above the main feature of a tax fraud investigation is its step-by-step nature with cycles of initial belief, action, evidence and belief update. Furthermore, it is dominated by a lack of full information, imprecision and uncertainty concerning the current delinquent tax, θ_1, and the remaining state variables $\theta_2, \theta_3, \ldots, \theta_6$. In this chapter we intend to embed the belief updating of the investigators during the steps of prosecution into the well-established Bayesian Learning Theory. It is worthwhile noting that there exist other methodologies like rule based systems, case based reasoning or social network analysis which may be used for investigation tax fraud. We limit ourself to the Bayesian approach (Fig. 5).

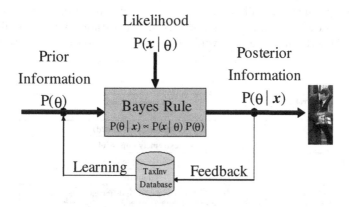

Fig. 5. Bayesian belief updates.

The kick-off is an initial suspicion issued by a stage holder or insider. This step can be conceived as the fixing of the prior distribution $p(\theta)$ on the (complete but still in detail unknown) tax liability $\theta \in \mathbf{R}^6$ of the tax betrayer. The next step at the authority's site is concerned with opening a new case, and getting access to the tax file of the suspect stored at the local tax authority of the taxpayer. It contains all tax declarations, assessments and notes of the previous years. More formally, the likelihood of the tax fraud, $l(x \mid \theta)$, is established. This allows the updating of the initial suspicion deriving the posterior distribution $p(\theta \mid x) \propto l(x \mid \theta)p(\theta)$. This cycle may be performed again if further step-by-step investigations deliver more information on the non-conforming suspect's life style related to the series of his annual taxable income. The necessary investigations are tricky for getting insight into the betrayer's life style, and make use of criminal investigator's good practice like, for instance, "Simple issues first!" or "All or nothing". The main step, however, of the tax fraud investigation is getting a search warrant from the court, and, consequently, starting inspection of business premises, home or summer house with "full strength". More formally, we take the former posterior $p(\theta \mid x))$ as a new prior $p^*(\theta)$ and combine it with the new unscrambled facts of the case, y, using the likelihood $l^*(y \mid \theta)$. We take $p^*(\theta \mid y)$ as the updated posterior. The investigation stops when p^* is "near to one" or conviction becomes impossible, and p^* drops down to zero. If p^* is large enough the charge is passed over to the judicial system to prosecute, judge and eventually arrest the susceptible. Truthful taxpayers will be satisfied in the long run reminding themselves that betrayers never will be able to construct a perfect manipulated world of figures, [2].

This framework of tax fraud investigation should not make the reader believe that the state space Θ is real valued and the probabilities, $p \in [0, 1]$, have a frequency interpretation. Quite opposite, Θ will have intrinsically a case dependent granularity based on binning, the probabilities are of subjective type, and linguistic terms will be used. This is not surprising since the tax investigators are professional tax consultants with some limit knowledge of law - and no notice of Probability Theory at all. Figure 6 shows a reference table between probabilities and its corresponding linguistic terms. For instance, when the likelihood $l(x \mid \theta) = 0.99$ the investigator would assess such evidence (x) by "extremely certain".

Probability 0-100%	Linguistic Term
0 %	impossible (excluded)
5 %	extremely impossible
10 %	fairly impossible
30 %	doubtful
50 %	odds are 1:1 (indifferent)
75 %	likely
90 %	almost certain
95 %	very certain (confident)
99 %	extremely certain
100 %	with certainty (totally sure)

Fig. 6. Reference table between probabilities and linguistic terms.

6   Case Studies

In the following we present some cases of tax fraud. They are sampled from [2], but are presented applying the framework of Bayesian Learning described above. Our first case is of historical interest and concerns Al Capone (1899–1947). He was the boss of the "Chicago Outfit", became responsible for killing and murder and a broad variety of further criminal actions, but the FBI was unable to prove it. Finally they got him due to tax fraud (sic!).

Case I: Al Capone

- Initial suspicion: The FBI observed investments of illegal revenues in laundries in Chicago, cf. "Money Laundering". $\theta_1 = 200000$ USD with a prior belief "Extremely certain" $(p(\theta_1) = 0, 99)$.
- Evidence: Business of illegal gambling (x_1), prostitution (x_2), protection racket (x_3), alcohol deals (x_4). All observed but not sufficient for his conviction by a criminal court, i.e. $p(\theta_1 \mid x_1, x_2, x_3, x_4) \approx 0$.
- Assessment: His declared total income until T, $\sum_\tau e_{T-\tau}$, was less than the wealth value added, $V_T - V_0$ with $p(\theta \mid e_T, e_{T-1}, \ldots) > 0, 99$.
- Punishment: Tax fine 50.000 USD, 11 years (132 months) of jail, and legal charges of 8000 USD charged by the tax authorities, i.e. $\theta_{AC} = (null, 50.000, 0, 8.000, 132, 0)$.

The second case is representative for betrayers like craftsmen. Privacy and enterprise seem to have no stiff borderline. The black market worldwide has an estimated volume of order billions USD.

Case II: Manipulated business data of a plumber and heating installer

- Initial suspicion: Self-denunciation by the deceived wife reporting about moonlighting, manipulated accounts and missing invoices. The spouse was responsible for bookkeeping but became not subject to prosecution due to self-denunciation according §371 AO in Germany. We have a-priori $p(\theta_1 >> 0) = 95\%$.
- Evidence: 1st phase: Illicit actions, private acquisitions of antiques, entertainment electronics etc. and home repairs booked as operating costs of the firm; damage $x_1 = 300.000$ DM with $p^{(1)}(\theta_1) \mid x_1) > p(\theta_1 >> 0)$.
  2nd phase: Increasing expenditures of the firm, (x_2), by depreciation of antiques and a fictitious car pool. Belief update leads to $p^{(2)}(\theta_1) \mid x_1, x_2) > p^{(1)}(\theta_1 \mid x_1)$.
  3rd phase: Identifying a (hidden) safe at home, jewelry, the number of a foreign private giro bank account, and a notebook with black money entries lead the fact $x_2 \approx 90.000$ DM, and, consequently, $p^{(3)}(\theta_1) \mid x_1, x_2, x_3) = 1 > p^{(2)}(\theta_1 \mid x_1, x_2)$.
- Punishment: The installer was sentenced to an arrear of 500.000 DM and a fine of 280.000 DM, i.e. $\theta = (500.000, 280.000, 0, 0, 0, 0)$ with certainty.

Our final case is funny in so far as it is a matter of fact that all of us already have suffered from a negligent error, or as the Romans' put it "Errare humanum est". However, the difficult discrimination between intention and negligence can be used to be protected just as in the following case.

Case III: Error based tax saving

- Initial suspicion: A doctor makes a lot of money by his flourishing surgery and renting apartments in his inherited houses while his wife manages the bookkeeping. All preceding annual income tax declarations of both people were accepted by the local tax authority. An excise officer confirms the current annual tax balance sheet and the profit and loss account. As he felt that the taxable income was possibly downsized he called the tax fraud investigation authority. Formally, we have $x = 0$ with $1 : 1$ odds or prior belief $p(\theta_1 > 0) = 50\%$.
- Evidence: Although the business figures on the aggregate level of the balance sheet and revenues and expenditures of the current case and in the past were seemingly correct the examination of all bookkeeping single transactions of the current year showed an inconsistency due to a single transposed digit of a return item, i.e. 149.000 instead of 194.000 DM. We have $x_1 = 45.000$ with $p^{(1)}(\theta_1 > x_1 \mid x_1) = 99\%$. Because the spouse could have intentionally made this error a complete audit of the last eight years was launched. It was found out that in each year one and only one transposed digit existed reducing the taxable income. Intention became evident, but no fine was fixed because the tax investigation bureau thought it difficult to prove intention. The delinquent tax summed up to $\theta_1 = 450.000$ with the belief "Total sure". In the following years no audit has shown any evidence of an ongoing fraud corresponding the couple's income declaration.
- Punishment: $\theta = (450.000, 0, 0, 0, 0, 0)$ with certainty or $p(\theta_1) = 1$.

7   Outlook

Tax fraud like data fraud is omnipresent, and happened in the past and will happen in the future. It seems impossible to stop it completely although it is no longer considered to be a peccadillo in most civilized countries. What can be done is to improve the education of the present and next generation of tax investigators as well as the use of modern IT. International, cross-border cooperation is mandatory. *Fermi Assessments* and the more universal *Model Conformity Methodology* using linear models with errors in the variables, cf. [1], should be available as tools with which young investigators are to be trained in the beginning of their career.

From a pessimistic point of view tax fraud on large scale will become the "Big Challenge" of this decade. The drivers of this development are the globalization, virtual markets, virtual currency and global, orchestrated actions of criminal social networks, cf. carousel fraud.

Let us close with some aphorisms. Di Trocchio made the conjecture: "Fraud has been since ever an art. Recently it has become a science." A more pessimistic view is due to B. Brecht: "First comes the food and later the ethics". The author prefers the slogan of Germany's most prominent tax investigator, Frank Wehrheim: "In the long run we get them all".

References

1. Müller, R.M., Lenz, H.-J.: Business Intelligence. Springer, Heidelberg (2013)
2. Wehrheim, F., Gösele, M.: Inside Steuerfahndung. Riva Verlag, München (2011)
3. Jensen, F.V., Nielsen, T.D.: Bayesian Networks and Decision Graphs, 2nd edn. Springer, New York (2007)
4. Taschner, R.: Die Zahl, die aus der Kälte kam. Hanser Verlag, München (2013)
5. Köppen, V.: Improving the Quality of Indicator Systems by MoSi - Methodology and Evaluation. Doctoral Dissertation, Freie Universität Berlin (2013)
6. Kurpjuweit, K.: Am Finanzamt vorbeigefahren. Tagesspiegel, Nr. 22821, 18. Juli, S.7 (2016)

Empirical Research and Research Ethics in Information Security

Edgar Weippl[1][(✉)], Sebastian Schrittwieser[2], and Sylvi Rennert[1]

[1] SBA Research, Vienna, Austria
eweippl@sba-research.org
[2] JRC Target, FH St. Poelten, Sankt Pölten, Austria
sebastian.schrittwieser@fhstp.ac.at

Abstract. Applied and empirical research in information security not only observes and probes technical systems but people are also always involved in these experiments. Therefore ethical considerations are important. Based on our experience and an analysis of well-known papers, we propose the method of ethics case discussions to include ethics considerations in empirical research.

Keywords: Information security · Ethics

1 Empirical Research

Applied research in information security is becoming increasingly important as many large-scale cloud systems and complex decentralized networked systems are used by millions of people today. This complexity is amplified in the engineering of future cyber-physical systems, where the established enterprise perspective of information security needs to be replaced with risk management approaches that balance and trade off needs in safety, reliability, privacy, cybersecurity, and resiliency. In addition, validation of research results is also important for cyber-insurance and aspects of accountability and liability. While many of the applied research conferences happily accept empirical papers, there is too much focus on the reported results and too little emphasis on the methods used to derive the results and build confidence in them.

There are often technical challenges related to the application of empirical research methods to the software development projects. These challenges show the limitations of existing methods when applied to different domain contexts. The use of this research approach in information security is evolving and many of the earlier well-known empirical research findings are hard to reproduce for two main reasons: First, the original data is no longer available (if it ever was) or may have been altered. Second, research ethics have changed and experiments such as, e.g., the social phishing of early days, are no longer an acceptable practice.

We use methods of empirical research and applied computer science:

– We collect data to observe networked systems in order to support the identification of yet unknown and evolving threats.

O. Camp et al. (Eds.): ICISSP 2016, CCIS 691, pp. 14–22, 2017.
DOI: 10.1007/978-3-319-54433-5_2

- Based on these findings, we research methods that can mitigate risks and protect assets in the short and medium term. These methods are evaluated together with our partner companies.
- By identifying the root causes, we work on new approaches that address the weaknesses by fundamentally rethinking existing protocols and implementations.

However, in most cases, people are part of the system that we observe and that we influence through our experiments. For instance, we analyzed how social networks can be attacked [20] or which information is leaked in anonymization networks [19,21]. Therefore considering ethical implications is important, in particular in cases where users express that privacy is important.

2 Ethics

In the era of "big data", research based on the enormous amount of data that are more or less easily accessible online—e.g., on social networks, data clouds, and file sharing networks – is becoming increasingly common. The volume of data combined with advances in computing also amplifies the potential ramifications of such research. Therefore, it is important to consider the ethical implications of research that are directly influences real people and real data and to develop ethical principles governing such research efforts.

While in the past, many researchers discussed threats from a theoretical viewpoint (e.g. Thompson et al.'s famous "Trusting Trust" [6] from 1984), the trend is now going towards quantitative analysis of security issues (e.g. [1–5]). From an empirical viewpoint, it would make sense to validate your research into attacks by implementing and testing an attack "in the wild". From an ethical perspective, however, the situation is more complex and we have to consider two major aspects: Can the results of our research be used to harm others, and do our research activities in themselves harm others?

As for the first question, we have to be aware that our research has applications, some of which we may not approve of. Although it is not always possible to anticipate all the ways in which research can be used, it should be our responsibility to try to think about how the results could be misused, e.g., by oppressive regimes or criminals. Would it be ethical to develop analysis methods for Tor [5] or similar anonymization networks considering regimes might use our work to deanonymize people using them to circumvent censorship?

The second question, which will be the focus of this paper, is one that is familiar from medical and psychological research. While the potential direct impact of security research methods is not usually as dramatic as in those disciplines, the use of unethical methods may nevertheless cause substantial damage. It is all the more important as the line between white hats and black hats can easily become blurred and is only defined by the researcher's personal ethics.

In light of the growing popularity of empirical computer security research we believe it is important to encourage a serious discussion of ethics in the research community and to develop ethical standards similar to those governing research other disciplines.

2.1   Rules Discussed at Cyber-Security Resarch Ethics Dialog

The principles discussed in this paper are not directly derived from any particular ethical guideline or borrowed from other scientific disciplines. We base our discussion on the paper of [18]. Our aim is to suggest fundamental ethical principles based on common sense, as we believe it is of the utmost importance to achieve a broad consensus on such principles across the information security community. Without such a fundamental agreement, the development of detailed guidelines or frameworks would be ineffectual. We discuss this idea further in the following section.

Do Not Harm Humans Actively. Today, this is one of the fundamental principles of research and, from a common sense perspective, it seems obvious. However, even disciplines where today it is an immutable principle, such as medical research, have historically ignored this apparently obvious moral imperative (for an example, see the Tuskegee syphilis experiment[1]). It was only after decades of unethical medical research where patients were not informed or even actively misinformed about available treatments, not treated at all, or infected on purpose and used as vectors for further infections, that rules were drawn up to define which lines should not be crossed in medical research, such as the Declaration of Helsinki [9]) – a set of ethical principles governing medical research involving human subjects as well as identifiable human material and data2, which is widely regarded the cornerstone of medical research ethics.

Today, few would argue against the need for such rules in the field of medical research, where human lives are directly and often dramatically affected. The impact in information security research may not usually be as drastic, but over the past years, there have been studies and experiments that still had a dramatic impact on the individuals involved (often without their knowledge or consent). Although not academic research, the "Craigslist Experiment"[2] showed what a serious impact unethical studies can have on individuals, and depending on the setup, an academic study on privacy-impacting behavior (perhaps similar to [10]) or cyber-bullying in social networks might have a similar impact on those involved. Ensuring that no humans come to harm in any way must therefore be a priority in academic research in information security. This can be complicated by unpredictable effects on complex systems — how can we ensure that our analysis of, e.g., a botnet does not interfere with the system and its involuntary participants in a harmful way?

Do Not Watch Bad Things Happening. This, again, seems like an obvious principle, but even more so than the previous one, following it can seem like a hindrance to information security research. The underground economy with its spam networks, malware, credit card and identity theft, and a host of other illegal activities is an environment that can generally only be observed in the wild.

---

[1] http://en.wikipedia.org/wiki/Tuskegeesyphilisexperiment.

[2] The trolls among us. New York Times. Aug 3, 2008. http://www.nytimes.com/2008/08/03/magazine/03trolls-t.html.

However, if we observe a botnet without informing the victims or trying to get it shut down, we are standing by as others – network operators, mail service providers, innocent victims who lose money or buy counterfeit pharmaceutical products that may constitute a serious health threat — are harmed.

How, then, can such environments be studied in an ethical way? And would not collecting or deleting identifying data of victims of a botnet absolve one of the moral duty to inform the victims or enforcement agencies? And thinking further, how can we ensure that informing a user that their computer is infected would not cause further harm, e.g. in the form of consequences at work for someone who allowed the workstation to become infected through negligence?

Do Not Perform Illegal Activities to Harm Illegal Activities. A seemingly more complex question is whether it is unethical to use unethical or illegal methods to harm those engaging in illegal activities. For example, a researcher seeking to avoid violating the two previously stated principles, might want to test the effectiveness of botnets by sending spam to prepared test accounts. However, paying for botnet resources would mean funding illegal activity (i.e. maintaining and renting out botnets) with research funds, which is clearly not ethical. To solve this problem, the researcher might decide to use a stolen credit card number and then have it locked, so that the credit card company would revoke the payment. However, even using a stolen credit card would be illegal and unethical. The same goes for botnets: hacking into a distributed network is illegal, whether it is a legal network like SETI@home [12] or Folding@home [13] or an illegal botnet. Unless such an activity is sanctioned by law enforcement, it is not only unethical but also in violation of the law. From a philosophical perspective, this issue may seem complex, but from a legal point of view, it is clear that the end does not justify the means.

Do Not Conduct Undercover Research. This is closely linked to the previous point. Undercover work may require simulation of or actual participation in illegal activities, which is why undercover work by law enforcement officers is strictly regulated (e.g., when it comes to induction rituals in gangs or performing illegal activities as part of an undercover operation). Therefore, some investigations by third parties can only be carried out legally in cooperation with law enforcement. However, in many countries, this is not yet common practice in academic research. Nevertheless, it would be not only unethical but illegal to buy illegal drugs, botnets, stolen credit card numbers or any other illegal goods in the name of science. In addition to the legal ramifications of such activities, researchers should also consider the ethical implications of paying for such goods and thus funneling money into the underground economy.

Despite the general and seemingly common-sense nature of these four principles proposed here, they may seem like serious obstacles to research in the information security domain. If we follow these rules, some empirical studies that previously seemed perfectly acceptable may, in retrospect, fall into a morally grey area or even be completely unethical. This is not unlike the rules governing research in the medical field: while it might be interesting to observe infection rates and patterns of diseases under real conditions, or compare different therapies the complete absence of treatment, such research is unthinkable today, as it would cause avoidable harm and suffering to humans. Despite these strict ethical rules in medicine and psychology, valuable research is still being conducted. In our opinion, this is what we need in the field of information security: that research that harms or does not help humans becomes unthinkable and we develop new ways of studying important security issues. As these principles can be difficult to implement and it may be daunting to make a decision on the ethics of a given research proposal unaided, we have applied a method from healthcare to security research: ethical case deliberations. The following section describes the background as well as our adaptation of the method for our work at SBA Research.

3   Ethical Case Deliberation

The discussion of ethical issues in security research is relatively recent, particularly in the German-speaking region. Although some articles have been published on the topic in the Anglophone countries and some efforts have been made by security researchers to develop guidelines for research [4,24], we are still a far cry from the situation in the field of medicine, where ethics committees, ethics guidelines, and ethical case deliberations are par for the course [22,23].

This paper focuses on ethical case deliberations and how this tool could be adapted to security research. We believe this method could benefit security researchers, who often work it with sensitive personal data, such as private messages, photos, and documents. The data owners have the right to expect an ethically sound treatment of their data, whatever the setting.

If we apply the method of ethical case deliberation, researchers would present their project to an audience of colleagues, lawyers, non-experts, etc., and discuss its ethical implications with them. This allows them to gather opinions, questions, and reservations from people with different perspectives at backgrounds in order to make an ethical decision. Doubts regarding the way in which research is conducted and legal questions should be raised in these deliberations.

To our knowledge, the method of ethical case deliberations has so far never been used in security research, making this a completely novel approach. In this section, we will first lay out the background of ethical case deliberations, then show how we plan to adapt them to the field of security research, and finally, describe and example of such a deliberation and its results at our research Institute.

3.1   Background

Ethical case deliberations come from the healthcare sector, where they support clinical staff in making ethical decisions in their work. Should ethical questions or uncertainties arise in the course of the treatment of a patient, or should there be conflicting opinions about the welfare of a patient and the – e.g., between the nursing staff and physicians – an ethical case deliberation is convened. It can help reach decisions on whether or not to administer or continue a treatment and other ethically controversial situations [26]. The participants of an ethical case deliberation are people interested in joint decision-making [26, 27] – mainly the clinical staff involved, but depending on the case, it may also include the patient or their relatives. The discussion is moderated by a neutral third party [26]. One frequently used method is the Nijmegen method, but there are also others that can be used [26, 28].

The Nijmegen method consists of four consecutive steps: In the first two, the ethical dilemma as presented and the facts about all relevant aspects are collected. This is followed by an evaluation of the ethical dilemma taking into account all the facts based on ethics guidelines, and finally, the participants reach a joint decision [28, 29].

It has proven useful to base the evaluation and decision on set of ethics guidelines from the medical field, such as the "Principles of biomedical ethics", which consist of the four principles of respect of autonomy, non-maleficence, beneficence, and justice [22].

The outcome of an ethical case deliberation should be seen as a good decision in as specific case under certain conditions, but it should not be generalized: a change in circumstances, such as other results from other research or new pharmaceuticals could change that situation drastically. In a clinical setting, the results of an ethical case deliberation should be considered a good possible decision that is supported by those involved, but the final decision still rests with the attending physician.

3.2 Approach

Our objective is to adapt the method of ethical case deliberations to the field of security research. This requires a number of changes and decisions regarding participants, moderation, ethics guidelines, method, time frame, and logging. Our recommendations are provided as a starting point only – individual security researchers and the community as a whole can need to come to find a method that works for them. Our recommendations have been tested and appear promising, but alternatives are certainly possible and, where they appear sensible to us, we have noted them.

Participants. We would suggest having no more than ten participants: the more people are involved in the discussion, the longer it gets and the harder it becomes to keep track of individual points. We found six to be an ideal number, as this allows a diversity of opinions without becoming too confusing.

The list of participants should, of course, include the researcher(s) whose project is to be evaluated, as well as their peers. Other important participants are representatives of an ethics committee on security research, if there is one, and a lawyer, should there be any question about the legality of methods used in research. If the proposal is not too technically complex, it could be interesting to also hear the views of laypeople who might be affected by the research.

A balanced ethical case deliberation group should consist of a good mix of internal and external, female and male, as well as expert and non-expert participants. However, it should be noted that recruiting laypeople may delay the start of the discussion, and may therefore not always be an option.

Moderation. The discussion should be moderated by a neutral third party. This person should have experience in the moderation of discussions, particularly when it comes to communication skills and comp tenses in process control, and they should be able to move the discussion forward. The moderator should have at least a basic knowledge of the topic at hand in order to be able to follow the discussion and document the opinions and results (e.g., on a flipchart or whiteboard).

Ethics Guidelines. It would make no sense to use ethics guidelines from the medical field for ethical case deliberations in security research, as the requirements and risks are very different, as discussed in the previous section. However, the four principles we suggested there are very general, making a detailed discussion of a case hard. Therefore, we decided to use the principles defined in the Menlo Report, which were developed specifically for information and community technology (ICT) research [24]. The four core Menlo Principles are respect for persons, beneficence, justice and respect for law and public interest. Each of these principles is divided into several subsections where all aspects of the principles and how to apply them are described in detail. Although there are other suggestions and drafts for ethics guidelines in ICT research, none of them have the scope or specificity of the Menlo Report [30]. Additionally, it is a reasonable assumption that the authors of the Menlo Report will continue to develop and update it.

Method. We suggest the following structure for the discussion: The moderator explains the purpose and method of ethical case deliberations and specifies the time frame for the discussion (see below). If necessary, the participants should introduce themselves (e.g., if an external expert has been recruited who does not know the researchers of the organization). If necessary, the moderator can explain the rules of the discussion, e.g., that only one person should speak at a time or that participants should address each other directly. Whether or not any rules are introduced, it is important to stress that every contribution is useful.

After the moderator explains the process, the actual discussion can start. We found it useful to first present the ethical dilemma and then evaluate it using the four Menlo Principles as a guideline, discussing the dilemma with respect to one principle after the other. If there are severe disagreements concerning one principle, the research question can be changed and the process repeated. After the discussion of the ethical aspects is completed, the participants should try to find a joint decision. All arguments presented should be included in the documentation which, like the decision, should have the support of all participants. At the end of the meeting, moderator should thank everyone for their participation.

We have designed a short presentation guiding the ethical case discussion in SBA Research, which you may adapt freely for your purposes.

Time Frame. We recommend a discussion time of three hours, as this allows plenty of time to discuss all aspects in detail and come to an agreement. Should a conclusion be reached before the end of the allotted time, the discussion can naturally end early.

Logging. It is important to document the process and results of the ethical case deliberation. Depending on the purpose of the discussion, this could be done either by a person not involved in the discussion taking minutes or by recording the entire discussion and using the audio file as a log of the results.

References

1. Kanich, C., Kreibich, C., Levchenko, K., Enright, B., Voelker, G.M., Paxson, V., Savage, S.: Spamalytics: an empirical analysis of spam marketing conversion. Commun. ACM **52**(9), 99–107 (2009)
2. Stone-Gross, B., Cova, M., Cavallaro, L., Gilbert, B., Szydlowski, M., Kemmerer, R., Kruegel, C., Vigna, G.: Your botnet is my botnet: analysis of a botnet takeover. In: Proceedings of the 16th ACM Conference on Computer and Communications Security, pp. 635–647. ACM (2009)
3. Jagatic, T.N., Johnson, N.A., Jakobsson, M., Menczer, F.: Social phishing. Commun. ACM **50**(10), 94–100 (2007)
4. Bilge, L., Strufe, T., Balzarotti, D., Kirda, E.: All your contacts are belong to us: automated identity theft attacks on social networks. In: Proceedings of the 18th International Conference on World Wide Web, pp. 551–560. ACM (2009)
5. McCoy, D., Bauer, K., Grunwald, D., Kohno, T., Sicker, D.: Shining light in dark places: understanding the tor network. In: Borisov, N., Goldberg, I. (eds.) PETS 2008. LNCS, vol. 5134, pp. 63–76. Springer, Heidelberg (2008). doi:10.1007/978-3-540-70630-4_5
6. Thompson, K.: Reflections on trusting trust. Commun. ACM **27**(8), 761–763 (1984)
7. Kanich, C., Kreibich, C., Levchenko, K., Enright, B., Voelker, G., Paxson, V., Savage, S.: Spamalytics: an empirical analysis of spam marketing conversion. In: Proceedings of the 15th ACM Conference on Computer and Communications Security, pp. 3–14. ACM (2008)
8. McCoy, D., Pitsillidis, A., Jordan, G., Weaver, N., Kreibich, C., Krebs, B., Voelker, G., Savage, S., Levchenko, K.: Pharmaleaks: understanding the business of online pharmaceutical affiliate programs. In: Proceedings of the 21st USENIX Conference on Security Symposium, p. 1. USENIX Association (2012)
9. Kimmelman, J., Weijer, C., Meslin, E.: Helsinkidiscords: FDA, ethics, and international drug trials. Lancet **373**(9657), 13–14 (2009)
10. Plc, S.: (2007) Sophos facebook ID probe shows 41 percent of users happy to reveal all to potential identity thieves. http://www.sophos.com/pressoffice/news/articles/2007/08/facebook.html. Accessed 07 Feb 2013
11. Commtouch: Internet threats trend report (2012)
12. Anderson, D.P., Cobb, J., Korpela, E., Lebofsky, M., Werthimer, D.: Seti@home: an experiment in public-resource computing. Commun. ACM **45**(11), 56–61 (2002)

13. Beberg, A.L., Ensign, D.L., Jayachandran, G., Khaliq, S., Pande, V.S.: Folding@home: lessons from eight years of volunteer distributed computing. In: Parallel & Distributed Processing, IPDPS 2009 (2009)
14. Wondracek, G., Holz, T., Platzer, C., Kirda, E., Kruegel, C.: Is the internet for porn? An insight into the online adult industry. In: Proceedings (online) of the 9th Workshop on Economics of Information Security, Cambridge, MA (2010)
15. Thomson, J.A., Itskovitz-Eldor, J., Shapiro, S.S., Waknitz, M.A., Swiergiel, J.J., Marshall, V.S., Jones, J.M.: Embryonic stem cell lines derived from human blastocysts. Science **282**(5391), 1145–1147 (1998)
16. Dittrich, D., Kenneally, E.: The Menlo Report: Ethical Principles Guiding Information and Communication Technology Research, US Department of Homeland Security (2011)
17. Bailey, M., Dittrich, D., Kenneally, E., Maughan, D.: The Menlo report. IEEE Secur. Priv. **10**(2), 71–75 (2012)
18. Schrittwieser, S., Weippl, E.: Ethics in security research – which lines should not be crossed? In: Proceedings of the Cyber-Security Research Ethics Dialog & Strategy Workshop (CREDS 2013) at IEEE Symposium on Security and Privacy (S&P). IEEE, San Francisco, May 2013
19. Winter, P., Köwer, R., Mulazzani, M., Huber, M., Schrittwieser, S., Lindskog, S., Weippl, E.: Spoiled onions: exposing malicious tor exit relays. In: Cristofaro, E., Murdoch, S.J. (eds.) PETS 2014. LNCS, vol. 8555, pp. 304–331. Springer, Cham (2014). doi:10.1007/978-3-319-08506-7_16
20. Huber, M., Mulazzani, M., Weippl, E.: Who on earth is "Mr. Cypher": automated friend injection attacks on social networking sites. In: Rannenberg, K., Varadharajan, V., Weber, C. (eds.) SEC 2010. IAICT, vol. 330, pp. 80–89. Springer, Heidelberg (2010). doi:10.1007/978-3-642-15257-3_8
21. Huber, M., Mulazzani, M., Weippl, E.: Tor HTTP usage and information leakage. In: De Decker, B., Schaumuller-Bichl, I. (eds.) CMS 2010. LNCS, vol. 6109, pp. 245–255. Springer, Heidelberg (2010). doi:10.1007/978-3-642-13241-4_22
22. Beauchamp, T.L., Childress, J.F.: Principles of Biomedical Ethics. Oxford University Press, Oxford (2001)
23. Dörries, A.: Mixed feelings: Physicians' concerns about clinical ethics committees in Germany, HEC Forum, no. 15, pp. 245–257 (2003)
24. Dittrich, D., Kenneally, E., Bailey, M.: Applying Ethical Principles to Information and Communication Technology Research: A Companion to the Menlo Report, US Department of Homeland Security (2011)
25. Carpenter, J., Dittrich, D.: Bridging the distance: removing the technology buffer and seeking consistent ethical analysis in computer security research. In: Digital Ethics: Research and Practice (2012)
26. Dörries, A.: The 4-Step approach - ethics case discussion in hospitals. Diametros **22**, 39–46 (2009)
27. Hahn, B., Schulz, M., Hansen, U., Stöcker, R., Kobert, K.: Ethische Fallbesprechungen als Instrument in Psychiatrischen Kliniken - Erfahrungen aus der Klinik. In: Depressivität und Suizidalität – Prävention, Früherkennung, Plegeinterventionen, Selbsthilfe, Unterostendorf, Ibicura, pp. 76–83 (2010)
28. Steinkamp, N., Gordijn, B.: Ethical case deliberation on the ward. A comparison of four methods. Med. Health Care Philos. **6**, 235–246 (2003)
29. Steinkamp, N., Gordijn, B.: Die Nimwegener Methode für ethische Fallbesprechungen. Rheinisches Ärzteblatt **5**, 22–23 (2000)
30. Carle, S.: Crossing the Line — Ethics for the Security Professional. SANS Institute (2003)

Papers

Online Handwritten Signature Verification for Low-End Devices

Nilakantha Paudel[1]([⊠]), Marco Querini[2], and Giuseppe F. Italiano[2]

[1] Department of Mathematics, Roma Tre University,
Largo San Leonardo Murialdo, 1, 00146 Roma, Italy
paudel@mat.uniroma3.it, nilu.paudel@gmail.com
[2] University of Rome "Tor Vergata", via del Politecnico 1, 00133 Roma, Italy
{marco.querini,giuseppe.italiano}@uniroma2.it,
querini.marco@gmail.com

Abstract. Handwritten Signature Verification (HSV) systems are widely used to verify the authenticity of a user signature automatically. In offline systems, the handwritten signature (represented as an image) is taken from a scanned document, while in online systems, pen tablets are used to register the signature, characterized by several dynamics (e.g., its position, pressure and velocity). The main contribution of this work is to present a new online HSV system that is designed to run on low-end mobile devices. Towards this end, we report the results of an experimental evaluation of our system on different online handwritten signature datasets with low-end mobile devices.

Keywords: Handwritten signature · Signature verification · Mobile signature · Identity verification · Biometric security

1 Introduction

Biometrics examine the physical or behavioral traits that can be used to determine a person's identity. Biometric recognition allows for the automatic recognition of an individual based on one or more of these traits. This method of authentication ensures that the person is physically present at the point-of-identification and makes unnecessary to remember a password or to carry a token. The most popular biometric traits used for authentication are face, voice, fingerprint, iris and handwritten signature.

In this paper, we focus on handwritten signature verification (HSV), which is a natural and trusted method for user identity verification. HSV can be classified into two main classes, based on the device used and on the method used to acquire data related to the signature: online and offline signature verification. Offline methods process handwritten signatures taken from scanned documents, which are, therefore, represented as images. This means that offline HSV systems

---

A preliminary version of this paper was presented at the 2nd International Conference on Information Systems Security and Privacy [13].

O. Camp et al. (Eds.): ICISSP 2016, CCIS 691, pp. 25–43, 2017.
DOI: 10.1007/978-3-319-54433-5_3

only process the 2D spatial representation of the handwritten signature (i.e., its shape). Conversely, online systems use specific hardware, such as pen tablets, to register pen movements during the act of signing. For this reason, online HSV systems are able to process dynamic features of signatures, such as the time series of the pen's position and pressure.

Online HSV has been shown to achieve higher accuracy than offline HSV [4, 5,15] but unfortunately it suffers from several limitations. In fact, handwritten signatures are usually acquired by means of digitizing tablets connected to a computer, because common low-end mobile devices (such as mobile phones) may not be able to support the verification algorithms (due to their hardware configuration capacity to compute the algorithm) or may be too slow to run the verification algorithm (due to limited computational power). As a result, the range of possible usages of the verification process is strongly limited by the hardware needed. To overcome this limitation, one needs techniques capable of verifying handwritten signatures acquired by smartphones and tablets in mobile scenarios with very high accuracy.

Online HSV systems (such as [1,8,16–18]) are able to address only partially these issues: they are supported by mobile devices, but they are not inherently designed for common low-end mobile devices such as mobile phones; several approaches make use of pen pads (special purpose hardware for handwriting), signature tablets (special purpose desktop and mobile hardware for signing), interactive pen displays (complete instruments for working in digital applications), Kiosk systems and PC Tablets.

As for the online HSV systems described in [2,6,10], even if experiments related to online HSV were carried out on low-end devices in order to evaluate the verification accuracy, no analysis addressing the computational time is used in the algorithm design (which is particularly important, due to the limited computational power of mobile devices).

The goal of this paper is to address the above challenges by designing a new online HSV system that can be run on low-end devices too. The novelties of our approach lie mainly in the following aspects. First, we propose a method for the verification of signature dynamics which is compatible to a wide range of low-end mobile devices (in terms of computational overhead and verification accuracy) so that no special hardware is needed. Secondly, our new method makes use of several technical features that, to the best of our knowledge, have not been previously used for handwritten signature recognition. Finally, in order to assess the verification accuracy of our HSV system, along with the average computational time, we conduct an experimental study whose results are reported for different data sets of signatures.

2   Features of the Online Signatures

2.1   Dynamics

An online handwritten signature on a digital device is a series of points, and each point is represented by a vector in four dimensions, X, Y, Pressure and Time. We

Fig. 1. Handwritten signature

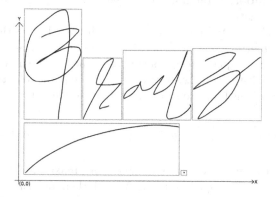

Fig. 2. Strokes of the signature shown in Fig. 1, blocks are in left to right and top to bottom order.

define these series of points as dynamics of the signature. When the user writes the signature, s/he might do pen-up and pen-down moves rather than moving the pen tip continuously. We define a stroke (ST) as the trajectory of a pen tip between a pen-down and a pen-up. A signature can be can be partitioned into multiple strokes as shown in Figs. 1 and 2.

- **X, Y:** The x and y coordinates of each sampled point that is captured from the device screen. Since the user may put his/her signature on any region of the screen, a translated mean origin point is computed and all the X-Y coordinates are translated into the new coordinates with the reference of that new origin point.
- **Pressure (P):** The pressure with which the screen is pressed. When the pen is down, or when the user draws the line continuously, then the pressure value becomes 1 (maximum value) for that points. Similarly, when the pen is released from the screen, then the pressure value becomes 0 (minimum value) for that specific point.

– **Time Series (TS):** The sequence of equispaced sampling time instants. The sampling period, i.e., the time difference between two consecutive samples, is constant and exactly equal to the inverse of the device sampling frequency.

2.2   Features

We use the features to study the structure of the signature and of its strokes from the various perspectives. Each feature is important for both the registration and verification steps. Sections 3.1 and 3.2 explain why they are important and how they do the work for the signature registration and verification steps. Features are computed over the dynamics by means of mathematical tools as follows.

Features of the Signature

(i) **Pen-Up Number:** Total number of pen-ups done by the user while writing his/her full signature.

(ii) **Path Length (PL):** The total path length travelled by the user pen tip during the signature creation. The device sampling frequency gives the value of all dynamics in equal interval of time, and the Euclidean distance formula calculates the distance between two consecutive points of each interval. So, the total path length of the signature (PL) is defined by the equation

$$\sum_{i=2}^{n} \sqrt{(x_i - x_{i-1})^2 + (y_i - y_{i-1})^2} \text{ where } x_i \in X \text{ and } y_i \in Y$$

(iii) **Diagonal Length (DL):** We take the maximum(x_{max}, y_{max}) and minimum(x_{min}, y_{min}) points in X, Y and then by using the Euclidean distance formula for two-dimensional plane, the equation that defines the diagonal length (DL) is

$$\sqrt{(x_{max} - x_{min})^2 + (y_{max} - y_{min})^2}$$

(iv) **Time Length (TL):** The total time in milliseconds that has taken by the user to write his/her complete signature (the time duration between the first pen down and last pen up).

(v) **Mean Speed (MS):** The average speed of the signature. We have four different dynamics sets (X, Y, TS and P) of equal size. All the points in these sets are sequential and tracked on the same time interval from the devices screen. We calculate the velocity between two consecutive points and then make a sum. After that, we divide the total sum of the velocities by the total number of points. The mean speed (MS) is defined by the equation

$$\frac{1}{n} \sum_{i=2}^{n} \frac{\sqrt{(x_i - x_{i-1})^2 + (y_i - y_{i-1})^2}}{(t_i - t_{i-1})}, \text{ where } x_i \in X, y_i \in Y \text{ and } t_i \in TS.$$

(vi) **Covariance-XY (CXY):** In order to measure the scatteredness of the points in signature path, we calculate the Covariance-XY (CXY) by using the statistical variance equation

$$\frac{1}{n} \sum_{i=1}^{n} \sqrt{(x_i)^2 + (y_i)^2}, \text{ where } x_i \in X \text{ and } y_i \in Y.$$

(vii) **Vector Length Ratio (VLR):** Each point of the signature captured by the acquiring device has a 4 dimensional representation (X, Y, TS and P), but for the Vector length ratio (VLR), we only focus on x-axis and y-axis and calculate the sum of the length of all the vectors drawn from the origin to each point of (X, Y). Finally, the sum is divided by (PL). So, the VLR is given by the equation

$$\frac{1}{PL} \sum_{i=1}^{n} \sqrt{(x_i - x_{origin})^2 + (y_i - y_{origin})^2}, \text{ where } x_i \in X \text{ and } y_i \in Y.$$

Features of the Strokes. As previously mentioned, a stroke is a part of a signature. So, it is the subsequence of a signature sequence and has the same features and dynamics that the signature has (except the pen-up number because it's a trajectory between the pen down and pen up). Our goal is to find the ratio between each stroke's feature to the corresponding signature's feature. That gives us an idea how much amount (regarding feature's unit) does a single stroke takes to form the full signature.

(i) **Path Length Ratio (PLR):** The ratio between the total path length of the stroke over the total path length of the signature that is given by the equation:

$$\frac{\text{PL of the stroke}}{\text{PL of the signature}}$$

(ii) **Time Length Ratio (TLR):** The ratio between the total time taken by the user to write the stroke (part of the signature) over the total time length of the signature. It is given by the equation:

$$\frac{\text{TL of the stroke}}{\text{TL of the signature}}$$

(iii) **Diagonal Length Ratio (DLR):** We find a single block for the whole signature after having the maximum(x_{max}, y_{max}) and minimum(x_{min}, y_{min}) points in X, Y. Similarly, we find the same kind of block for a stroke. After that, the ratio between the diagonal length of a stroke block over the signature block is calculated by the equation

$$\frac{\text{DL of the stroke}}{\text{DL of the signature}}$$

(iv) **Mean Speed Ratio (MSR):** The user may move his pen tip with different speed to write the signature. Most of the users write the signature with different starting and ending speed. So, the mean speed is different for each stroke. Our target is to calculate the ratio between the mean speed of a stroke and the mean speed of the full signature, that is given by the following equation:

$$\frac{\text{MS of the stroke}}{\text{MS of the signature}}$$

(v) **Covariance XY Ratio (CXYR):** It gives the scatteredness of the point within a block. So, in some stroke's the points may be close each other and dense as well. Whereas in some block may not be. So, we calculate the ratio of the scatteredness of the points in each block over the full signature by using the following equation:

$$\frac{\text{CXY of the stroke}}{\text{CXY of the signature}}$$

(vi) **Stroke Vector Length Ratio (STVLR):** It gives the ratio between the vector length ratio of a stroke over the vector length ratio of a full signature by means of the following expression:

$$\frac{\text{VLR of the stroke}}{\text{VLR of the signature}}$$

3   The Signature Verification Algorithm

We describe next the registration and verification process from a technical perspective.

3.1   Signature Registration Phase

In this phase, the system takes the user's genuine signatures as input and generates the biometric template of the features with the following steps.

Acquisition and Pre-processing. In the acquisition phase, the user has to write the signatures with the same number of pen ups for three rounds as input. In each round, whenever the signature is captured from the screen, the pre-processing starts immediately. Then, the system eliminates the noise, normalizes the path and all kind of features are calculated and then checked with the features of existing signatures. In the checking process, the signature should have exactly the same number of pen ups. The area covered by the signature and its length depend on the screen sizes. Since various devices may have different screen sizes, the feature values PL, DL, TL, MS, CXY, VLR, PLR, DLR, TLR, MSR, CXYR, STVLR depend on the screen pixel density.

In addition, it's almost impossible to write the signature with the same dynamics and features as before. But it's possible to write a signature, that is similar to the previous signature up to a certain percentage. So, for the very first time, the user is totally free to write the signature as he/she wants. But at the second time, the signature has to match the first signature up to a certain level. Similarly, the third signature has to match the first and the second signature up to the certain tolerance factor. For example, during the first signature, the user may write a vertical line and at the second time, instead of writing a vertical line he/she may write a horizontal line with same speed, length and time. Topologically both of those lines are similar, but in practice, they are different. The X-length, Y-length and diagonal length take the control and reject the second signature. For this reason, each feature should be similar to the features of existing signatures and their corresponding strokes up to a certain tolerance factor. Otherwise, the user has to write the signature again for that round (Fig. 3).

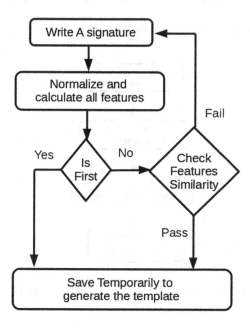

Fig. 3. Flowchart for signature registration.

Template Generation and Store. Once the pre-processing is completed, then the system has the features and dynamics of three different signature samples. So in this step, we calculate the average of each feature as follows: $\frac{1}{3}\sum_{i=1}^{3} Feature_{(i)}$ and create an interval for each feature with its average value up to a certain threshold factor.

We also use the dynamic time warping (DTW) for the template generation and signature verification process. In time series analysis, dynamic time warping

[12] is an algorithm for measuring similarity between two temporal sequences which may vary in time or speed. In addition it has also been used for partial shape matching applications. Moreover, it has been successfully used in literature for both on-line and off-line HSV [3,11,14].

There are different kinds of algorithms to check the similarity between the sequences like Frèchet distance but we use DTW. This is because of its high accuracy and efficiency (in terms of computational time) which is well suited for our algorithm that is specially designed for mobile devices (Fig. 5).

Fig. 4. Maximum match between two different time series by using DTW, source [12]

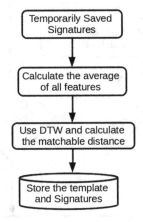

Fig. 5. Flowchart for template generation phase.

3.2 Signature Verification Phase

In the verification phase, the system makes the decision on whether the claimed signature is genuine or forged (Fig. 4). We already calculated the accepted interval for each feature in the template generation phase. The steps for the verification process are as follows:

Check with Global Features of the Signature

(i) Check with Pen up Number: If the claimed signature has a different number of pen-ups, then it will be rejected.

(ii) Check with all features of the signature, PL, DL, TL, MS, CXY and VLR respectively:

If each feature of the claimed signature does not fall in its corresponding interval generated by template generation step, then it will be rejected.

Check with Features of the Strokes. The claimed signature may have more than a single stroke. For every stroke, the system checks all the features, TLR, DLR, MSR, CXYR and STVLR. Each feature should lie in the corresponding interval that was generated at the template generation phase. The system counts how many strokes pass the test. If this percentage is lower than a certain threshold then the signature is rejected.

Check with DTW. If the claimed signature passes all the above verification steps, then DTW is applied on it as follows.

Let m be the total number of strokes in a single signature. Then by using the feature of each signature, the following m-dimensional vector is computed. Let the ith stroke (related to feature f of signature) of the jth signature in a 1D time series be denoted as S_j^i. $DTW(S_j^i, S_k^i)$ denotes the 1D DTW method applied to the ith segments of the jth and k^{th} signatures.

$$
\left\| \begin{matrix} f^1 \\ f^2 \\ ... \\ f^m \end{matrix} \right\| = \left\| \begin{matrix} \frac{DTW(S_1^1,S_2^1)+DTW(S_1^1,S_3^1)+DTW(S_2^1,S_3^1)}{3} \\ \frac{DTW(S_1^2,S_2^2)+DTW(S_1^2,S_3^2)+DTW(S_2^2,S_3^2)}{3} \\ ... \\ \frac{DTW(S_1^m,S_2^m)+DTW(S_1^m,S_3^m)+DTW(S_2^m,S_3^m)}{3} \end{matrix} \right\|
$$

When $\|f\|$ vector is computed for each feature f, we get a $\|X\|$ vector (x coordinates), a $\|Y\|$ vector (y coordinates), a $\|P\|$ vector (P coordinates), and a $\|T\|$ vector (TS coordinates).

Finally, we combine the metrics with the following sums,

$$
\left\| \begin{matrix} d^1 \\ d^2 \\ ... \\ d^m \end{matrix} \right\| = \left\| \begin{matrix} X^1 + Y^1 + P^1 + ... + T^1 \\ X^2 + Y^2 + P^2 + ... + T^2 \\ ... \\ X^m + Y^m + P^m + ... + T^m \end{matrix} \right\|
$$

The output distance vector $\|d\|$ represents the "distance" among the three signatures. The whole process is repeated twice; the first time between the genuine registered signatures ($\|d_g\|$ as output, which is already calculated during the template generation phase) and the second time between the claimed signature and registered signatures ($\|d_v\|$ as output). In the template generation phase, we also calculated the interval by using the threshold factor in $\|d_g\|$. So if $\|d_v\|$ does not lie in that interval, then the claimed signature is rejected, otherwise accepted.

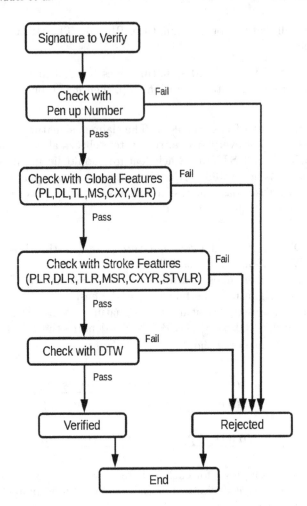

Fig. 6. Flow chart for the verification process.

Now, we describe our algorithm. We present several samples of genuine and forges signatures by Fig. 7. First, the total pen up number is considered. If the signature to be verified has a different number of pen-ups, then the signature is assumed to be a forgery. If the forger writes the signature very fast then he/she produces the better line quality with less accuracy. Similarly, if he/she writes very slowly then the signature may be more accurate but the line quality is poor, and the time length is unnaturally high. So in either case, our algorithm works because of **TL**.

During the template generation phase, the user is totally free to write the genuine signature on the device screen. So, we calculate the **Features** and **DL** for his/her signature from the device perspective. Now, if the forger writes the signature on all the available area then it has a very high value in **Features**

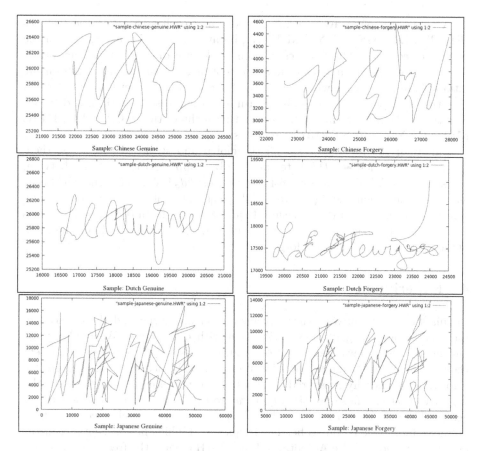

Fig. 7. Samples of genuine and forgery signatures.

and **DL**. Similarly, if he/she writes in a small area then it will have very low **Features** and **DL**. In either case the algorithm works to rejects it.

Even if the forger writes the signature within a given area with expected length and time. Still, it is tough to write the signature with tolerable **MS**. Whereas the real user can write his/her signature within the acceptable interval of **MS**. So our algorithm can easily recognize the forger's speed and rejects his/her attempt.

CXY measures the scatter value of all points in a signature that are distributed on the device screen. So, even if the forger writes a signature matching **PL, TL, MS**, it is unlikely to match the distribution of the points with the genuine signatures. So, whenever his/her signature does not match the **CXY** then our algorithm detects that it is a forgery. The **VLR** tides the signature points with its path length and measures the trend of the points and its quality. If the signature to be checked has a different trend as compared to the registered template, then it is rejected (Fig. 6).

A signature may have multiple strokes, and each stroke has the features (**PL, TL, DL, MS, CXY and VLR**), because it is just a subsequence of the signature sequence. The features of each stroke are different from each other. So, our algorithm calculates all the features of each stroke and then finds out its ratio with respect to the whole signature. So, even if the forger is able to write a signature that passes the all global features test successfully, still, if it does not pass the stroke ratio verification process, that includes the (**PLR, TLR, DLR, MSR, CXYR and STVLR**) then the signature is rejected.

Finally, if the forgery passes all the global and stroke feature tests, then, the signature undergoes *DTW* testing. *DTW* compares the similarity between two sequences. We find out two distance vectors: $\|d_g\|$ represents the "distance" among the three genuine signatures, while $\|d_v\|$ represents the "distance" among three genuine with claimed signature. If $\|d_v\|$ does not lie in the interval which is calculated on the basis of $\|d_g\|$ by a certain threshold at the template generation phase, then it is rejected as a forgery.

4 Experiment

In this section, we present the implementation prototype and the experimental results concerning identity verification with our system. We implemented our algorithms in Java and tested on Android version ≥ 4.0. Figure 8 represent the class diagram for implementation prototype. The accuracy of a recognition algorithm is generally measured in terms of two potential types of errors: false negatives (*fn*) and false positives (*fp*). *fp* are cases where a claimed identity is accepted, but it should not be, while *fn* are cases where a claimed identity is not accepted, while it should be. The frequency at which false acceptance errors occur is denoted as False Acceptance Rate (**FAR**), while the frequency at which false rejection errors occur is denoted as False Rejection Rate (**FRR**). Two metrics building on true/false positives/negatives (*tp,fp,tn,fn*) are widely adopted: precision and recall. Recal (**RCL**) $= tp/(tp + fn)$ is the probability that a valid identity is accepted by the system (i.e., true positive rate) while precision (**PCR**) $= tp/(tp + fp)$ is the probability that a claimed identity which is accepted by the system is valid. F-measure (**FMR**) $= (2 \times prec \times recall)/(prec + recall)$, which is the harmonic mean of precision and recall, that combines both metrics into a global measure.

Table 1. PCR, RCL, FMR, FAR and FRR as a functions of a tolerance factor (**TF**).

TF	PCR	RCL	FMR	FRR	FAR
34%	0.983	0.919	0.943	0.008	0.008
35%	0.969	0.934	0.945	0.014	0.065
36%	0.953	0.936	0.936	0.021	0.063

A threshold on the similarity score must be identified for determining whether two signatures are similar (accept the identity) or significantly different (reject the identity). The higher the threshold, the higher the precision (i.e., the lower the risk of accepting invalid identities). However, a high threshold also decreases the recall of the system (i.e., the higher the risk to reject valid identities).

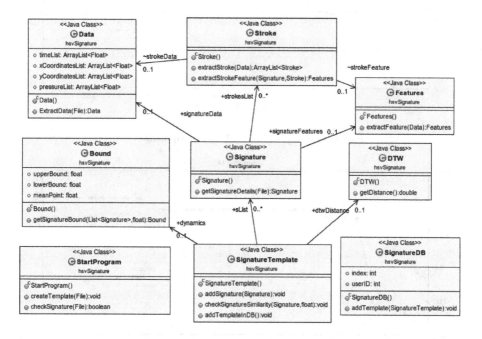

Fig. 8. Implementation prototype of our algorithm.

The performance of the proposed scheme has been assessed in terms of PCR, RCL, FAR, FRR and FMR on three different datasets: on the SigComp2011 Dutch and Chinese datasets [7]; on the SigComp2013 Japanese dataset [9]. We start by describing the experimental set-up. Several mobile devices have been involved in our experiments (i.e., Google Nexus 5, GalaxyS2, XperiaZ2 and ZTE Blade A430), along with several standard datasets. The specification of the datasets involved are as follows:

– The SigComp2011 [7] competition involved (online) dutch and chinese data. The purpose of using these two data sets was to evaluate the validity of the participating systems on both Western and Chinese signatures. Signature data were acquired using a WACOM Intuos3 A3 Wide USB Pen Tablet and collection software, i.e., MovAlyzer.
  • **Dutch Dataset.** The dataset is divided in two non-overlapping parts, a training set (comprised of 10 authors with 330 genuine signatures and 119 forgeries) and a test set (comprised of 10 authors with 648 genuine signatures and 611 corresponding forgeries).

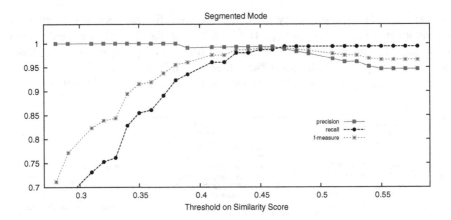

Fig. 9. Average value for Chinese signature.

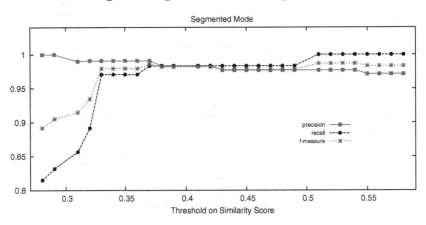

Fig. 10. Average value for Dutch signature.

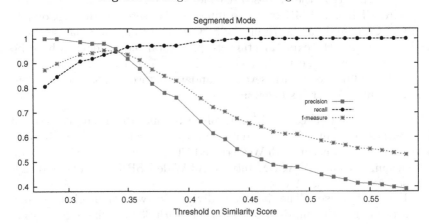

Fig. 11. Average value for Japanese signature.

- **Chinese Dataset.** The dataset is divided in two non-overlapping parts, a training set (comprised of 10 authors with 230 genuine signatures and 430 forgeries) and a test set (comprised of 10 authors with 120 genuine signatures and 461 corresponding forgeries).
– The SigComp2013 [9] competition involved (online) data collected by PRresearchers at the Human Interface Laboratory, Mie University Japan.
  - **Japanese Dataset.** The signature data were acquired using a HP EliteBook 2730p tablet PC and self-made collection software built with Microsoft INK SDK. The whole dataset consists of 1260 genuine signatures (42 specimens/individual) and 1080 skilled forgeries (36 specimens/forgery). The dataset is divided in two non-overlapping parts, a training set (comprised of 11 authors with 42 genuine signatures of each author and 36 forgeries per author) and a test set (comprised of 20 authors with 42 genuine signatures each and 36 corresponding forgeries per author).

The experimental results in terms of PCR, RCL and FMR (that vary according to the chosen thresholds) have been used for tuning the thresholds in order to get better performance. We did the experiment from 5% to 150% threshold to find the best solution. In the datasets, single users have genuine signatures with a different Pen-Up numbers. We grouped the genuine signature by the number of Pen-Ups and then generate a template. Later on, when we perform the signature testing operation, we identify the corresponding group for that user by Signature Pen-Up number. The main results of our findings are discussed in the remainder of this section.

Table 2. Computational time of datasets in different mobile devices, time is in seconds

Datasets	Samsung Galaxy S2 Plus	Sony-Xperia Z2	ZTE Blade A430	LG-Nexus 5	Average
Chinese	0.47	0.08	0.10	0.04	0.17
Dutch	0.98	0.22	0.27	0.11	0.40
Japanese	4.36	1.00	1.94	0.80	2.03
Average	1.94	0.43	0.77	0.32	0.87

Figure 7 is the samples of genuine and forgery signatures for different datasets. The algorithm is based on the signature pattern. We observed that, in general, signatures from the same language have similar patterns. So, the average value for a dataset from one language may differ to datasets from other languages. Figures 9, 10 and 11 plot the average of Chinese, Dutch and Japanese datasets respectively. As it can be seen from those figures, the best tolerance factor for Chinese dataset is 47%. Similarly, 37% and 33% for Dutch and Japanese

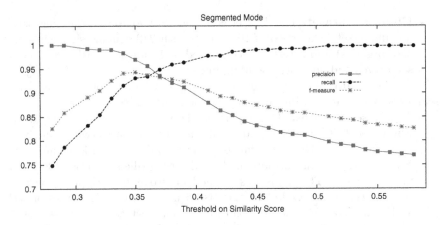

Fig. 12. PCR, RCL, FMR, FAR and FRR as a functions of a tolerance factor (**TF**).

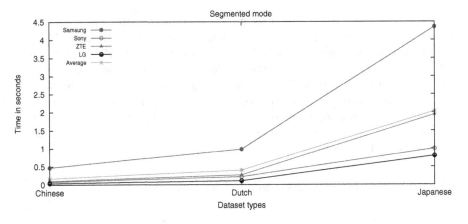

Fig. 13. Computational time of datasets in different mobile devices, time is in seconds.

datasets respectively. The average for each dataset has calculated from the sample of both genuine and forgery signatures of users. After that, we calculated the best threshold for overall datasets.

Figure 12 plots the PCR, RCL and FMR as a function of the chosen tolerance factor, i.e., the threshold reported in Table 1. That shows the results related to precision, recall, f-measure, FAR, and FRR for values which maximize the f-measure. The best results for average were achieved using a 35% tolerance factor. Claimed identities are accepted whenever the score is above the threshold, rejected otherwise. The higher the threshold, the higher the precision, but the lower the recall.

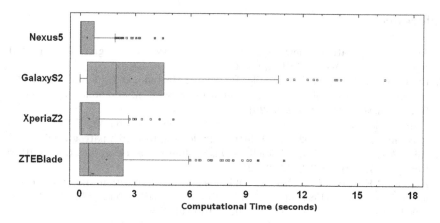

Fig. 14. Computational time for different mobile devices.

Finally, we address the computational overhead. We stress that the overall running time is important, since in many applications handwritten signatures could be decoded on low-end devices, such as mobile phones or tablets. Figure 13 plots the average of computational time taken by different devices for all datasets reported in Table 2. Similarly, The plots of Fig. 14 represent the scatterplot matrix of the computational time for different mobile devices, box indicates the lower quartile, median, upper quartile, and whisker represents the smallest and largest observation (Graph is generated by the Statgraphics Software). It shows that even low-end devices (such as Samsung Galaxy S2) are able to verify the signature quickly (i.e., in a few seconds), while devices with high performance (such as Google Nexus 5) are really fast in verifying signatures (i.e., in a few hundreds of milliseconds).

5   Conclusions

In this paper, we have presented a new HSV system for document signing and authentication, whose novelties lie mainly in the following aspects. First, we proposed a method for the verification of signature features which is compatible to a wide range of low-end mobile devices (in terms of computational overhead and verification accuracy) so that no special hardware is needed. Secondly, our new method makes use of several technical features that, to the best of our knowledge, have not been previously used for handwritten signature recognition. In our experiments, precision and recall cross at 94%. As for the overall computational time, the average verification time is under 1 s for devices such as Nexus 5 or Xperia Z2. This is an interesting result, especially when the limited computational power of mobile devices is considered.

References

1. Andxor Corporation: View2sign (2013). http://www.view2sign.com/supported-signatures.html. Accessed 01 Apr 2014
2. Blanco-Gonzalo, R., Sanchez-Reillo, R., Miguel-Hurtado, O., Liu-Jimenez, J.: Performance evaluation of handwritten signature recognition in mobile environments. IET Biometrics **3**(3), 139–146 (2013)
3. Faundez-Zanuy, M.: On-line signature recognition based on VQ-DTW. Pattern Recognit. **40**(3), 981–992 (2007). http://dx.doi.org/10.1016/j.patcog.2006.06.007
4. Jain, A.K., Griess, F.D., Connell, S.D.: On-line signature verification. Pattern Recognit. **35**(12), 2963–2972 (2002)
5. Kalera, M.K., Srihari, S., Xu, A.: Offline signature verification and identification using distance statistics. Int. J. Pattern Recognit. Artif. Intell. **18**(07), 1339–1360 (2004). http://dx.doi.org/10.1142/S0218001404003630
6. Krish, R.P., Fierrez, J., Galbally, J., Martinez-Diaz, M.: Dynamic signature verification on smart phones. In: Corchado, M., et al. (eds.) PAAMS 2013. CCIS, vol. 365, pp. 213–222. Springer, Heidelberg (2013). doi:10.1007/978-3-642-38061-7_21
7. Liwicki, M., Malik, M.I., van den Heuvel, C.E., Chen, X., Berger, C., Stoel, R., Blumenstein, M., Found, B.: Signature verification competition for online and offline skilled forgeries (sigcomp 2011). In: International Conference on Document Analysis and Recognition (ICDAR), pp. 1480–1484. IEEE (2011)
8. Mailah, M., Lim, B.H.: Biometric signature verification using pen position, time, velocity and pressure parameters. Jurnal Teknologi **48**(1), 35–54 (2012). http://dx.doi.org/10.11113/jt.v48.218
9. Malik, M.I., Liwicki, M., Alewijnse, L., Ohyama, W., Blumenstein, M., Found, B.: ICDAR 2013 competitions on signature verification and writer identification for on-and offline skilled forgeries (SigWiComp 2013). In: 2013 12th International Conference on Document Analysis and Recognition (ICDAR), pp. 1477–1483. IEEE (2013)
10. Mendaza-Ormaza, A., Miguel-Hurtado, O., Blanco-Gonzalo, R., Diez-Jimeno, F.J.: Analysis of handwritten signature performances using mobile devices. In: 2011 IEEE International Carnahan Conference on Security Technology (ICCST), pp. 1–6. IEEE (2011)
11. Miguel-Hurtado, O., Mengibar-Pozo, L., Lorenz, M.G., Liu-Jimenez, J.: On-line signature verification by dynamic time warping and Gaussian mixture models. In: International Carnahan Conference on Security Technology, pp. 23–29. IEEE (2007). http://dx.doi.org/10.1109/CCST.2007.4373463
12. Müller, M.: Information Retrieval for Music and Motion, vol. 2. Springer, Heidelberg (2007)
13. Paudel, N., Querini, M., Italiano, G.F.: Handwritten signature verification for mobile phones. In: 2nd International Conference on Information Systems Security and Privacy, pp. 46–52 (2016)
14. Shanker, A.P., Rajagopalan, A.: Off-line signature verification using DTW. Pattern Recognit. Lett. **28**(12), 1407–1414 (2007)
15. Qiao, Y., Liu, J., Tang, X.: Offline signature verification using online handwriting registration. In: IEEE Conference on Computer Vision and Pattern Recognition (CVPR 2007), pp. 1–8. IEEE (2007). http://dx.doi.org/10.1109/CVPR.2007.383263

16. SutiDSignature. http://www.sutisoft.com/sutidsignature (2013). Accessed 01 Apr 2014
17. Trevathan, J., McCabe, A.: Remote handwritten signature authentication. In: ICETE, pp. 335–339. Citeseer (2005)
18. Xyzmo: Xyzmo signature solution (2013). http://www.xyzmo.com/en/products/Pages/Signature-Verification.aspx. Accessed 01 Apr 2014

Easing the Burden
of Setting Privacy Preferences:
A Machine Learning Approach

Toru Nakamura[1], Shinsaku Kiyomoto[1(✉)],
Welderufael B. Tesfay[2], and Jetzabel Serna[2]

[1] KDDI R&D Laboratories Inc., Saitama, Japan
{tr-nakamura,kiyomoto}@kddilabs.jp
[2] Chair of Mobile Business and Multilateral Security, Goethe University Frankfurt,
Theodor-W.-Adorno-Platz 4, 60323 Frankfurt am Main, Germany
{welderufael.tesfay,jetzabel.serna}@m-chair.de

Abstract. Setting appropriate privacy preferences is both a difficult
and cumbersome task for users. In this paper, we propose a solution to
address users' privacy concerns by easing the burden of manually configuring appropriate privacy settings at the time of their registration into
a new system or service. To achieve this, we implemented a machine
learning approach that provides users personalized privacy-by-default
settings. In particular, the proposed approach combines prediction and
clustering techniques, for modeling and guessing the privacy profiles associated to users' privacy preferences. This approach takes into consideration the combinations of service providers, types of personal data and
usage purposes. Based on a minimal number of questions that users
answer at the registration phase, it predicts their privacy preferences
and sets an optimal default privacy setting. We evaluated our approach
with a data set resulting from a questionnaire administered to 10,000
participants. Results show that with a limited user input of 5 answers
the system is able to predict the personalised privacy settings with an
accuracy of 85%.

Keywords: Privacy · Privacy-by-default · Privacy policy · Privacy
preferences

1 Introduction

Default privacy settings play a major role in restricting or revealing person-
ally identifiable information of online service users. On the one hand, highly
restrictive privacy settings limit the information sharing utilities of online services, while on the other hand less restrictive privacy settings can significantly
damage the privacy of users. The best case scenario is to have a personalised
privacy and utility optimal preference setting that meets the user's particular
needs. The challenge is that service providers do not provide privacy optimal

O. Camp et al. (Eds.): ICISSP 2016, CCIS 691, pp. 44–63, 2017.
DOI: 10.1007/978-3-319-54433-5_4

and tailored preference settings by default, and most users are not capable of establishing such settings by themselves. The extent to which users are capable of setting their preferences depends on their skill level and understanding of the setting [1]. According to [2], typical preferences, e.g., those set by social network sites such as Facebook on behalf of users, meet the expectations of users only 37% times. Moreover, authors in [3] stated that users exhibit a privacy paradox behaviour, in that, despite their increasing privacy concerns most of them are reluctant to take further steps and alter the default settings set by the service providers that do not take individual preferences into account. Furthermore, not having properly and optimally set privacy preferences greatly increases the privacy concerns of end users. In particular, the new direction of commercial services such as O2O (Online-to-Offline), are attended by a series of privacy concerns that have become a serious issue, mainly due to the expansion of service collaborations [4,5]. In this regard, situations such as being diverted to services users were previously totally unaware of having a relationship with, have resulted in even more privacy concerns among users. An example of this is Internet ads. Studies conducted by [6,7], have suggested that Internet ads, which are personalised through the use of private data, may be responsible for leaking users' private information. As a result, privacy is an increasingly important aspect that might hinder users' willingness to publish personal data. Therefore, to properly address users' privacy concerns, they need to be aware of what data are being collected and for what purposes. To accomplish this aim, access control mechanisms based on users' privacy preferences are a key function for providing personal data without creating anxiety in users. However, it is difficult to manually configure appropriate privacy settings where the combinations of service providers, types of personal data, and the purposes to which personal data are put, become huge.

Hence, it is important to simplify this task of setting privacy-preserving default preferences by providing tailoring mechanisms that will address individual privacy concerns, and provide personalised privacy settings to users.

In this paper, we propose an intelligent mechanism for automatic generation of personalised privacy settings. It aims to provide optimised privacy preference settings by default to support users' online interactions, while minimising individual's privacy risks. To this aim, our proposed approach consists of delivering a minimal set of questions to each user at the time of registration to a new service, and from the users' answers predict the personalised default privacy settings for each user. We consider a set of 80 different parameters associated with different types of data for 16 different utilisation purposes. First, we formulated a questionnaire that allowed us to find out the privacy concerns of users, and their acceptability of providing personal data for different purposes. The questionnaire was carried out in the form of web survey with approximately 10,000 participants. Second, we propose a guessing scheme based on machine learning. The basic scheme implements *SVM (Support Vector Machine)*. In this scheme we first generate the SVM models for a full set of settings by considering only a few answers for the privacy settings. Finally, in order to improve the overall performance, we propose an extension of the basic scheme by using SVM combined with clustering algorithms.

The rest of the paper is organised as follows, Sect. 2 gives an overview of privacy policy management. Section 3 describes the main methodology used in this research work. Section 4 introduces the proposed approach, which is evaluated in Sect. 5. Section 6 discusses the advantages and limitation of this approach. Section 7 provides an overview of related work in the area of privacy preferences while Sect. 8 draws the main conclusions and points out future directions of research.

2   Privacy Policy Management

In this section we discuss the different dimensions of privacy policy settings and management tools.

Privacy policy management has become the common approach adopted by online service providers in order to specify, communicate and enforce privacy rights of online users. In this model, each online service provider delivers a privacy policy associated to each of its online services, and, users are required to read and accept the privacy policy right before starting to use the corresponding service. If a user does not agree with the privacy policy of the service, the user simply cannot use the service. Furthermore, because it is presumable that users would need to check a large number of privacy policies, it becomes a tedious task that most users find difficult to understand. An experimental study conducted by Acquisti and Grossklags [8], demonstrated that, when confirming privacy policies, users lack knowledge about technological and legal forms of privacy protection. Their observations suggested that several difficulties obstruct individuals in their attempts to protect their own private information, even those concerned about and motivated to protect their privacy. These findings were reinforced by authors in [9] who also supported the presumption that users are not familiar with technical and legal terms related to privacy. Moreover, it was suggested that users' knowledge about privacy threats and technologies that help to protect their privacy is inadequate [10]. Furthermore, Solove also suggested that, even though, privacy law has been relying too heavily upon the privacy self-management model [11], this model simply could not achieve its objectives, and stated that, it has been pushed beyond its limits.

In this regard, the Platform for Privacy Preferences Project (P3P) [12,13] was designed to enable online services to express their privacy policies in a standard format. In this way, privacy policies could be retrieved automatically and interpreted easily by user agents. The user agent modules will then enable users to be informed of site practices and to try to automate the decision-making process. In this direction, the Privacy Bird [14,15] was designed to automatically retrieve the P3P policies of a web site. Other approaches to describe privacy policies were also introduced in [13,18,19]. Backes *et al.* presented a comparison of enterprise privacy policies using formal abstract syntax and semantics to express the policy contents [17], while Tondel and Nyre [20] proposed a similarity metric for comparing machine-readable privacy policies. Furthermore, a privacy policy checker for online services was introduced by authors in [21]. The checker compared the user privacy policy with the provider privacy policy and then automatically determined whether the service could be used. However, according to authors in [22] this type of approaches resulted in inadequate user acceptance for real world scenarios.

Worth to note that interpreting a privacy policy is just the first step, afterwards, users need to manually configure a set of privacy settings designed to match a given privacy policy. Furthermore, even though some browsers have a privacy module that tries to match privacy preferences to privacy policies, in practice, it has not been widely adopted by online services [16]. That is, mainly due to its complex policy definitions and because the module is to be implemented only on web browsers. Thus, until recently, many research works have focused on studying privacy policy specification, while fewer studies have dedicated efforts to simplify the task of setting privacy preferences, which is the main focus of our research work.

3   Methodology

This section introduces the methodology used for data collection and provides and insight of the distribution of participants and their privacy preferences.

3.1   Data Collection

In this study, we first have developed a questionnaire that allowed us to learn about users' willingness to share different types of personal data, considering different services and utilisation purposes, and consequently allowed us to map those preferences to the user privacy preference setup. For this purpose, we first identified different kinds utilisation purposes (Table 1) and personal data (Table 2), as defined in P3P [12].

Table 1. Utilization purposes.

No	Data purpose
A	Providing the service
B	System administration
C	Marketing
D	Behaviour analysis
E	Recommendation

We published the questionnaire as an online survey and collected the answers from 10,000 participants recruited by a research service company. While the main goal of the questionnaire was to identify users' privacy preferences, we also raise

Table 2. Kinds of personal data.

No	Data type
1	Addresses and telephone numbers
2	Email addresses
3	Service accounts
4	Purchase records
5	Bank accounts
6	Device information (e.g., IP addresses, OS)
7	Browsing histories
8	Logs on a search engine
9	Personal info (e.g., age, gender, etc.)
10	Contents of email, blog, twitter etc.
11	Session information (e.g., Cookies)
12	Social information (e.g., religion, volunteer records)
13	Medical information
14	Hobby
15	Location information
16	Official ID (e.g., national IDs or license numbers)

privacy awareness by delivering information about the potential benefits and risks of providing access to certain data for each service.

3.2 Descriptive Results

The distribution of the participants was uniform (see Table 3), and each participant answered an 80 item questionnaire corresponding to the 80 combinations resulting from online services, types of personal data and utilisation purposes, each on a Likert scale of 1 to 6 ("1" for strongly disagree, and "6" for strongly agree.). Figure 1 summarizes the distribution of the results grouped by digital nativity[1] of users. As it can be observed, the percentage of participants decreases with the increasing acceptance of providing personal data, however, apparently the digital nativity of participants had no influence.

Finally, we used the collected data as an input for our proposed guessing schemes (Sect. 4). Furthermore, in order to simplify our models, we merged the obtained results into the following three classes on a scale from 0 to 2, i.e., (i) 1 & 2 into scale 0; (ii) 3 & 4 into scale 1; and, (iii) 5 & 6 into scale 2.

---

[1] Individuals born after 1980, raised in a digital, media-saturated world - Prensky 2001.

Table 3. Distribution of participants.

Gender	Age	Ratio (%)
Male	20s	10.0
Male	30s	10.0
Male	40s	10.0
Male	50s	10.0
Male	Over 60	10.0
Female	20s	10.0
Female	30s	10.0
Female	40s	10.0
Female	50s	10.0
Female	Over 60	10.0

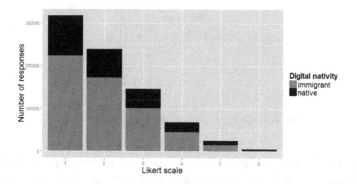

Fig. 1. Distribution of responses according to the willingness of sharing personal data and digital nativity of participants.

4   Approach

This section introduces our initial approach, which, considers two guessing schemes, both implementing SVM as a basis. We selected SVM because it is considered a powerful learning system, although mainly for binary-class problems [38]. Nevertheless, we consider that SVMs can also efficiently perform non-linear classification by implicitly mapping their inputs into high-dimensional feature spaces through a nonlinear mapping chosen a priori. Therefore, for the purpose of our experiments, we used a multilabel and multiclass SVM approach.

4.1   Overview of the Achitecture

The proposed approach consists of *a predictor generator* and *a privacy setting prediction engine*, and a *privacy settings database*. The predictor generator, generates a question set, by selecting a minimum (optimal) number of relevant

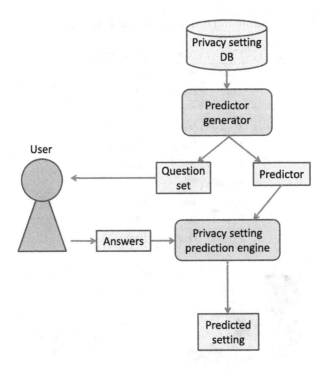

Fig. 2. High level view of the proposed system.

questions, which, are associated to the online service, data type and utilisation purpose from the database. The prediction engine, also generates the corresponding predictor from the modeling of existing privacy settings. The optimal question set is provided to the user, and, once the user provides the answers to the delivered question set, his/her responses are used by the privacy setting prediction engine, which, generates the predicted settings for the user. Once the personalised settings have been generated, they are communicated to the user. The high level view of the system is shown in Fig. 2.

4.2   Experimental Approach

In order to demonstrate the applicability of the proposed system, we implemented a proof of concept of both the predictor generator and the privacy setting prediction engine. We evaluated them in terms of accuracy using the collected data, i.e., results of the questionnaire introduced in the previous section. In particular, the items of the questionnaire corresponded to the privacy settings in our proposed approach. Collected data was split in training data and test data. Concretely, the training data corresponded to the privacy setting database of our proof of concept. In the evaluation scheme, we first fixed a question set. Next, we regarded the values of the answers of the fixed questions as the feature vector, and we generated the optimal prediction model using the training data with our predictor generator. Afterwards, this step (previous evaluations) had been repeated for all the candidates of question sets. As a result, we obtained the question set that achieved the best accuracy and its corresponding prediction model. Finally, we evaluated the accuracy for a test data by comparing each of the predicted values generated with the answers to the fixed questions and the prediction model with real values in the test data. An abstract view of the evaluation scheme is shown in Fig. 3.

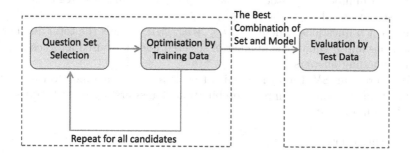

Fig. 3. Evaluation scheme.

Finally, our approach was designed taking into consideration two different schemes: the first based on the sole use of SVM; while the second scheme implemented an additional layer that included clustering techniques. Both schemes, i.e., the SVM-based, and the combined scheme (SVM and clustering) consisted of two phases; the *learning phase* and *guessing phase*.

4.3   SVM-based Scheme

The learning and guessing phases performed by the SVM-based scheme are explained next.

[Learning Phase]

– We select n questions where $1 \leq n \leq Max$. Max equals the total number of questions and n equals the number of selected questions used for training the corresponding answers.
– Using the selected n questions, we generated the SVM privacy preference model. In this model, the class labels represent the acceptance level for each of the unselected $Max - n$ questions using a combination of answers for n as sample points in the training data.

[Guessing Phase]

– For each unknown point, i.e., a combination of answers to selected n questions, we use the SVM models generated in the learning phase for each unselected question and calculate the guessed values of the answers to those $Max - n$ unselected questions.

4.4 Combined Scheme

Similar to Sect. 4.3, the combined scheme consisted of two phases: the learning phase and guessing phase, the main steps of each phase are introduced next.

[Learning phase]

- We generate clusters from the training data with the corresponding clustering algorithm. Each cluster is assigned a cluster ID $i(1 \leq i \leq k)$, where k is the total number of clusters. A gravity point of a cluster is regarded as the representative values of the cluster.
- We select n questions, where $1 \leq n \leq Max$. Max equals the total number of questions and n equals the number of selected questions used for guessing the corresponding answers.
- We generate an SVM model in which the class label is mapped to the cluster ID by using as sample points, a combination of answers to selected n questions in the training data.

[Guessing Phase]

- For each unknown point (i.e., a combination of answers to selected n questions), we calculated the guessed values of a cluster ID to which the unknown point belongs. We regarded the representative values (i.e., the gravity point of the cluster) as the guessed values of answers to the $Max - n$ unselected questions.

5 Results

The proposed approach (Sect. 4) was implemented in a proof of concept and evaluated with real user data collected from the questionnaires. Hence, this section introduces our initial experimental results. We implemented the proposed scheme with R, and "e1071" package of SVM [39]. We evaluated each scheme by running the experiments 10 times. The data samples were chosen randomly, and were split into training data and testing data. Table 4 shows the summary of parameters used in our experimental setup.

We performed two different experiments for each of the schemes. We first selected the top combinations, $TC = 15$ of n questions that achieved the highest accuracy considering 150 entries randomly selected; i.e., 100 entries for the training data, 50 entries for the testing data. We limited the experiment to 150 entries in order to decrease the running time when evaluating all possible combinations. We used the same top combinations, $TC = 15$ of n questions and evaluated the scheme using 10,000 entries (i.e., 9,000 for training data, and 1000 for testing data). Note that in the second experiment we cannot claim that the selected 15 combinations provide the highest accuracy.

The experiment's main steps for each of the schemes are explained in the following subsections.

Table 4. Experimental settings.

Parameter	Value
Max	80
n	5
Top Combinations (TC)	$TC = 15$
Training Data (TRD)	$TRD = 100, TRD = 9000$
Test Data (TED)	$TED = 50, TED = 1000$

5.1 SVM-based Scheme

In what follows, we explain the procedures of evaluation of the model with the training data set.

- As shown in Table 4, we first defined that n equals 5 as the number of selected questions, from a total number of $Max = 80$;
- We generated the corresponding SVM models in which the class labels were the acceptance level for each of the unselected $Max - n$ questions. We used as sample points a combination of answers for the selected n questions in the training data.
- For all 80 answers of each instance (participant) in the training data, we used the SVM models for each of the unselected $Max - n$ questions (i.e., 75), and n answers to selected n questions for each instance. Afterwards, we calculated the guessed values of the answers to the unselected questions.
- We calculated all the participants' guessed values of answers to unselected $Max - n$ questions by repeating Step 3 for all the participants in the training data.
- We compared the original values of answers to the 75 unselected questions in the training data with the guessed values of those calculated in Step 4. Finally, we regard the percentage of correctly guessed values as the accuracy of the proposed scheme.

  The procedure of evaluation of the generated privacy by default preference model with the testing data is described as follows.

- We considered the SVM models generated in the learning phase.
- For all the 80 answers of a participant in the testing data, we calculated the guessed values of answers to the 75 unselected questions.
- We calculated all participants' guessed values of answers to the 75 unselected questions by repeating step 3 for each participant in the testing data.
- We compared the original values of the answers to the 75 unselected questions in the testing data with the guessed values of those calculated in step 4. We regard the percentage of correctly guessed values as the accuracy of the proposed scheme.

Table 5. Results of SVM-scheme with optimization.

Combination					Accuracy (TRD = 100, TED = 50)		Accuracy (TRD = 9000, TED = 1000)	
					TRD	TED	TRD	TED
A-8	B-12	C-16	D-14	E-11	0.894	0.83296	0.858903111	0.85662
B-7	C-12	D-6	D-14	D-15	0.88928	0.832106667	0.853968889	0.851904
B-12	B-15	D-5	D-8	E-6	0.88828	0.832293333	0.85102637	0.846982667
B-7	C-16	D-11	D-14	E-11	0.887986667	0.835893333	0.854038815	0.85178
B-4	B-15	D-14	E-6	E-11	0.887613333	0.832506667	0.852193333	0.849068
B-8	C-16	D-14	E-10	E-11	0.887186667	0.83728	0.854693481	0.852498667
A-8	B-12	D-6	D-14	E-11	0.884493333	0.83064	0.854496148	0.853093333
B-4	B-15	D-6	D-14	E-11	0.884226667	0.83424	0.852772296	0.85098
A-3	A-16	C-12	D-11	E-3	0.883733333	0.830426667	0.850421926	0.84796
B-7	B-12	D-14	D-15	E-6	0.883586667	0.83272	0.853168444	0.850312
B-7	C-14	D-10	D-16	E-11	0.88356	0.832106667	0.852408296	0.849949333
B-7	C-12	D-10	D-16	E-11	0.883373333	0.83552	0.851519259	0.848646667
A-2	B-7	D-14	D-16	E-11	0.8832	0.839066667	0.854657037	0.853193333
A-12	B-7	C-14	D-6	D-15	0.88316	0.8348	0.853704741	0.85178
A-12	B-8	C-16	E-10	E-11	0.882986667	0.832533333	0.852644741	0.849993333

Table 5 shows the average of results obtained from 10 experiment runs considering the top 15 combinations (i.e., highest accuracy) of selected n questions. Each parameter of the SVM model was optimised by a grid search on the parameters C and γ. The results show a guessing accuracy of 83% for all top 15 combinations for 150 entries and 85% for 9 of the 15 top combinations.

5.2   Combined Scheme

The accuracy of the combined scheme was evaluated considering the guessed values of participants as the gravity points of the clusters to which participants belonged. The evaluation procedure consisted of the following steps.

- Using a clustering technique, we first generated clusters of participants, that corresponded to the combinations of answers of the $Max = 80$ questions. As a result, each participant was assigned a cluster ID.
- For each of the participants, we regarded the gravity point of his/her cluster as his/her guessed values for the Max answers.
- We compared the original values with the guessed values in the training data, and we regarded the percentage of the correctly guessed values as the accuracy of the selected clustering algorithm.

We run the experiments using K-means [40], Ward's method [41] and DB-Scan [42] as the selected clustering algorithm. For K-means and Ward's method, we evaluated them considering different number of clusters from 1 to 30. In the case of DB-Scan, we evaluated it considering different parameters pts from 2 to 6, and eps from 1 to 4. While K-means provided better accuracy (i.e., 77%) than Ward's method, for both the accuracy is increased by increasing the number of clusters; we evaluated the combination scheme with K-means using a total of 5 clusters. In the case of DB-Scan, it was difficult to directly compare it with K-means or Ward's method because in the DB-Scan algorithm the number of clusters cannot be decided in advance; however, in almost all cases, the accuracy of the DB-Scan algorithm was lower than K-means and Ward's method. Therefore, in the rest of the paper we focus only on K-means.

An overview of the main results for K-means, Ward's method and DB-Scan are shown in Table 6 and in Table 7 respectively.

The evaluation procedure of the combined scheme with training data is as follows.

- We generated clusters from training data using K-means. Each cluster was assigned a cluster ID $i(1 \le i \le 5)$.
- We chose n equals 5 questions from a total number of $Max = 80$ questions.
- We generated an SVM model in which the class labels corresponded to the cluster ID by using a combination of answers to selected $n = 5$ questions in training data as sample points.
- For all the 80 answers of each participant in the training data, we calculated the guessed values of a cluster ID using the SVM model and the 5 answers of each participant to selected questions. We regarded the gravity point of the cluster as the guessed values of $Max - n$ i.e., 75 answers to unselected questions.
- We calculated all the participants' guessed values of answers to the 75 unselected questions by repeating step 3 for each participant in the training data.
- We compared the original values of answers to the 75 unselected questions in the training data with the guessed values of those calculated in step 4. We regarded the percentage of correctly guessed values as the accuracy of the proposed scheme.

The evaluation procedure of the combined scheme with testing data is as follows.

- We used the SVM model generated in the learning phase. The class label of the model was associated with the cluster ID by using a combination of answers to the 5 selected questions in the training data as sample points.
- For all the 80 answers of a participant in the testing data, we calculated the guessed values of a cluster ID for the participant with the SVM model and the 5 answers of the participant to selected questions. We regarded the gravity point of the cluster as the guessed values of the 75 answers to the unselected questions.
- We calculated all the participants' guessed values of answers to 75 unselected questions by repeating step 3 for all the participants in the testing data.
- We compared the original values of answers to the 75 unselected questions in the training data with the guessed values of those calculated in step 4. Afterwards, we considered the percentage of correctly guessed values as the accuracy of this scheme.

Table 6. Accuracy of K-means and Ward.

#Clusters	K-means	Ward's
1	68.01362	68.01
2	81.67737	80.11
3	82.44963	80
4	83.05238	82.07
5	83.51137	82.17
6	83.83588	82.17
7	84.4875	82.92
8	85.29425	83.16
9	84.98512	83.73
10	85.576	83.9
11	85.82725	84.18
12	86.26325	84.23
13	86.19075	84.47
14	86.46462	84.51
15	86.64112	84.74
16	86.9585	84.79
17	86.91762	84.84
18	86.8855	84.98
19	87.18925	85.2
20	86.96225	85.25
21	87.20975	85.23
22	87.20163	85.31
23	87.25513	85.5
24	87.44513	85.51
25	87.50288	85.67
26	87.41025	85.76
27	87.74637	85.94
28	87.6485	86.04
29	87.64587	86.11
30	87.79313	86.12

The result is shown in Table 8. "Cluster accuracy for training data" means the percentage of correctly guessed values for the cluster ID calculated in step 4 of the evaluation procedure for the training data.

The best accuracy achieved by the combined scheme was 82%. This accuracy was achieved using 8 of the top 15 combinations for 150 entries, and 12 of the top 15 combinations for 10,000 entries.

Table 7. DB scan.

pts	eps	#Clusters	Accuracy
2	1	76	0.767654
2	2	61	0.789983
2	3	44	0.709418
2	4	15	0.697803
3	1	41	0.764831
3	2	31	0.788213
3	3	17	0.707174
3	4	5	0.696771
4	1	34	0.762885
4	2	21	0.786394
4	3	11	0.802324
4	4	2	0.702045
5	1	28	0.761396
5	2	21	0.786629
5	4	2	0.702076
5	4	2	0.702076
6	1	19	0.759063
6	2	16	0.785908
6	3	7	0.802275
6	4	2	0.702083

Table 8. Accuracy of the combined scheme (TRD = 100, TED = 50).

Combination					Cluster accuracy - TRD	Accuracy - TRD	Accuracy - TED
A-11	A-15	B-4	C-2	D-6	0.744	0.8245	0.819975
A-12	B-7	B-8	D-11	E-9	0.76	0.83405	0.8238
B-6	B-7	D-7	E-10	E-11	0.752	0.83355	0.8188
A-10	B-4	D-4	E-6	E-8	0.724	0.822475	0.81155
A-10	B-4	D-6	D-9	E-6	0.73	0.82835	0.82105
A-10	B-4	D-6	D-9	E-7	0.736	0.8317125	0.820525
A-10	B-4	D-7	D-9	E-6	0.725	0.828875	0.821175
A-10	B-4	D-9	E-4	E-6	0.711	0.8275	0.8192
A-11	B-4	B-8	D-10	E-6	0.721	0.828625	0.822875
A-11	B-4	D-10	E-6	E-13	0.7	0.8228	0.8152
A-13	B-4	D-11	E-6	E-11	0.712	0.827275	0.820375
A-16	B-6	B-10	D-8	E-6	0.775	0.8337875	0.8232
B-4	B-10	D-4	D-13	E-7	0.761	0.8310375	0.819125
B-4	D-4	D-6	D-13	E-12	0.754	0.8316375	0.8213
B-4	D-6	D-9	E-4	E-7	0.705	0.8225	0.8181

6   Discussion

The proposed default privacy preference setting guessing scheme based on SVM, and its extension, which included a combination of SVM with clustering techniques has achieved a reasonably high level of precision for guessing the default privacy setting with minimal user input. Specifically, we had 80 questionnaire items out of which only five were used to guess for the remaining 75 questions. These automated default settings not only relieve users of the burden of carrying out tiresome privacy setting tasks, but also relieve them from having to make information disclosure decisions later on.

Results show that the first scheme offers better accuracy (i.e., 85%) than the combined scheme (i.e., 82%). However, when compared to the combined scheme, the SVM only scheme performs more slowly due to the number of models that need to be created (i.e., 75). Thus, considering a minimum difference in accuracy (3%), one could decide to implement the combined scheme and have better performance, in particular considering that the additional time for clustering with K-means for 9,000 entries is minimal (i.e., 0.3 s) and therefore, could be neglected. To the best of our knowledge, this result demonstrates the first personalised privacy by default setting generated using SVM and clustering algorithms applicable to web services in general. Authors [43], introduced a user preference predicting approach for common preferences. Their study used similarity-based clustering to group users with similar interests achieving 80% of accuracy. Additionally, they introduced an error correcting procedure to boost the accuracy to 98%. However, the results from the error correcting procedure have been achieved using simulated data (Table 9).

Even though our approach demonstrated the applicability of machine learning algorithms in privacy by default settings with a considerably high accuracy, it has some limitations that should be considered in future research. The guessing precision of the algorithms is dependent on the training and testing input data provided to it by the user-answered questionnaire items. However, the correctness and genuineness of the answers is dependent on the user providing rational and intentionally correct answers. In addition, the user study was carried out in Japan, and cultural attributes may influence the extent to which the results can be generalised and applied to other societies. Furthermore, we limited our study to 5 questions considering the top 15 combinations of 150 entries, therefore, additional research is needed in order to determine both the optimal number and best combination of questions that are sufficient to have an acceptable accuracy of prediction. In our future work, we plan to run more number of experiments with varying learning algorithms. Finally, the proposed approach only focused on default privacy preference settings and, not on the multi-dimensional privacy issues that users face when using Internet services and making data disclosure and non-disclosure decisions.

Table 9. Accuracy of combination scheme (#Training data = 9,000, #Test data = 1,000).

Combination					Cluster accuracy - TRD	Accuracy - TRD	Accuracy - TED
A-11	A-15	B-4	C-2	D-6	0.731411111	0.81693	0.81735875
A-12	B-7	B-8	D-11	E-9	0.748988889	0.82109125	0.82167
B-6	B-7	D-7	E-10	E-11	0.724666667	0.822432917	0.823305
A-10	B-4	D-4	E-6	E-8	0.744133333	0.820498889	0.8205675
A-10	B-4	D-6	D-9	E-6	0.746	0.81941375	0.81997875
A-10	B-4	D-6	D-9	E-7	0.763822222	0.823401111	0.8250475
A-10	B-4	D-7	D-9	E-6	0.759411111	0.822305694	0.82301125
A-10	B-4	D-9	E-4	E-6	0.751011111	0.819230278	0.8195725
A-11	B-4	B-8	D-10	E-6	0.743255556	0.820663889	0.820705
A-11	B-4	D-10	E-6	E-13	0.755888889	0.821184306	0.821355
A-13	B-4	D-11	E-6	E-11	0.743044444	0.821143889	0.82237
A-16	B-6	B-10	D-8	E-6	0.757722222	0.82313375	0.823545
B-4	B-10	D-4	D-13	E-7	0.7456	0.8230475	0.82392625
B-4	D-4	D-6	D-13	E-12	0.749477778	0.823683889	0.82439125
B-4	D-6	D-9	E-4	E-7	0.7408	0.823176528	0.8243375

7   Related Work

With the advent of privacy violations and increased user privacy concerns, significant efforts have been put on privacy policy representation. However, approaches to end user privacy preference settings management are still limited. In this regard, Kolter and Pernul highlighted the importance of privacy preferences and proposed a user-friendly, P3P-based privacy preference generator [22] for service providers that included a configuration wizard and a privacy preference summary. In a similar form, the research approach proposed by Biswas [23] focused on privacy settings and consisted of an algorithm to detect the conflicts in privacy settings, specifically, between user preferences and application requirements in smart phone ecosystems.

Authors in [24] proposed Privacy Butler; a personal privacy manager to monitor a user's online presence based on a privacy policy. This concept focuses only on content related to user's online presence in a social network; and it monitors whether third parties have disclosed user's information without consent, this mechanisms verifies the content satisfactorily matches the privacy preference of the user; and, in case of a mismatch it attempts to modify or delete the corresponding content. Srivastava and Geethakumari [25,26] proposed a privacy settings recommender system also focused on online social network services. Berendt et al. [27] emphasised the importance of automatic privacy preference generation and Sadah et al. [28] suggested that machine learning techniques have the power to generate more accurate preferences than users themselves and relieve them from the complex task of specifying their privacy preferences. This issue has been supported by Madejski *et al.* [29], whose study focused in online social networks and demonstrated that there exists a serious mismatch between intentions for privacy settings and real settings. Preference modelling for eliciting preferences was studied by Bufett and Fleming [30]. Mugan *et al.* [31] proposed a method for generating persona and suggestions intended to help users incrementally refine their privacy preferences over time. Fang *et al.* [32,33] have proposed a privacy wizard for social networking sites. The purpose of the wizard is to automatically configure a users' privacy settings with minimal effort required by the user. The wizard is based on the underlying observation that real users conceive their privacy preferences based on an implicit structure. Thus, after asking the user a limited number of carefully chosen questions, it is usually possible to build a machine learning model that accurately predicts the users' privacy preferences. Although, similar work is presented, our approach is applicable to general online services, while theirs is limited in scope (i.e., used to restrict privacy of friends in social media, namely, Facebook). Moreover, their model works similar to an access control list where users put restrictions on their Facebook friends while ours sets the privacy preference of web services.

Furthermore, Lin *et al.* [34] applied hierarchical clustering techniques to analyse and understand users' mobile app privacy presences. The authors analysed mobile apps privacy behaviours using static analysis tools, and also crowdsourced users' mobile app privacy preferences using Amazon Mechanical Turk. While the results are interesting, their privacy preference clustering is more focused to mobile apps, i.e. Android permission model. Guo and Chen [35] proposed an algorithm to optimise privacy configurations based on desired privacy level and utility preference of users, in this approach users are still required to set up a preference level. Contrary to this, Tondel *et al.* [36] proposed a conceptual architecture for learning privacy preferences based on the decisions that users make in their normal interactions on the web. Authors suggested that learning of privacy preferences has the potential to increase the accuracy of preferences without requiring users to have a high level of knowledge or willingness to invest time and effort in their privacy. Although interesting work, its design is based on the assumption that users are privacy conscious and are expected to be willing to take part in the preference generation by installing a user agent. Additionally, no practical implementation or experimentation has been provided.

Authors [37] designed a fine-grained privacy preference model using ontologies that enables users to set privacy preferences on their data. Even though their approach presents a light weight solution, the user will have to run the privacy preference ontology every time she wants to affect the setting. Further more, their approach is also dependent on the Web Access Control vocabulary.

8   Conclusions and Future Work

In this paper we introduced a machine learning approach in order to provide personalised default privacy settings. We argue that the complexity of setting privacy preferences is a burden that shouldn't be put on to users especially under the assumption that users are able to choose the best privacy setting for themselves. While this may be true in for some cases, it has been shown that ordinary online users fall far short of being able to do this. This calls for the need to help users with efficient and tailored privacy preference mechanisms. Therefore, in this study, we have designed and implemented a proof of concept based on machine learning in order to facilitate the privacy settings of users by asking them a minimum number of questions. The results show that machine learning algorithms have great potential to automate privacy preference setting with minimal input from users. Future work will include further enhancing the accuracy of the preference setting results. To this end, we plan to investigate techniques for finding the combination of questions that will maximise the accuracy of the prediction scheme. Furthermore, repeating the experiment with different user group and experimental setup could enrich the conclusions and generalisations drawn in this paper, therefore, in the research roadmap, we plan to collect data from European users as well. Finally, we plan to evaluate the proof of concept with real users and enable the system to learn from users' privacy preferences when they begin interacting with the associated service.

Acknowledgments. This paper is an extension of the paper published in the ICISSP2016 conference. Authors would like to thank anonymous reviewers for their insightful comments, which, allow us to improve the overall quality of the paper.

References

1. Hargittai, E., et al.: Facebook privacy settings: who cares? First Monday **15**(8) (2010)
2. Liu, Y., Gummadi, K.P., Krishnamurthy, B., Mislove, A.: Analyzing facebook privacy settings: user expectations vs. reality. In: Proceedings of the 2011 ACM SIGCOMM Conference on Internet Measurement Conference (IMC 2011), pp. 61–70, New York, NY, USA. ACM (2011)
3. Deuker, A.: Addressing the privacy paradox by expanded privacy awareness – the example of context-aware services. In: Bezzi, M., Duquenoy, P., Fischer-Hübner, S., Hansen, M., Zhang, G. (eds.) Privacy and Identity 2009. IAICT, vol. 320, pp. 275–283. Springer, Heidelberg (2010). doi:10.1007/978-3-642-14282-6_23
4. Basu, A., Vaidya, J., Kikuchi, H.: Efficient privacy-preserving collaborative filtering based on the weighted slope one predictor. J. Internet Serv. Inf. Secur. (JISIS) **1**(4), 26–46 (2011)
5. Scipioni, M.P., Langheinrich, M.: Towards a new privacy-aware location sharing platform. J. Internet Serv. Inf. Secur. (JISIS) **1**(4), 47–59 (2011)
6. Guha, S., Cheng, B., Francis, P.: Challenges in measuring online advertising systems. In: Proceedings of the 10th ACM SIGCOMM Conference on Internet Measurement (IMC 2010), pp. 81–87 (2010)
7. Korolova, A.: Privacy violations using micro targeted ads: a case study. In: Proceedings of the 2010 IEEE International Conference on Data Mining Workshops (ICDMW 2010), pp. 474–482 (2010)
8. Acquisti, A., Grossklags, J.: Privacy and rationality in individual decision making. IEEE Secur. Priv. **3**(1), 26–33 (2005)

9. Pollach, I.: What's wrong with online privacy policies? Commun. ACM **50**(9), 103–108 (2007)
10. Jensen, C., Potts, C., Jensen, C.: Privacy practices of internet users: self-reports versus observed behavior. Int. J. Hum. Comput. Stud. **63**(1–2), 203–227 (2005)
11. Solove, D.J.: Privacy self-management and the consent paradox. Harv. Law Rev. **126**, 1879–1903 (2013)
12. W3C. The platform for privacy preferences 1.0 (P3P1.0) specification. In: Platform for Privacy Preferences (P3P) Project (2002)
13. Cranor, L.F.: P3p: making privacy policies more useful. IEEE Secur. Priv. **1**(6), 50–55 (2003)
14. Cranor, L.F., Arjula, M., Guduru, P.: Use of a P3P user agent by early adopters. In: Proceedings of the 2002 ACM Workshop on Privacy in the Electronic Society (WPES 2002), pp. 1–10 (2002)
15. Cranor, L.F., Guduru, P., Arjula, M.: User interfaces for privacy agents. ACM Trans. Comput. Hum. Interact. **13**(2), 135–178 (2006)
16. Pedersen, A.: P3 - problems, progress, potential. Priv. Laws Bus. Int. Newslett. **2**, 20–21 (2003)
17. Backes, M., Karjoth, G, Bagga, W, Schunter, M.: Efficient comparison of enterprise privacy policies. In: Proceedings of the 2004 ACM Symposium on Applied Computing (SAC 2004), pp. 375–382 (2004)
18. Dehghantanha, A., Udzir, N.I., Mahmod, R.: Towards a pervasive formal privacy language. In: 2010 IEEE 24th International Conference on Advanced Information Networking and Applications Workshops (WAINA), pp. 1085–1091 (2010)
19. Bekara, K., Mustapha, Y.B., Laurent, M.: XPACML extensible privacy access control markup langua. In: 2010 Second International Conference on Communications and Networking (ComNet), pp. 1–5 (2010)
20. Tøndel, I.A., Nyre, Å.A.: Towards a similarity metric for comparing machine-readable privacy policies. In: Camenisch, J., Kesdogan, D. (eds.) iNetSec 2011. LNCS, vol. 7039, pp. 89–103. Springer, Heidelberg (2012). doi:10.1007/978-3-642-27585-2_8
21. Yee, G.O.M.: An automatic privacy policy agreement checker for e-services. In: International Conference on Availability, Reliability and Security (ARES 2009), pp. 307–315 (2009)
22. Kolter, J., Pernul, G.: Generating user-understandable privacy preferences. In: International Conference on Availability, Reliability and Security (ARES 2009), pp. 299–306 (2009)
23. Biswas, D.: Privacy policies change management for smartphones. In: 2012 IEEE International Conference on Pervasive Computing and Communications Workshops (PERCOM Workshops), pp. 70–75 (2012)
24. Wishart, R., Corapi, D., Madhavapeddy, A., Sloman, M.: Privacy butler: a personal privacy rights manager for online presence. In: 2010 8th IEEE International Conference on Pervasive Computing and Communications Workshops (PERCOM Workshops), pp. 672–677 (2010)
25. Srivastava, A., Geethakumari, G.: A framework to customize privacy settings of online social network users. In: 2013 IEEE Recent Advances in Intelligent Computational Systems (RAICS), pp. 187–192 (2013)
26. Srivastava, A., Geethakumari, G.: A privacy settings recommender system for online social networks. In: Recent Advances and Innovations in Engineering (ICRAIE), pp. 1–6 (2014)
27. Berendt, B., Günther, O., Spiekermann, S.: Privacy in e-commerce: stated preferences vs. actual behavior. Commun. ACM **48**(4), 101–106 (2005)

28. Sadeh, N., Hong, J., Cranor, L., Fette, I., Kelley, P., Prabaker, M., Rao, J.: Understanding and capturing people's privacy policies in a mobile social networking application. Pers. Ubiquit. Comput. **13**(6), 401–412 (2009)

29. Madejski, M., Johnson, M., Bellovin, S.M.: A study of privacy settings errors in an online social network. In: 2012 IEEE International Conference on Pervasive Computing and Communications Workshops (PERCOM Workshops), pp. 340–345 (2012)

30. Buffett, S., Fleming, M.W.: Applying a preference modeling structure to user privacy. In: Proceedings of the 1st International Workshop on Sustaining Privacy in Autonomous Collaborative Environments (2007)

31. Mugan, J., Sharma, T., Sadeh, N.: Understandable learning of privacy preferences through default personas and suggestions (2011)

32. Fang, L., LeFevre, K.: Privacy wizards for social networking sites. In: Proceedings of the 19th International Conference on World Wide Web, pp. 351–360. ACM (2010)

33. Fang, L., Kim, H., LeFevre, K., Tami, A.: A privacy recommendation wizard for users of social networking sites. In: Proceedings of the 17th ACM Conference on Computer and Communications Security, pp. 630–632. ACM (2010)

34. Lin, J., Liu, B., Sadeh, N., Hong, J.I.: Modeling users? Mobile app privacy preferences: restoring usability in a sea of permission settings. In: Symposium on Usable Privacy and Security (SOUPS 2014), pp. 199–212 (2014)

35. Guo, S., Chen, K.: Mining privacy settings to find optimal privacy-utility tradeoffs for social network services. In: 2012 International Conference on Privacy, Security, Risk and Trust (PASSAT), and 2012 International Confernece on Social Computing (SocialCom), pp. 656–665 (2012)

36. Tondel, I.A., Nyre, A.A., Bernsmed, K.: Learning privacy preferences. In: 2011 Sixth International Conference on Availability, Reliability and Security (ARES), pp. 621–626 (2011)

37. Sacco, O., Passant, A.: A privacy preference ontology (ppo) for linked data. In: LDOW. Citeseer (2011)

38. Gunn, S.R., et al.: Support vector machines for classification and regression. ISIS Technical report 14 (1998)

39. Meyer, D., Dimitriadou, E., Hornik, K., Weingessel, A., Leisch, F., Chang, C.-C., Lin, C.-C.: Package 'e1071' (2015). https://cran.r-project.org/web/packages/e1071/e1071.pdf

40. MacQueen, J., et al.: Some methods for classification and analysis of multivariate observations. In: Proceedings of the Fifth Berkeley Symposium on Mathematical Statistics and Probability, Oakland, CA, USA, vol. 1, pp. 281–297 (1967)

41. Ward Jr., J.H.: Hierarchical grouping to optimize an objective function. J. Am. Stat. Assoc. **58**(301), 236–244 (1963)

42. Ester, M., Kriegel, H.-P., Sander, J., Xiaowei, X.: A density-based algorithm for discovering clusters in large spatial databases with noise. KDD **96**, 226–231 (1996)

43. Qin, M., Buffett, S., Fleming, M.W.: Predicting user preferences via similarity-based clustering. In: Bergler, S. (ed.) AI 2008. LNCS (LNAI), vol. 5032, pp. 222–233. Springer, Heidelberg (2008). doi:10.1007/978-3-540-68825-9_22

Differential Analysis on Simeck and SIMON with Dynamic Key-Guessing Techniques

Kexin Qiao[1,2,3(✉)], Lei Hu[1,2], and Siwei Sun[1,2]

[1] State Key Laboratory of Information Security,
Institute of Information Engineering,
Chinese Academy of Sciences, Beijing 100093, China
{qiaokexin,hulei,sunsiwei}@iie.ac.cn
[2] Data Assurance and Communication Security Research Center,
Chinese Academy of Sciences, Beijing 100093, China
[3] University of Chinese Academy of Sciences, Beijing 100049, China

Abstract. In CHES 2015, a new lightweight block cipher Simeck was proposed that combines good design components of SIMON and SPECK, two lightweight ciphers designed by NSA. As a great tool to improve differential attack, dynamic key-guessing techniques were proposed by Wang *et al.* that work well on SIMON. In this paper, we convert the dynamic key-guessing techniques to a program that can automatically give out the data in dynamic key-guessing procedure. With our tool, the differential security evaluation of SIMON and Simeck like block ciphers becomes very convenient. We apply the method to Simeck and four members of SIMON family. With a differential of lower Hamming weight we find by Mixed Integer Linear Programming method and differentials in Kölbl *et al.*'s work, we launch attacks on 21, 22-round Simeck32, 28-round Simeck48 and 34, 35-round Simeck64. Besides, by use of newly proposed differentials in CRYPTO 2015 we get new attack results on 22-round SIMON32/64, 24-round SIMON48/96, 28, 29-round SIMON64/96 and 29, 30-round SIMON64/128. As far as we are concerned, our results on SIMON64 are currently the best results.

Keywords: Simeck · SIMON · Dynamic Key-guessing · Differential cryptanalysis

1 Introduction

In 2013, NSA proposed two lightweight block ciphers called SIMON and SPECK. SIMON is optimized for hardware implementation and SPECK is optimized for software. Since their publication, various cryptanalysis have been launched on reduced versions of these two ciphers [1–7]. In CHES 2015, a new lightweight block cipher family Simeck [8] was proposed that combine good components of SIMON and SPECK. The Simeck family applies a slightly modified version of SIMON's round function and reuses it in the key schedule which is how SPECK

© Springer International Publishing AG 2017
O. Camp et al. (Eds.): ICISSP 2016, CCIS 691, pp. 64–85, 2017.
DOI: 10.1007/978-3-319-54433-5_5

does. The hardware implementations of Simeck block cipher family are even smaller than that of SIMON in terms of area and power consumption [8].

Differential cryptanalysis is one of the most powerful attack method on ciphers. In 2014, a new differential attack with dynamic key-guessing techniques was proposed to work on the reduced versions of SIMON family [7]. The key idea of the attack is to combine the classic differential attack and the modular differential attack that is widely used in hash function attacks [9–13]. This technique applies to ciphers that contain bitwise AND operator. Some subkey bits can be calculated from differences of state bits due to properties of differential propagation of AND operator. With differentials of high probability in previous papers [1,4,14], dynamic key-guessing techniques were used to improve the best previous cryptanalysis results by 2 to 4 rounds on family of SIMON block ciphers [7]. Dynamic key-guessing techniques extend the number of rounds in differential attacks dramatically.

The designers of Simeck give out security analysis results including differential attacks [15], linear attacks [16], impossible differential attacks [17], *etc.*, mainly following the attack procedure of SIMON due to their similarity. But they didn't estimate the security regarding dynamic key-guessing techniques. Recently, cryptanalysis covering more rounds are given [18,19]. Kölbl and Roy give differentials with high probability of all three versions and launch differential attacks covering 19, 26 and 33 rounds of Simeck32/64, Simeck48/96 and Simeck64/128 respectively [19]. Though they noticed the dynamic key-guessing method, they did not implement it.

Differential cryptanalysis is closely related to diferentials. Differentials that cover more rounds or that are with higher probability result in improved attacks with lower data and time complexity and more rounds. In CRYPTO 2015, Kölbl *et al.* [20] found out new differentials on round-reduced versions of SIMON32, SIMON48 and SIMON96 which can be used to improved previous differential attacks in terms of rounds attacked or time and data complexity.

In this paper, we demonstrate details of dynamic key-guessing techniques and implement this method by programming. Given the differential of high probability and the number of rounds to be added before and after the differential, the data in dynamic key-guessing procedure are output automatically. The time and data complexities are then calculated conveniently. We apply this method on Simeck family and four members of SIMON family block ciphers. Specifically, we find a 13-round differential of Simeck32/64 with lower hamming weight with probability $2^{-29.64}$. Applying this differential and those in Kölbl *et al.*'s work [19], we give differential cryptanalysis results on 21, 22-round Simeck32/64, 28-round Simeck48/96 and 34, 35-round Simeck64/128. Besides, with newly proposed differentials [20], we launch the same attack on 22-round SIMON32/64, 24-round SIMON48/96, 28, 29-round SIMON64/96 and 29, 30-round SIMON64/128. As far as we are concerned, out results on SIMON64 outperform previous results in terms of number of rounds attacked or time and data complexity. The comparisons of the cryptanalysis results of Simeck and SIMON are in Tables 1 and 2 respectively.

Table 1. Comparison of cryptanalysis results of Simeck.

Versions	Total rounds	Attacked rounds	Time complexity	Data complexity	Success prob	Reference
Simeck32/64	32	18	$2^{63.5}$	2^{31}	47.7%	[18]
		19	2^{36}	2^{31}	-	[19]
		20	$2^{62.6}$	2^{32}	-	[8]
		20	$2^{56.65}$	2^{32}	-	[21]
		21	$2^{48.5}$	2^{30}	41.7%	Sect. 4.2
		22	$2^{57.9}$	2^{32}	47.1%	Sect. 4.2
		23	$2^{61.78}$	$2^{31.91}$	-	[22]
Simeck48/96	36	24	2^{94}	2^{45}	47.7%	[18]
		24	$2^{94.7}$	2^{48}	-	[8]
		24	$2^{91.6}$	2^{48}	-	[21]
		26	2^{62}	2^{47}	-	[19]
		28	$2^{68.3}$	2^{46}	46.8%	Sect. 4.2
		30	$2^{92.2}$	$2^{47.66}$	-	[22]
Simeck64/128	44	25	$2^{126.6}$	2^{64}	-	[8]
		27	$2^{120.5}$	2^{61}	47.7%	[18]
		27	$2^{112.79}$	2^{64}	-	[21]
		33	2^{96}	2^{63}	-	[19]
		34	$2^{116.3}$	2^{63}	55.5%	Sect. 4.2
		35	$2^{116.3}$	2^{63}	55.5%	Sect. 4.2
		37	$2^{121.25}$	$2^{63.09}$	-	[22]

Table 2. Comparison of cryptanalysis results of SIMON.

Cipher	Key size	Total rounds	Attacked rounds	Time complexity	Data complexity	Success prob	Reference
SIMON32	64	32	21	$2^{55.25}$	2^{31}	51%	[7]
			22	$2^{58.76}$	2^{32}	31.5%	Sect. 5
			23	2^{50}	$2^{30.59}$	-	[23]
SIMON48	96	36	24	$2^{87.25}$	2^{47}	48%	[7]
			24	$2^{83.10}$	$2^{47.78}$	-	[23]
			24	$2^{78.99}$	2^{48}	47.5%	Sect. 5
SIMON64	96	42	28	$2^{84.25}$	2^{63}	46%	[7]
			28	$2^{75.39}$	2^{60}	50.3%	Sect. 5
			29	$2^{86.94}$	2^{63}	47.5%	Sect. 5
	128	44	29	$2^{116.25}$	2^{63}	46%	[7]
			29	$2^{101.40}$	2^{60}	50.3%	Sect. 5
			30	$2^{110.99}$	2^{63}	47.5%	Sect. 5

The organization of the paper is as follows. In Sect. 2 we give a brief introduction of the Simeck and SIMON block ciphers. In Sect. 3 we describe Wang *et al.*'s dynamic key-guessing techniques in a general way and demonstrate details in implementing the techniques. In Sect. 4 we give a 13-round differential of Simeck32/64 found by Mixed Integer Linear Programming (MILP) method and use it as well as differentials in references to launch differential attack with dynamic key-guessing techniques on Simeck. In Sect. 5 we give our results on SIMON32/64, SIMON48/96, SIMON64/96 and SIMON64/128 by applying the same method. We conclude the paper in Sect. 6.

2   The Simeck and SIMON Lightweight Block Cipher

2.1   Notations

In this paper, we use notations as follows.

X^{r-1}	input of the r-th round
L^{r-1}	left half of X^{r-1}
R^{r-1}	right half of X^{r-1}
K^{r-1}	subkey used in r-th round
X_i	i-th bit of X, indexed from left to right
$X \ggg r$	right rotation of X by r bits
$\oplus$	bitwise exclusive OR (XOR)
$\wedge$	bitwise AND
ΔX	$X \oplus X'$, difference of X and X'
$+$	addition operation
$\%$	modular operation
$\cup$	union of sets
$\cap$	intersection of sets

2.2   Description of Simeck and SIMON

Simeck and SIMON both apply Feistel structure and are denoted by Simeck$2n/mn$ and SIMON$2n/mn$ respectively where $2n$ is the block size and mn the master key size. Simeck family includes three members: Simeck32/64, Simeck48/96 and Simeck64/128 with number of rounds $n_r = 32$, 36 and 44 respectively. SIMON family includes 10 members among which we focus on SIMON32/64, SIMON48/96, SIMON64/96 and SIMON64/128 in this paper. The round function of Simeck and SIMON are very similar. Suppose the left half of input texts to the i-th round is $L^{i-1} = \{X_n^{i-1}, X_{n+1}^{i-1}, \cdots, X_{2n-1}^{i-1}\}$ and the right half is $R^{i-1} = \{X_0^{i-1}, X_1^{i-1}, \cdots, X_{n-1}^{i-1}\}$ and the subkey is $K^{i-1} = \{K_0^{i-1}, K_1^{i-1}, \cdots, K_{n-1}^{i-1}\}$. The round function is

$$(L^i, R^i) = (R^{i-1} \oplus F(L^{i-1}) \oplus K^{i-1}, L^{i-1})$$

where

$$F(x) = ((x \lll a) \wedge (x \lll b)) \oplus (x \lll c)$$

for $i = 1, \cdots n_r$. In Simeck, we have $a = 0$, $b = 5$, $c = 1$ and in SIMON, $a = 1$, $b = 8$, $c = 2$.

The key schedule is irrelevant to our differential analysis as our method concentrate on single key model where all plaintexts are encrypted under same master key. We refer the readers to [8,24] for details of the ciphers.

3   Differential Attack with Dynamic Key-Guessing Techniques

Differential attack [15] is one of the most powerful attacks on iterative block ciphers. If there is an input difference that results in an output difference with high probability against a reduced-round block cipher (such a structure is called a differential), by adding extra rounds before and after the differential, an attacker can choose and encrypt an amount of plaintext pairs that may satisfy the input difference, and then guess the subkey bits in the added rounds that influence the differential. Right guess will lead conspicuous number of plaintext and ciphertext pairs to be consistent to the differential.

In 2014, Wang *et al.* proposed dynamic key-guessing techniques to greatly reduce the number of secret key bits that need to be guessed in differential cryptanalysis [7]. These techniques were based on observations that some subkey bits can be deduced from equations invoked by certain input differences of AND operator. Different input differences of AND operator result in different conditions of subkey bits involved in the equations. Before using these observations, attackers should find out the sufficient bit conditions that act as equations in the extended rounds to make the differential hold. Thus the preprocessing phase of differential cryptanalysis with dynamic key-guessing techniques is divided into two stages when a differential with high probability of the cipher has been found: firstly, generate the extended path and identify the sufficient bit conditions to be processed and secondly generate the related subkey bits corresponding to each bit condition in the first stage. In the following we illustrate the differential attacks with dynamic key-guessing techniques in a general way and reveal some details of the implementation of the technique. We refer the readers to Wang *et al.*'s work [7] for some principles of the technique.

3.1   Generate the Extended Path with Sufficient Bit Conditions

Suppose that a differential with probability p covering R rounds has been found, we prefix r_0 rounds on the top and append r_1 rounds at the bottom. To get the differential path of the prefixed r_0 rounds, "decrypt" the input difference of the differential according to the rules that the output differences of AND operator is 0 if and only if its input differences are $(0, 0)$. Otherwise set the output difference of AND operator to "$*$". For the appended r_1 rounds, "encrypt" the output difference of the differential according to the same rules.

The bit conditions to be processed in the extended paths are sufficient bit-difference conditions that make the differential path hold. Specifically, when the input differences of AND operator are not $(0,0)$ and its output difference is definite (0 or 1, not $*$), then this output difference is a sufficient bit condition. Note that the prefixed r_0 rounds should be processed in encryption direction to lable sufficient bit conditions and the appended r_1 rounds should be processed in decryption direction. In this step, we get an extended path table with sufficient conditions labeled (see Table 5 for example).

3.2 Data Collection

Suppose there are l_0 definite conditions in the plaintext differences and l_1 sufficient bit conditions in ΔX^1 according to the extended path table. Divide the plaintexts into $2^{l_0+l_1}$ structures with $2^{2n-l_0-l_1}$ plaintexts in each structure. In each structure, the $(l_0 + l_1)$ bits are constants.

For two structures with different bits in positions in which the differences are 1 among the above $(l_0 + l_1)$ bit positions in the extended path table, save the corresponding ciphertexts into a table indexed by ciphertext bits in positions where the differences are 0 in the last row of the path table. Suppose there are l_2 ciphertext bits with difference 0, then for each such structure pair, there are about $2^{2(2n-l_0-l_1)-l_2}$ plaintext pairs remaining.

We build 2^t plaintext structures, and filter out the remaining pairs by decrypting one round. Suppose there are another k bit conditions to be satisfied in $\Delta X^{r_0+R+r_1-1}$ after one round decryption of the ciphertexts, then there are $2^{t-1+2(2n-l_0-l_1)-l_2-k}$ pairs left. Store them in a table T. At the same time, we expect to get $\lambda_r = 2^{t-1+2n-l_0-l_1} \cdot p$ right pairs.

The plaintext pairs in the table T can still be filtered by bit conditions in ΔX^2 and $\Delta X^{r_0+R+r_1-2}$ as some plaintext pairs may result in no subkey bit solution to equations regarding sufficient bit conditions in ΔX^2 and $\Delta X^{r_0+R+r_1-2}$. The procedure of generating subkey bits related to each sufficient bit condition is described in next subsection.

3.3 Generate Related Subkey Bits for Each Sufficient Bit Condition

For each sufficient bit condition, we get two kinds of subkey bits related to this bit - the subkey bits as variables of the equation and subkey bits that need to be guessed to get the specific equation. In encryption direction, we have an equation for sufficient bit condition $\Delta X^i_{j+n} = 0$ or 1 where $j \in [0, n-1]$ and

$$
\begin{aligned}
\Delta X^i_{j+n} = &\Delta X^{i-1}_{(j+a)\%n+n} \wedge X^{i-1}_{(j+b)\%n+n} \oplus \Delta X^{i-1}_{(j+b)\%n+n} \\
&\wedge X^{i-1}_{(j+a)\%n+n} \oplus \Delta X^{i-1}_{(j+a)\%n+n} \wedge \Delta X^{i-1}_{(j+b)\%n+n} \\
&\oplus \Delta X^{i-1}_{(j+c)\%n+n} \oplus \Delta X^{i-2}_{j+n},
\end{aligned}
\tag{1}
$$

where

$$
\begin{aligned}
X^{i-1}_{(j+b)\%n+n} =& X^{i-2}_{(j+b+a)\%n+n} \wedge X^{i-2}_{(j+b+b)\%n+n} \\
& \oplus X^{i-2}_{(j+b+c)\%n+n} \oplus X^{i-2}_{(j+b)\%n} \oplus K^{i-2}_{(j+b)\%n}, \\
X^{i-1}_{(j+a)\%n+n} =& X^{i-2}_{(j+a+a)\%n+n} \wedge X^{i-2}_{(j+a+b)\%n+n} \\
& \oplus X^{i-2}_{(j+a+c)\%n+n} \oplus X^{i-2}_{(j+a)\%n} \oplus K^{i-2}_{(j+a)\%n}.
\end{aligned}
\tag{2}
$$

When $(\Delta X^{i-1}_{(j+a)\%n+n}, \Delta X^{i-1}_{(j+b)\%n+n}) = (0,0)$ and $\Delta X^{i-1}_{(j+c)\%n+n} \oplus \Delta X^{i-2}_{j+n} \neq \Delta X^{i}_{j+n}$, it is an invalid equation and we get no subkey bit solution. Therefore, for sufficient bit conditions in ΔX_2 and $\Delta X^{r_0+R+r_1-2}$, this property can be used to filter out the wrong plaintext pairs as ΔX^1, ΔX^0 and $\Delta X^{r_0+R+r_1-1}$, $\Delta X^{r_0+R+r_1}$ are independent of keys. For remaining plaintext pairs in the table T, filter out the wrong ones with sufficient bit conditions in ΔX^2 and $\Delta X^{r_0+R+r_1-2}$. Put the remaining plaintext pairs in a table T_1.

We refer to $\Delta X^{i-1}_{(j+a)\%n+n}, \Delta X^{i-1}_{(j+b)\%n+n}, \Delta X^{i-1}_{(j+c)\%n+n} \oplus \Delta X^{i-2}_{j+n}$ as parameter differences for equation $\Delta X^{i}_{j+n} = 0$ or 1. For valid equations, the subkey bits related to the equation $\Delta X^{i}_{j+n} = 0$ or 1 are divided into the following 3 conditions:

1. When

$$
(\Delta X^{i-1}_{(j+a)\%n+n}, \Delta X^{i-1}_{(j+b)\%n+n}) = (1,0),
$$

the variables of the equation are the subkey bits that are linear to $X^{i-1}_{(j+b)\%n+n}$ and the subkey bits to be guessed are those that influence

$$
X^{i-2}_{(j+b+a)\%n+n}, X^{i-2}_{(j+b+b)\%n+n}, X^{i-2}_{(j+b+c)\%n+n}, X^{i-2}_{(j+b)\%n}
$$

and have not been deduced or guessed before;

2. When

$$
(\Delta X^{i-1}_{(j+a)\%n+n}, \Delta X^{i-1}_{(j+b)\%n+n}) = (0,1),
$$

the variables of the equation are the subkey bits that are linear to $X^{i-1}_{(j+a)\%n+n}$ and the subkey bits to be guessed are those that influence

$$
X^{i-2}_{(j+a+a)\%n+n}, X^{i-2}_{(j+a+b)\%n+n}, X^{i-2}_{(j+a+c)\%n+n}, X^{i-2}_{(j+a)\%n}
$$

and have not been deduced or guessed before;

3. When

$$
(\Delta X^{i-1}_{(j+a)\%n+n}, \Delta X^{i-1}_{(j+b)\%n+n}) = (1,1),
$$

the variables of the equation are the linear combination of subkey bits linear to $X^{i-1}_{(j+b)\%n+n}$ and subkey bits linear to $X^{i-1}_{(j+a)\%n+n}$ and the subkey bits to be guessed are those that influence

$$
X^{i-2}_{(j+b+a)\%n+n}, X^{i-2}_{(j+b+b)\%n+n}, X^{i-2}_{(j+b+c)\%n+n}, X^{i-2}_{(j+b)\%n},
$$

$$
X^{i-2}_{(j+a+a)\%n+n}, X^{i-2}_{(j+a+c)\%n+n}, X^{i-2}_{(j+a)\%n}
$$

and have not been deduced or guessed before.

For each text bit, we use a recursive algorithm to determine the subkey bits that influence it and subkey bits that are linear to it. The pseudo code is in Algorithm 1.

For sufficient key bits in the appended r_1 rounds, we process each bit in the decryption direction and give the formulas and pseudo code in Appendix Eq. 6. After processing all sufficient bit conditions in the prefixed and appended rounds, we get a table of subkey bits variables corresponding to different parameter conditions for each sufficient bit condition (see Table 6 for example).

It can be seen that whether a specific subkey bit can be deduced in an equation corresponding to a sufficient bit condition depends on the other three parameter bit differences. Some bit differences may act as parameters in more than one sufficient bit conditions and therefore we should process such sufficient bit conditions together. Specifically, we gather sufficient bit conditions with related parameters into one group and calculate the average number of subkey bits values for the group. In each round, suppose we put the original order of sufficient bit conditions in $Index\_order$ and the corresponding parameter sets in $Para\_sets$, we use Algorithm 2 to group sufficient bit conditions.

Algorithm 1. Generate related key bits for X_j^i in encryption direction.

1: **Input:** Round i and bit position j
2: **Output:** $[Influent\_keys, Linear\_keys]$
3: **function** RELATEDKEYS(i, j)
4:     $Influent\_keys = [\ ]$, $Linear\_keys = [\ ]$
5:     **if** $i = 0$ **then**
6:         **return** $[Influent\_keys, Linear\_keys]$
7:     **else**
8:         **if** $j < n$ **then**
9:             **return** RELATEDKEYS$(i - 1, j + n)$
10:        **else**
11:            $[I_0, L_0]$=RELATEDKEYS$(i - 1, (j + a)\%n + n)$
12:            $[I_1, L_1]$=RELATEDKEYS$(i - 1, (j + b)\%n + n)$
13:            $[I_2, L_2]$=RELATEDKEYS$(i - 1, (j + c)\%n + n)$
14:            $[I_3, L_3]$=RELATEDKEYS$(i - 1, j\%n)$
15:            $Linear\_keys = L_2 \cup L_3 \cup K_{j\%n}^{i-1}$
16:            $Influent\_keys = I_0 \cup I_1 \cup I_2 \cup I_3 \cup K_{j\%n}^{i-1}$
17:            **return** $[Influent\_keys, Linear\_keys]$
18:        **end if**
19:    **end if**
20: **end function**

In an actual attack, for each round, firstly guess the subkey bits to get the specific equations in this round. Then deduce the values of subkey bit variables in the equations according to parameter difference values group by group. In the j-th group, if we guess g_j subkey bits to get specific equations that totally

---

Algorithm 2. Group sufficient bit conditions in one round.

1: **procedure** GROUP($Index\_order, Para\_sets$)
2:     **Assert** length($Index\_order$)=length($Para\_sets$)
3:     k=0
4:     **while** k <length($Index\_order$) **do**
5:         flag=0
6:         j=k+1
7:         **while** j <length($Index\_order$) **do**
8:             **if** $Para\_sets[j] \cap Para\_sets[k]$ is not empty **then**
9:                 $Index\_order[k]=Index\_order[k] \cup Index\_order[j]$
10:                 Remove $Index\_order[j]$ from $Index\_order$
11:                 $Para\_sets[k] = Para\_sets[k] \cup Para\_sets[j]$
12:                 Remove $Para\_sets[j]$ from $Para\_sets$
13:                 flag=1
14:             **else**
15:                 j++
16:             **end if**
17:         **end while**
18:         **if** flag=0 **then**
19:             k++
20:         **end if**
21:     **end while**
22: **end procedure**

---

involve k_j subkey bit variables and there are $t_{j,i}$ parameter conditions in each of which we correspondingly get $v_{j,i}$ values of the subkey bit variables, the average number of values for the $(g_j + k_j)$ subkey bits in this group is $2^{g_j} \cdot \frac{\sum_i t_{j,i} v_{j,i}}{\sum_i t_{j,i}}$. For all groups, we get $\prod_j (2^{g_j} \cdot \frac{\sum_i t_{j,i} v_{j,i}}{\sum_i t_{j,i}})$ values of $\sum_j (g_j + k_j)$ subkey bits. For all extended rounds (or say groups), if the number of involved subkey bits (include the guessed ones and deduced ones) is less than the length of the master key, we are able to launch an attack with time complexity less than exhaustive search.

Note that there are two types of repeats in subkey bit variables and guessed subkey bits when combining the numbers of values of subkey bits in all groups. The first type is due to that some subkey bits are variables of more than one group. The second type is that a linear combination of some subkey bits is a variable of an equation that may be deduced and then each of the subkey bits is again need to be guessed and thus one bit is repeated. When launching an actual attack, all these bits should be preserved as there are conditions that no specific value of the subkey bit variable is get from an equation. These repeats don't influence calculating the complexity as when there is a repeated key bit, there is a correspondingly doubled number of solutions and thus the average number of solutions for key bits stays the same as that when we eliminate the repeated bits. In our program we only eliminate the repeats of the first type.

3.4 Calculate Complexity of the Attacks

Given the differential with high probability and number of rounds that we add before and after the differential, the program can give out the number of all subkey bits involved in the extended rounds $|sk|$ and the number of solutions to these subkey bits for each pair in T_1, say C_s. A wrong subkey occurs with probability $p_e = \frac{C_s}{2^{|sk|}}$ and the expected count of a wrong subkey for all pairs in T_1 is $\lambda_e = N_r \times p_e$. Combining the complexity of searching subkey bits involved in the extended paths that get more than $s = \lfloor \lambda_r \rfloor$ hits and the complexity of traversing the remaining subkey bits, the time complexity of the attack is dominated by

$$T_{es} = 2^{mn} \times (1 - Poisscdf(s, \lambda_e)), \tag{3}$$

where $Poisscdf(\cdot, y)$ is the cumulative distribution function of Poisson distribution with expectation y. The success probability is

$$1 - Poisscdf(s, \lambda_r), \tag{4}$$

where $Poisscdf(s, \lambda_r)$ denotes the probability that there is no subkey bits with more than s hits.

4 Differential Attacks on Simeck with Dynamic Key-Guessing Techniques

4.1 A Differential of Simeck32/64

Though several differentials with high probability of Simeck family were given [19], we want to get new differentials with lower hamming weight. Using automatic search method with MILP techniques [6,14,25,26], we find a 13-round differential characteristic of Simeck32/64 with probability 2^{-38} (see Table 3). Then we search for all differential characteristics with the same input and output differences and with probability q such that $2^{-50} \leq q \leq 2^{-38}$. The distribution of the differential characteristics is given in Table 4. Combing all the differential characteristics we get that the probability of the differential $(0x0, 0x2) \rightarrow (0x2, 0x0)$ is about $2^{-29.64}$.

4.2 Results on Simeck

We use differentials with high probability to evaluate the security of Simeck family regarding differential attacks with dynamic key-guessing techniques. The outputs of our program provide all information about the subkey bits corresponding to all sufficient bit conditions. Take 21-round Simeck32/64 which applies a 13-round differential $(0x8000, 0x4011) \rightarrow (0x4000, 0x0)$ as an example, we give a description of the output of our program. We provide details of prefixed 3 rounds and appended 5 rounds separately. Firstly we give the prefixed path with sufficient bit conditions labeled by black fonts (reorganized in Table 5). Then we give sufficient bit condition indexes in group from the second round to the third round and the parameters corresponding to each group:

Table 3. A differential characteristic of 13-round Simeck32/64 with probability 2^{-38}.

Rnds	The input differences
0	0000000000000000 0000000000000010
1	0000000000000010 0000000000000000
2	0000000000000100 0000000000000010
3	0000000000001010 0000000000000100
4	0000000000010000 0000000000001010
5	0000000000111010 0000000000010000
6	0000000000001100 0000000000111010
7	0000000000101010 0000000000001100
8	0000000000010000 0000000000101010
9	0000000000001010 0000000000010000
10	0000000000000100 0000000000001010
11	0000000000000010 0000000000000100
12	0000000000000000 0000000000000010
13	0000000000000010 0000000000000000

Table 4. The distribution of the characteristics of Simeck32 in the differential with input and output difference $(0000, 0002) \rightarrow (0002, 0000)$. The invalid characteristics is due to the special property of the dependent inputs of the AND operations in Simeck [4,6,14].

Prob	2^{-38}	2^{-40}	2^{-41}	2^{-42}	2^{-43}	2^{-44}	2^{-45}	2^{-46}	2^{-47}	2^{-48}	2^{-49}	2^{-50}	Invalid
#Char	4	62	52	427	637	2427	4384	12477	22742	48324	62039	50411	169458

```
[[{17, 27, 28, 22, 23}, {26, 21, 31}, {25}, {30}], [{17},
    {22}, {26}, {27}, {28}, {31}]]
[[{'\\Delta x^1_17','\\Delta x^1_28','\\Delta x^1_28 xor \\
    Delta x^0_27','\\Delta x^0_22','\\Delta x^1_22','\\Delta
    x^0_28','\\Delta x^1_27','\\Delta x^0_17','\\Delta x^0_23
    '}, {'\\Delta x^1_22 xor \\Delta x^0_21','\\Delta x^1_27
    xor \\Delta x^0_26','\\Delta x^1_31','\\Delta x^0_31','\\
    Delta x^1_26'}, {'\\Delta x^1_26 xor \\Delta x^0_25'}, {'
    \\Delta x^1_31 xor \\Delta x^0_30'}], [{'\\Delta x^1_17'
    }, {'\\Delta x^1_22'}, {'\\Delta x^1_26'}, {'\\Delta x^1
    _27'}, {'\\Delta x^1_28'}, {'\\Delta x^1_31'}]]
```

which means the sufficient bit conditions in the second round are divided into 4 groups and the sufficient bit conditions in the third round are divided into 6 groups. The first group of the second round is related to 9 parameters and the second group of the second round is related to 5 parameters and the rest goes the same way.

Then we provide the subkey bits corresponding to each bit condition in a python directory structure:

```
{'expand': '\\Delta x^1_17&x^1_22 xor \\Delta x^1_22&x^1_17
    xor \\Delta x^1_17&\\Delta x^1_22 xor 0 xor \\Delta x^0
    _17 = I', 'guessed key': set(), 'related key': ['\\Delta
    x^1_17 not zero', {'K^0_6'}, '\\Delta x^1_22 not zero', {
    'K^0_1'}], 'bit condition': '\\Delta x^2_17=I'}
```

where each item has the follow meaning:

`'expand'`	the equivalent expansion of sufficient bit condition
`'guessed key'`	subkey bits that need to be guessed to get the specific sufficient bit condition equation
`'related key'`	subkey variables corresponding to different parameter conditions(actually the subkey bit variable is the linear combination of the listed subkey bits)
`'bit condition'`	the sufficient bit condition

Then we give the details of dynamic key-guessing procedure of each group including subkey bit variables in this group, patterns of parameters for invalid equations and the parameter variables, number of key bit solutions and number of conditions that result in it, all solution numbers, all conditions and valid conditions. Take Group 1 of the second round for example:

```
Group  1
['K^0_15', 'K^0_10', 'K^0_5', 'K^0_4']
['*10*0', '1***0', '**00*']
{'\\Delta x^1_22 xor \\Delta x^0_21', '\\Delta x^1_27 xor \\
    Delta x^0_26', '\\Delta x^1_31', '\\Delta x^0_31', '\\
    Delta x^1_26'}
number of key bits solutions number of conditions
0 15
16 1
2 8
4 8
all solution numbers 64
all conditions 32
valid conditions 17
```

The average number of subkey bit values we are expected to get in this group is all solution numbers divided by all conditions. After each round we give the subkey bits that need to be guessed to get the specific equations in this round in

```
guessed key  [].
```

Then we list all subkey bit variables in all equations and set of all guessed key bits. The shading ones are repeated subkey bits that are eliminated in calculation of complexity.

```
K^0_6
K^0_1
K^0_0
. . .
```

Finally we give the number of values and number of subkey bits in the prefixed rounds after combining all groups:

```
we finally get 2^3.4729 values of 17 key bits
```

For the appended rounds, the data is the same as prefixed rounds.

For Simeck32/64, we adapt two differentials. The first one is $(0x8000, 0x4011) \rightarrow (0x4000, 0x0)$ that covers 13 rounds with probability $2^{-27.28}$ [19]. We prefix 3 rounds and append 5 rounds to the differential. Building 2^{14} structures with 2^{16} plaintexts in each structure we are expect to get $2^{31.2}$ pairs in T_1 and finally 3.29 right pairs. In the dynamic key-guessing procedure we are expect to get $2^{19.11}$ values of 53 subkey bits. According to the calculation method in Sect. 3.4, the time complexity and success probability of the attack are $2^{48.52}$ and 41.7%. The extended differential path of the 21-round Simeck32/64 is in Table 5. We demonstrate the solutions of subkey bits in Round 2 in Table 6.

Table 5. Sufficient conditions of extended differential Path of 21-round Simeck32/64.

Rounds	Input differences of each round
0	$1,*,0,0,0,*,*,*,0,*,*,*,*,1,*,*,*,*,*,*,0,*,*,*,*,*,*,*,*,*,*,*$
1	$0,*,0,0,0,0,*,0,0,0,*,*,*,0,1,*,1,*,0,0,0,*,*,*,0,*,*,*,*,1,*,*$
2	$0,1,0,0,0,0,0,0,0,0,0,1,0,0,0,1,0,*,0,0,0,0,*,0,0,0,*,*,*,0,1,*$
3	$1,0,0,0,0,0,0,0,0,0,0,0,0,0,0,0,0,1,0,0,0,0,0,0,0,0,0,0,1,0,0,0,1$
3→16	13-round differential
16	$0,1,0,0,0,0,0,0,0,0,0,0,0,0,0,0,0,0,0,0,0,0,0,0,0,0,0,0,0,0,0,0$
17	$1,*,0,0,0,0,0,0,0,0,0,0,*,0,0,0,0,0,1,0,0,0,0,0,0,0,0,0,0,0,0,0$
18	$*,*,0,0,0,0,0,*,0,0,0,*,*,0,0,1,1,*,0,0,0,0,0,0,0,0,0,0,*,0,0,0$
19	$*,*,*,0,0,0,*,*,0,0,*,*,*,0,1,*,*,*,0,0,0,0,0,*,0,0,0,*,*,0,0,1$
20	$*,*,*,0,0,*,*,*,0,*,*,*,*,*,*,*,*,*,*,0,0,0,*,0,0,*,*,*,0,1,*$
21	$*,*,*,0,*,*,*,*,*,*,*,*,*,*,*,*,*,*,*,0,0,*,*,*,0,*,*,*,*,*,*,*$

Due to page limits, we give the experimental data of other versions of our attacks in http://pan.baidu.com/s/1jGyBwj0 and give basic information of the attacks in the following. The second differential we use for Simeck32/64 is the one from Sect. 4.1. We add 4 rounds on the top and 5 rounds at the bottom. With 2^{18} structures containing 2^{14} plaintexts each, we are expected to get $2^{31.9}$ pairs in T_1 and finally 2.56 right pairs. We are expect to get $2^{21.09}$ values of 54 subkey bits in dynamic key-guessing procedure. The time complexity and success probability are $2^{57.88}$

Table 6. Solutions of subkey bits in round 2 of 21-round Simeck32/64.

Rounds	Bit Conditions	Solutions of Key Bits to Equations	Conditions Leading to Solutions	Pr	Pr^F
2(10)	$\Delta X_{17}^2 = 1 \Leftrightarrow$ $\Delta(X_{17}^1 \wedge X_{22}^1)$ $\oplus \Delta X_{17}^0 = 1$	Discard the pair	$(\Delta X_{17}^1, \Delta X_{22}^1, \Delta X_{17}^0) = (0,0,0)$		$\frac{1}{8}$
		$*$	$(\Delta X_{17}^1, \Delta X_{22}^1, \Delta X_{17}^0) = (0,0,1)$	$\frac{1}{8}$	
		K_1^0	$(\Delta X_{17}^1, \Delta X_{22}^1) = (0,1)$	$\frac{1}{4}$	
		K_6^0	$(\Delta X_{17}^1, \Delta X_{22}^1) = (1,0)$	$\frac{1}{4}$	
		$k_1^0 \oplus K_6^0$	$(\Delta X_{17}^1, \Delta X_{22}^1) = (1,1)$	$\frac{1}{4}$	
	$\Delta X_{27}^2 = 1 \Leftrightarrow$ $\Delta X_{27}^1 \wedge X_{16}^1$ $\oplus \Delta X_{28}^1 \oplus \Delta X_{27}^0 = 1$	Discard the pair	$(\Delta X_{27}^1, \Delta X_{28}^1 \oplus \Delta X_{27}^0) = (0,0)$		$\frac{1}{4}$
		$*$	$(\Delta X_{27}^1, \Delta X_{28}^1 \oplus \Delta X_{27}^0) = (0,1)$	$\frac{1}{4}$	
		K_0^0	$\Delta X_{27}^1 = 1$	$\frac{1}{2}$	
	$\Delta X_{28}^2 = 0 \Leftrightarrow$ $\Delta(X_{28}^1 \wedge X_{17}^1)$ $\oplus \Delta X_{28}^0 = 0$	Discard the pair	$(\Delta X_{28}^1, \Delta X_{17}^1, \Delta X_{28}^0) = (0,0,1)$		$\frac{1}{8}$
		$*$	$(\Delta X_{28}^1, \Delta X_{17}^1, \Delta X_{28}^0) = (0,0,0)$	$\frac{1}{8}$	
		K_{12}^0	$(\Delta X_{28}^1, \Delta X_{17}^1) = (0,1)$	$\frac{1}{4}$	
		K_1^0	$(\Delta X_{28}^1, \Delta X_{17}^1) = (1,0)$	$\frac{1}{4}$	
		$K_1^0 \oplus K_{12}^0$	$(\Delta X_{28}^1, \Delta X_{17}^1) = (1,1)$	$\frac{1}{4}$	
	$\Delta X_{22}^2 = 0 \Leftrightarrow$ $\Delta(X_{22}^1 \wedge X_{27}^1)$ $\oplus \Delta X_{22}^0 = 0$	Discard the pair	$(\Delta X_{22}^1, \Delta X_{27}^1, \Delta X_{22}^0) = (0,0,1)$		$\frac{1}{8}$
		$*$	$(\Delta X_{22}^1, \Delta X_{27}^1, \Delta X_{22}^0) = (0,0,0)$	$\frac{1}{8}$	
		K_6^0	$(\Delta X_{22}^1, \Delta X_{27}^1) = (0,1)$	$\frac{1}{4}$	
		K_{11}^0	$(\Delta X_{22}^1, \Delta X_{27}^1) = (1,0)$	$\frac{1}{4}$	
		$K_6^0 \oplus K_{11}^0$	$(\Delta X_{22}^1, \Delta X_{27}^1) = (1,1)$	$\frac{1}{4}$	
	$\Delta X_{23}^2 = 0 \Leftrightarrow$ $\Delta X_{28}^1 \wedge X_{23}^1$ $\oplus \Delta X_{23}^0 = 0$	Discard the pair	$(\Delta X_{28}^1, \Delta X_{23}^0) = (0,1)$		$\frac{1}{4}$
		$*$	$(\Delta X_{28}^1, \Delta X_{23}^0) = (0,0)$	$\frac{1}{4}$	
		K_7^0	$\Delta X_{28}^1 = 1$	$\frac{1}{2}$	
	$\Delta X_{26}^2 = 0 \Leftrightarrow$ $\Delta(X_{26}^1 \wedge X_{31}^1)$ $\oplus \Delta X_{27}^1 \oplus \Delta X_{26}^0 = 0$	Discard the pair	$(\Delta X_{26}^1, \Delta X_{31}^1, \Delta X_{27}^1 \oplus \Delta X_{26}^0) = (0,0,1)$		$\frac{1}{8}$
		$*$	$(\Delta X_{26}^1, \Delta X_{31}^1, \Delta X_{27}^1 \oplus \Delta X_{26}^0) = (0,0,0)$	$\frac{1}{8}$	
		K_{10}^0	$(\Delta X_{26}^1, \Delta X_{31}^1) = (0,1)$	$\frac{1}{4}$	
		K_{15}^0	$(\Delta X_{26}^1, \Delta X_{31}^1) = (1,0)$	$\frac{1}{4}$	
		$K_{10}^0 \oplus K_{15}^0$	$(\Delta X_{26}^1, \Delta X_{31}^1) = (1,1)$	$\frac{1}{4}$	
	$\Delta X_{21}^2 = 0 \Leftrightarrow$ $\Delta X_{26}^1 \wedge X_{21}^1$ $\oplus \Delta X_{22}^1 \oplus \Delta X_{21}^0 = 0$	Discard th pair	$(\Delta X_{26}^1, \Delta X_{22}^1 \oplus \Delta X_{21}^0) = (0,1)$		$\frac{1}{4}$
		$*$	$(\Delta X_{26}^1, \Delta X_{22}^1 \oplus \Delta X_{21}^0) = (0,0)$	$\frac{1}{4}$	
		K_5^0	$\Delta X_{26}^1 = 1$	$\frac{1}{2}$	
	$\Delta X_{31}^2 = 1 \Leftrightarrow$ $\Delta X_{31}^1 \wedge X_{20}^1$ $\oplus \Delta X_{31}^0 = 1$	Discard th pair	$(\Delta X_{31}^1, \Delta X_{31}^0) = (0,0)$		$\frac{1}{4}$
		$*$	$(\Delta X_{31}^1, \Delta X_{31}^0) = (0,1)$	$\frac{1}{4}$	
		K_4^0	$\Delta X_{31}^1 = 1$	$\frac{1}{2}$	
	$\Delta X_{25}^2 = 0 \Leftrightarrow$ X_{25}^1 $\oplus \Delta X_{26}^1 \oplus \Delta X_{25}^0 = 0$	K_9^0		1	
	$\Delta X_{30}^2 = 0 \Leftrightarrow$ X_{19}^1 $\oplus \Delta X_{31}^1 \oplus \Delta X_{30}^0 = 0$	K_3^0		1	

In the first column, 2(10) means there are 10 bit conditions in Round 2. In the third column, $*$ means the variables in this equation can take both values (0 and 1) and a specific subkey bit means this bit takes a definite value. The bold lines are group split lines.

and 47.1%. The extended differential path of 22-round Simeck32/64 is in Table 9 in Appendix.

Table 7. Differential attacks on reduced Simeck.

Versions	Attacked rounds	$|sk|$	λ_e	λ_r	Chosen count	Data complexity	Time complexity	Success Prob
Simeck32	21	53	$2^{-2.678}$	3.29	4	2^{30}	$2^{48.52}$	41.7%
	22	54	2^{-1}	2.56	3	2^{32}	$2^{57.88}$	47.1%
Simeck48	28	75	$2^{-8.365}$	2.54	3	2^{46}	$2^{68.31}$	46.8%
Simeck64	34	82	$2^{-1.678}$	3.94	4	2^{63}	$2^{116.34}$	55.5%
	35	118	$2^{-1.678}$	3.94	4	2^{63}	$2^{116.34}$	55.5%

For Simeck48/96, we use the differential $(0x400000, 0xe00000) \to (0x400000, 0x200000)$ that covers 20 rounds with probability $2^{-43.65}$ [19]. We append 4 rounds on top and 4 rounds at bottom. With 2^{18} structures with 2^{28} plaintexts in each, we are expected to get $2^{50.46}$ plaintext pairs in T_1 and finally 2.54 right pairs. There are $2^{32.89}$ values of 75 subkey bits in dynamic key-guessing procedure and the time complexity and success probability are $2^{68.31}$ and 46.8%. The extended differential path of the 28-round Simeck48/96 is in Table 10 in Appendix.

For Simeck64/128, we use the differential $(0x0, 0x4400000) \to (0x8800000, 0x400000)$ that covers 26 rounds with probability $2^{-60.02}$ [19]. We append 4 rounds on top and 4 rounds at bottom. With 2^{42} structures with 2^{21} plaintexts in each, we are expected to get $2^{38.59}$ plaintext pairs in T_1 and finally 3.94 right pairs. There are $2^{41.72}$ values of 82 subkey bits in dynamic key-guessing procedure and the time complexity and success probability are $2^{116.27}$ and 55.5%. If we add one more round on top, we are able to attack 35-round Simeck64/128 with the same data and time complexity and success probability. The difference is that we choose 2^{31} structures of 2^{32} plaintexts in each to encrypt, and expect to get $2^{49.05}$ pairs in T_1 and $2^{67.26}$ values of 118 subkey bits in the dynamic key guessing procedure. The extended differential path of the 35-round Simeck64/128 is in Table 11 in Appendix.

The data of the attacks on all reduced versions of Simeck are summarized in Table 7.

5   Results on SIMON

Our attacks on SIMON are based on differentials presented in Kölbl et al.'s new work in CRYPTO2015 [20]. The results are summarized in Table 8. Due to page limits, we give the experimental data in http://pan.baidu.com/s/1jGyBwj0 and give basic information of the attacks in the following.

For SIMON32/64, we add 3 rounds before and 5 rounds after the differential $(0x0, 0x8) \to (0x800, 0x0)$ that covers 14 rounds with probability $2^{-30.81}$. With 2^{25} structures of 2^7 plaintexts, we expect to get $2^{43.58}$ plaintext pairs in T_1 and finally 1.14 right pairs. There are $2^{26.33}$ values of 55 subkey bits in dynamic key-guessing procedure.

For SIMON48/96, we add 3 rounds before and 5 rounds after the differential $(0x80, 0x222) \rightarrow (0x222, 0x80)$ that covers 17 rounds with probability $2^{-46.32}$. With 2^{30} structures of 2^{18} plaintexts, we expect to get $2^{45.43}$ plaintext pairs in T_1 and finally 1.6 right pairs. There are $2^{25.56}$ values of 79 subkey bits in dynamic key-guessing procedure.

For SIMON64, we firstly apply the differential $(0x4000000, 0x11000000) \rightarrow (0x11000000, 0x4000000)$ that covers 21 rounds with probability $2^{-57.57}$. By adding 3 rounds before and 4 rounds after the differential, we are able to launch an attack on 28-round SIMON64/96 with 2^{48} structures of 2^{12} plaintexts. We are expected to get $2^{30.49}$ plaintext pairs in T_1 and finally 2.69 right pairs. There are $2^{37.5}$ solutions of 74 subkey bits in dynamic key-guessing procedure. If we add one more round on top, by constructing 2^{33} structures of 2^{27} plaintexts, we are able to launch an attack on 29-round SIMON64/128. There are $2^{53.35}$ values of 106 subkey bits in dynamic key-guessing procedure. These results on SIMON64 are better than previous best results [7] in terms of time and data complexity.

Another differential $(0x440, 0x1880) \rightarrow (0x440, 0x100)$ that covers 22 rounds with probability $2^{-61.32}$ will result in one more round attack on both SIMON64/96 and SIMON64/128. By adding 3 rounds before and 4 rounds after the differential, we are able to launch an attack on 29-round SIMON64/96 by constructing 2^{41} structures of 2^{22} plaintexts. There are $2^{37.41}$ values of 84 subkey bits in dynamic key-guessing procedure. By adding one more round on the top, we are able to launch an attack on 30-round SIMON64/128 with 2^{22} structures of 2^{41} plaintexts. There are about $2^{50.77}$ solutions of 118 subkey bits in dynamic key-guessing procedure. Thus we are able to attack one more round on SIMON64 than previous best results [7].

The sufficient conditions of extended differential paths of 22-round SIMON32, 24-round SIMON48 and 29, 30-round SIMON64 are demonstrated in Tables 12, 13, 14 and 15 in Appendix. The data of the attacks on all reduced versions of SIMON are summarized in Table 8.

Table 8. Differential attacks on SIMON.

Versions	Attacked rounds	$|sk|$	λ_e	λ_r	Chosen count	Data complexity	Time complexity	Success Prob
SIMON32/64	22	55	2^{-2}	1.14	1	2^{32}	$2^{58.76}$	31.5%
SIMON48/96	24	79	2^{-8}	1.6	1	2^{48}	$2^{78.99}$	47.5%
SIMON64/96	28	74	2^{-6}	2.69	2	2^{60}	$2^{75.39}$	50.3%
	29	84	2^{-4}	1.6	1	2^{63}	$2^{86.94}$	47.5%
SIMON64/128	29	106	2^{-8}	2.69	2	2^{60}	$2^{101.4}$	50.3%
	30	118	2^{-8}	1.6	1	2^{63}	$2^{110.99}$	47.5%

6   Conclusion

In this paper, we apply Wang *et al.*'s dynamic key-guessing techniques to a new lightweight block cipher family Simeck and four members of SIMON family block cipher and give new cryptanalysis results on them. We find a 13-round differential of low hamming weight and high probability of Simeck32 that is more suitable for differential cryptanalysis. We implement the dynamic key-guessing techniques in a program that can be used to automatically give the differential security estimation of SIMON and Simeck like block ciphers. For Simeck, our results include 21, 22-round Simeck32, 28-round Simeck48, 34, 35-round Simeck64. For SIMON, our results include 22-round SIMON32, 24-round SIMON48, 28, 29-round SIMON64/96 and 29, 30-round SIMON64/128. As far as we are concerned, our results on SIMON64 are the best results. Future work includes finding differentials with lower hamming weight that is more adaptable to dynamic key-guessing techniques and expand the dynamic key-guessing techniques to block ciphers of other structures.

Acknowledgements. Thanks to anonymous reviewers for their helpful comments and also organizers and audiences of ICISSP 2016. The work of this paper was supported by the National Key Basic Research Program of China (2013CB834203), the National Natural Science Foundation of China (Grants 61472417, 61472415 and 61402469), the Strategic Priority Research Program of Chinese Academy of Sciences under Grant XDA06010702, and the State Key Laboratory of Information Security, Chinese Academy of Sciences.

Appendix

Related Keys in Decryption Direction

For sufficient bit condition $\Delta X_j^i = 0$ or 1 and $j \in [0, n-1]$, in decrypt direction we have

$$
\begin{aligned}
\Delta X_j^i = \Delta X_{(j+b)\%n}^{i+1} \wedge X_{(j+a)\%n}^{i+1} \oplus \Delta X_{(j+a)\%n}^{i+1} \wedge X_{(j+b)\%n}^{i+1} \\
\oplus \Delta X_{j+b}^{i+1} \wedge \Delta X_{(j+a)\%n}^{i+1} \oplus \Delta X_{(j+c)\%n}^{i+1} \oplus \Delta X_j^{i+2},
\end{aligned}
\tag{5}
$$

where

$$
\begin{aligned}
X_{(j+a)\%n}^{i+1} &= X_{(j+a+b)\%n}^{i+2} \wedge X_{(j+a+a)\%n}^{i+2} \oplus X_{(j+a+c)\%n}^{i+2} \oplus \\
&\quad X_{(j+a)\%n}^{i+3} \oplus K_{(j+a)\%n}^{i+1}, \\
X_{(j+b)\%n}^{i+1} &= X_{(j+b+b)\%n}^{i+2} \wedge X_{(j+b+a)\%n}^{i+2} \oplus X_{(j+b+c)\%n}^{i+2} \oplus \\
&\quad X_{(j+b)\%n}^{i+3} \oplus K_{(j+b)\%n}^{i+1}.
\end{aligned}
\tag{6}
$$

Algorithm 3 demonstrates how to get subkey bits that influence X_j^i and that are linear to X_j^i.

Sufficient Conditions of Extended Differential Path for Simeck

We provide the sufficient conditions of extended differential paths of 22-round Simeck32/64, 28-round Simeck48/96 and 35-round Simeck64/128 in Tables 9, 10 and 11.

Algorithm 3. Generate related key bits for X_j^i in decryption direction.

1: **Input:** Round i and bit position j
2: **Output:** $[Influent\_keys, Linear\_keys]$
3: **function** RELATEDKEYS(i, j)
4:     $Influent\_keys=[\ ]$, $Linear\_keys=[\ ]$
5:     **if** $i = r_0 + R + r_1$ **then**
6:         **return** $[Influent\_keys, Linear\_keys]$
7:     **else**
8:         **if** $j \geq n$ **then**
9:             **return** RELATEDKEYS$(i + 1, j\%n)$
10:        **else**
11:            $[I_0, L_0]$=RELATEDKEYS$(i, (j + a)\%n + n)$
12:            $[I_1, L_1]$=RELATEDKEYS$(i, (j + b)\%n + n)$
13:            $[I_2, L_2]$=RELATEDKEYS$(i, (j + c)\%n + n)$
14:            $[I_3, L_3]$=RELATEDKEYS$(i + 1, j + n)$
15:            $Linear_keys=L_2 \cup L_3 \cup K_j^i$
16:            $Influent\_keys = I_0 \cup I_1 \cup I_2 \cup I_3 \cup K_j^i$
17:            **return** $[Influent\_keys, Linear\_keys]$
18:        **end if**
19:    **end if**
20: **end function**

Table 9. Extended differential path of 22-round Simeck32/64.

Rounds	Input differences of each round
0	$0,0,0,*,*,0,0,*,*,*,0,1,*,*,*,*,0,0,*,*,*,0,*,*,*,*,*,*,*,*,*,*$
1	$0,0,\mathbf{0},\mathbf{0},*,0,\mathbf{0},\mathbf{0},*,*,\mathbf{0},\mathbf{0},1,*,*,\mathbf{0},0,0,0,*,*,0,0,*,*,*,0,1,*,*,*,*$
2	$0,0,0,\mathbf{0},\mathbf{0},0,0,0,\mathbf{0},\mathbf{0},*,0,0,\mathbf{0},1,*,\mathbf{0},0,0,0,0,*,0,0,0,*,*,0,0,1,*,*,0$
3	$0,0,0,0,\mathbf{0},0,0,0,0,\mathbf{0},\mathbf{0},0,0,0,\mathbf{0},1,0,0,0,0,0,0,0,0,0,*,0,0,0,1,*,0$
4	$0,0,0,0,0,0,0,0,0,0,\mathbf{0},0,0,0,0,\mathbf{0},0,0,0,0,0,0,0,0,0,0,0,0,0,0,1,0$
4→17	13-round differential
17	$0,0,0,0,0,0,0,0,0,0,0,0,0,0,1,0,0,0,0,0,0,0,0,0,0,\mathbf{0},0,0,0,0,\mathbf{0},0$
18	$0,0,0,0,0,0,0,0,*,0,0,0,1,*,0,0,0,0,0,0,\mathbf{0},0,0,0,0,\mathbf{0},0,0,0,0,\mathbf{0},1,0$
19	$0,0,0,\mathbf{0},*,0,0,0,*,*,0,0,1,*,*,0,0,0,0,0,\mathbf{0},0,0,0,\mathbf{0},0,*,0,0,0,\mathbf{0},1,*,\mathbf{0}$
20	$0,0,0,*,*,0,0,*,*,*,*,0,1,*,*,*,*,0,0,\mathbf{0},\mathbf{0},*,0,\mathbf{0},\mathbf{0},*,*,\mathbf{0},0,1,*,*,\mathbf{0}$
21	$0,0,*,*,*,0,*,*,*,*,*,*,*,*,*,*,0,\mathbf{0},\mathbf{0},*,*,\mathbf{0},\mathbf{0},*,*,*,\mathbf{0},1,*,*,*,*$
22	$0,*,*,*,*,*,*,*,*,*,*,*,*,*,*,*,*,\mathbf{0},\mathbf{0},*,*,*,\mathbf{0},*,*,*,*,*,*,*,*,*$

Extended Differential Path for SIMON

We provide the sufficient conditions of extended differential paths of 22-round SIMON32, 24-round SIMON48 and 29, 30-round SIMON64 in Tables 12, 13, 14 and 15.

Table 10. Extended differential path of 28-round Simeck48/96.

Rounds	Input differences of each round
0	***000000***0***************0***0***************
1	***00000000000***0****1****000000***0**********
2	***0000000000000000***01***00000000000***0****1*
3	1110000000000000000000000***0000000000000000***01
4	0100000000000000000000001110000000000000000000000
4→24	20-round differential
24	01000000000000000000000000100000000000000000000000
25	1*1000000000000000000*000010000000000000000000000000
26	***000000000000*000***011*100000000000000000*000
27	***0000000*000***0****1****000000000000*000***01
28	***00*000***0***************0000000*000***0****1*

Table 11. Extended differential path of 34-round Simeck64/128.

Rounds	Input differences of each round
0	**********0000000*000**00***0*************00*000**00***0********
1	*0****1***000000000000*000**00***********0000000*000**00***0***
2	*00***01**000000000000000000*000**0****1***000000000000*000**00**
3	*000**001*000000000000000000000*00***01**0000000000000000*000*
4	0000010001000000000000000000000*000**001*00000000000000000000000
5	000000000000000000000000000000000000000010001000000000000000000000000
5→31	26-round differential
31	00001000100000000000000000000000000000000100000000000000000000000
32	000**001*1000000000000000000000*0000100010000000000000000000000000
33	00***01***00000000000000000*000**000**001*100000000000000000000000*
34	0****1****000000000000*000**00***00***01***0000000000000000*000**
35	**********000000*000**00***0****0****1****00000000000*000**00***

Table 12. Extended differential path of 22-round SIMON32.

Rounds	Input differences of each round
0	00**00001**0*000***0*01*****0000
1	0000*000001*000000**00001**0*000
2	000000000000010000000*000001*0000
3	00000000000000000000000000001000
3→17	14-round differential
17	00001000000000000000000000000000
18	001*00000000*0000000100000000000
19	1**0*00000**0000001*00000000*000
20	****0000***0*01*1**0*00000**0000
21	***0*0*******1*******0000***0*01*
22	******************0*0*******1***

Table 13. Extended differential path of 24-round SIMON48.

Rounds	Input differences of each round
0	00*0***01*1***11*00**0*0***************0******0
1	**000000*000*01**00*001*0000*0***01*1***11*00**0*0**
2	0000000000000001000100010000000*000*01**00*001*00
3	000000000000000010000000000000000000001000100010
3→20	17-round differential
20	00000000000000010001000100000000000000000010000000
21	000000*000*01**00*001*00000000000000000001000100010
22	00*0***01*1***11*00**0*0000000*000*01**00*001*00
23	***************0******000*0***01*1***11*00**0*0
24	***************1************************0******0

Table 14. Extended differential path of 29-round SIMON64.

Rounds	Input differences of each round
0	*0***1*0000*000*0**00*****0***********0*0**00*****0*************
1	**011*0100000000000*000*0**001*1*0***1*0000*000*0**00*****0*****
2	01*000*0000000000000000000*000***011*0100000000000*000*0**001*1
3	00010001000000000000000000000001*000*0000000000000000000*000*
4	0000010000000000000000000000000001000100000000000000000000000000
4→25	21-round differential
25	0001000100000000000000000000000000010000000000000000000000000000
26	01*000*0000000000000000000*000*00010001000000000000000000000000000
27	**011*0100000000000*000*0**001*101*000*00000000000000000000*000*
28	*0***1*0000*000*0**00*****0*******011*0100000000000*000*0**001*1
29	******0*0**00*****0***************0***1*0000*000*0**00*****0*****

Table 15. Extended differential path of 30-round SIMON64.

Rounds	Input differences of each round
0	****0****************010**000*********************0****0***
1	000**000****0******0***1*0000000****0****************010**000
2	00000000000**000*1**011*01000000000**000****0******0***1*0000000
3	0000000000000000000011000100000000000000000**000*1**011*01000000
4	00000000000000000000010001000000000000000000000000011000100000000
4→26	22-round differential
26	00000000000000000000010001000000000000000000000000000100000000
27	0000000000000*000*01*000*0000000000000000000000000010001000000
28	00000*000*0**001*1**011*0100000000000000000*000*01*000*0000000
29	0*0**00*****0******0***1*0000*0000000*000*0**001*1**011*01000000
30	****0****************0*0**00*0*0**00*****0******0***1*0000*00

References

1. Abed, F., List, E., Lucks, S., Wenzel, J.: Differential cryptanalysis of round-reduced SIMON and SPECK. In: Cid, C., Rechberger, C. (eds.) FSE 2014. LNCS, vol. 8540, pp. 525–545. Springer, Heidelberg (2015). doi:10.1007/978-3-662-46706-0_27

2. Alizadeh, J., Alkhzaimi, H.A., Aref, M.R., Bagheri, N., Gauravaram, P., Kumar, A., Lauridsen, M.M., Sanadhya, S.K.: Cryptanalysis of SIMON variants with connections. In: Saxena, N., Sadeghi, A.-R. (eds.) RFIDSec 2014. LNCS, vol. 8651, pp. 90–107. Springer, Cham (2014). doi:10.1007/978-3-319-13066-8_6

3. Alkhzaimi, H.A., Lauridsen, M.M.: Cryptanalysis of the SIMON family of block ciphers. IACR Cryptology ePrint Archive, Report 2013/543 (2013). http://eprint.iacr.org/2013/543

4. Alizadeh, J., Alkhzaimi, H.A., Aref, M.R., Bagheri, N., Gauravaram, P., Kumar, A., Lauridsen, M.M., Sanadhya, S.K.: Cryptanalysis of SIMON variants with connections. In: Saxena, N., Sadeghi, A.-R. (eds.) RFIDSec 2014. LNCS, vol. 8651, pp. 90–107. Springer, Cham (2014). doi:10.1007/978-3-319-13066-8_6

5. Shi, D., Hu, L., Sun, S., Song, L., Qiao, K., Ma, X.: Improved linear (hull) cryptanalysis of round-reduced versions of SIMON. In: Science China Information Sciences (to appear)

6. Sun, S., Hu, L., Wang, P., Qiao, K., Ma, X., Song, L.: Automatic security evaluation and (Related-key) differential characteristic search: application to SIMON, PRESENT, LBlock, DES(L) and other bit-oriented block ciphers. In: Sarkar, P., Iwata, T. (eds.) ASIACRYPT 2014. LNCS, vol. 8873, pp. 158–178. Springer, Heidelberg (2014). doi:10.1007/978-3-662-45611-8_9

7. Wang, N., Wang, X., Jia, K., Zhao, J.: Differential Attacks on Reduced SIMON Versions with Dynamic Key-guessing Techniques. Cryptology ePrint Archive, Report 2014/448 (2014). http://eprint.iacr.org/2014/448

8. Yang, G., Zhu, B., Suder, V., Aagaard, M.D., Gong, G.: The Simeck Family of Lightweight Block Ciphers (2015)

9. Cannière, C., Rechberger, C.: Finding SHA-1 characteristics: general results and applications. In: Lai, X., Chen, K. (eds.) ASIACRYPT 2006. LNCS, vol. 4284, pp. 1–20. Springer, Heidelberg (2006). doi:10.1007/11935230_1

10. Leurent, G.: Construction of differential characteristics in ARX designs application to skein. In: Canetti, R., Garay, J.A. (eds.) CRYPTO 2013. LNCS, vol. 8042, pp. 241–258. Springer, Heidelberg (2013). doi:10.1007/978-3-642-40041-4_14

11. Mendel, F., Nad, T., Schläffer, M.: Finding SHA-2 characteristics: searching through a minefield of contradictions. In: Lee, D.H., Wang, X. (eds.) ASIACRYPT 2011. LNCS, vol. 7073, pp. 288–307. Springer, Heidelberg (2011). doi:10.1007/978-3-642-25385-0_16

12. Theobald, T.: How to break Shamir's asymmetric basis. In: Coppersmith, D. (ed.) CRYPTO 1995. LNCS, vol. 963, pp. 136–147. Springer, Heidelberg (1995). doi:10.1007/3-540-44750-4_11

13. Wang, X., Yin, Y.L., Yu, H.: Finding collisions in the full SHA-1. In: Shoup, V. (ed.) CRYPTO 2005. LNCS, vol. 3621, pp. 17–36. Springer, Heidelberg (2005). doi:10.1007/11535218_2

14. Sun, S., Hu, L., Wang, M., Wang, P., Qiao, K., Ma, X., Shi, D., Song, L., Fu, K.: Towards finding the best characteristics of some bit-oriented block ciphers and automatic enumeration of (Related-key) differential and linear characteristics with predefined properties. Cryptology ePrint Archive, Report 2014/747 (2014). http://eprint.iacr.org/2014/747

15. Biham, E., Shamir, A.: Differential cryptanalysis of DES-like cryptosystems. J. Cryptology **4**, 3–72 (1991)
16. Matsui, M.: Linear cryptanalysis method for DES cipher. In: Helleseth, T. (ed.) EUROCRYPT 1993. LNCS, vol. 765, pp. 386–397. Springer, Heidelberg (1994). doi:10.1007/3-540-48285-7_33
17. Biham, E., Biryukov, A., Shamir, A.: Cryptanalysis of Skipjack reduced to 31 rounds using impossible differentials. In: Stern, J. (ed.) EUROCRYPT 1999. LNCS, vol. 1592, pp. 12–23. Springer, Heidelberg (1999). doi:10.1007/3-540-48910-X_2
18. Bagheri, N.: Linear cryptanalysis of reduced-round SIMECK variants. In: Biryukov, A., Goyal, V. (eds.) INDOCRYPT 2015. LNCS, vol. 9462, pp. 140–152. Springer, Heidelberg (2015). doi:10.1007/978-3-319-26617-6_8
19. Kölbl, S., Roy, A.: A Brief Comparison of Simon and Simeck. Cryptology ePrint Archive, Report 2015/706 (2015). http://eprint.iacr.org/2015/706
20. Kölbl, S., Leander, G., Tiessen, T.: Observations on the SIMON block cipher family. In: Gennaro, R., Robshaw, M. (eds.) CRYPTO 2015. LNCS, vol. 9215, pp. 161–185. Springer, Heidelberg (2015). doi:10.1007/978-3-662-47989-6_8
21. Zhang, K., Guan, J., Hu, B., Lin, D.: Security Evaluation on Simeck against Zero Correlation Linear Cryptanalysis. Cryptology ePrint Archive, Report 2015/911 (2015). http://eprint.iacr.org/2015/911
22. Qin, L., Chen, H.: Linear Hull Attack on Round-Reduced Simeck with Dynamic Key-guessing Techniques. Cryptology ePrint Archive, Report 2016/066 (2016). http://eprint.iacr.org/2016/066
23. Abdelraheem, M.A., Alizadeh, J., Alkhzaimi, H.A., Aref, M.R., Bagheri, N., Gauravaram, P.: Improved linear cryptanalysis of reduced-round SIMON-32 and SIMON-48. In: Biryukov, A., Goyal, V. (eds.) INDOCRYPT 2015. LNCS, vol. 9462, pp. 153–179. Springer, Heidelberg (2015). doi:10.1007/978-3-319-26617-6_9
24. Beaulieu, R., Shors, D., Smith, J., Treatman-Clark, S., Weeks, B., Wingers, L.: The SIMON and SPECK families of lightweight block ciphers. IACR Cryptology ePrint Archive, Report 2013/404 (2013). http://eprint.iacr.org/2013/404
25. Qiao, K., Hu, L., Sun, S., Ma, X., Kan, H.: Improved MILP modeling for automatic security evaluation and application to FOX. IEICE Trans. Fundam. Electron. Commun. Comput. Sci. **E98**(A), 72–80 (2015)
26. Sun, S., Hu, L., Song, L., Xie, Y., Wang, P.: Automatic security evaluation of block ciphers with S-bP structures against related-key differential attacks. In: Lin, D., Xu, S., Yung, M. (eds.) Inscrypt 2013. LNCS, vol. 8567, pp. 39–51. Springer, Heidelberg (2014). doi:10.1007/978-3-319-12087-4_3

Efficient Distribution of Certificate Chains in VANETs

Sebastian Bittl[(✉)] and Karsten Roscher

Fraunhofer ESK, 80686 Munich, Germany
sebastian.bittl@mytum.de, karsten.roscher@esk.fraunhofer.de

Abstract. Wireless car-to-X communication technology is about to enter the mass market within the next years. Thereby, security in created vehicular ad-hoc networks depends on digital signatures managed by a multi-level certificate hierarchy. Certificate distribution is critical in regard to channel usage and delay of data reception via security caused packet loss. These issues are even more significant in case not only pseudonym certificates, but also certificate authority certificates, have to be exchanged between nodes on demand. Prior work has not treated dissemination of higher level elements from a multi-level certificate chain in detail. Thus, this work provides a study on the recently standardized algorithms. Several drawbacks of the straight forward solution taken so far are identified, which include severe denial of service weaknesses. Solutions to the distribution problem are found to be similar to the ones of the packet forwarding problem encountered in position-based routing. Hence, we study several algorithms for efficient distribution of a certificate chain in regard to channel load, which are adapted from their counterparts in position-based routing. Thereby, a combination of pseudonym certificate buffering with requester based responder selection is found to be able to completely remove the requirement for certificate chain distribution in VANETs. The introduced design avoids the found denial of service weakness, while decreasing the worst case size of the security envelope of VANET messages by more than a third at the same time.

Keywords: Certificate distribution · VANET · Security

1 Introduction

Vehicular ad-hoc networks (VANETs) based on wireless data exchange are about to enter the mass market in upcoming years. In both Europe and the USA significant progress is being made within the European Telecommunications Standards Institute Intelligent Transport Systems (ETSI ITS) and Wireless Access in Vehicular Environments (WAVE) frameworks [2,21]. Thereby, system security is a core point of concern, as the main use cases are safety critical advanced driver assistance systems (ADAS). Hence, a security system based on digital signatures and a multi-level certificate hierarchy has been designed.

© Springer International Publishing AG 2017
O. Camp et al. (Eds.): ICISSP 2016, CCIS 691, pp. 86–107, 2017.
DOI: 10.1007/978-3-319-54433-5_6

Within ETSI ITS, the certificate hierarchy consists of three levels. These include the root certificate(s) authorizing so called authorization authority certificates (AACs), which are used to authorize pseudonym certificates (PSCs, or authorization tickets) [8]. Thus, an authorization authority acts as a certificate authority. WAVE does not limit the amount of certificate hierarchy levels, but the minimum number is three. PSCs are used to sign an ITS-station's (ITS-S's) messages, e.g., Cooperative Awareness Messages (CAMs) or Basic Safety Messages (BSMs). In order to verify messages, the receiver requires to know the certificate chain of the sender. In order to avoid tracking of vehicles, PSCs are changed rapidly by each ITS-S. Thus, it is required to exchange certificates, except of the root certificate(s) known to all stations, on demand between ITS-S's.

Prior work has shown that, the increase in message size caused by certificate dissemination leads to increased channel load, which can significantly decrease VANET performance [23]. Therefore, bandwidth saving strategies for certificate distribution are required. Nonetheless, recent work has focused on distribution strategies of PSCs. In contrast, AAC distribution, as required by a hierarchical certificate chain approach, has not been studied in detail so far.

A fully centralized scheme distributing all certificate authority (CA) certificates to every ITS-S from a backbone network, without ITS-S to ITS-S dissemination, is proposed in [27]. To avoid dependence on a backbone network handled distribution, which also requires cooperation between all CAs, both ETSI ITS and WAVE use a fully decentralized scheme. Thereby, an AAC is distributed by every ITS-S using it within its certificate chain, like it is done for PSCs [5,8].

The maximum size of the security envelope, which is added at the network layer of VANET protocol stacks, greatly influences overall system design. It limits the size of higher layer data sets, as the size of packets which can be handed over to the lower level access layer is limited [13]. Increasing this limit is unsuitable, as this would significantly deteriorate overall system performance, e.g., due to an increase in collisions on the wireless channel.

AAC dissemination among ITS-Ss in VANETs following ETSI ITS and WAVE standards is specified in [5,8]. However, we find that the straight forward approach for certificate chain dissemination taken there can lead to significant peaks in channel load. Moreover, the maximum size of the security envelope gets increased significantly by more than a half compared to the preceding standard version using only PSC distribution [6,8]. This is because an included certificate accounts for more than 50% of the size of the entire security envelope [11].

Furthermore, the specified request mechanism for AACs can be (mis-)used by an attacker to perform a serious denial of service (DOS) attack on the VANET. Thus, we propose an alternative AAC distribution strategy. It combines multiple concepts like temporary buffering of unauthorized PSCs and AAC emission strategies inspired by packet forwarding algorithms taken from position-based routing (often called GeoNetworking within ETSI ITS).

A first look on the impact of outlined issues has been provided in [12]. This work extends the one given in [12], especially regarding the DOS weakness of the standardized way of distributing AACs.

The further outline of this work is as follows. Firstly, Sect. 2 provides a review of prior work. The problems addressed in this work are defined in Sect. 3. New algorithms for efficient AAC dissemination are introduced in Sect. 4. Section 5 gives an evaluation of the proposed concepts. Finally, a conclusion about achieved results is provided in Sect. 6 together with possible topics of future work.

2   Related Work and Attacker Model

Security mechanisms within ETSI ITS and WAVE use digital signatures to secure authenticity and integrity of messages. Required parameters, e.g., public keys, are contained in certificates, which are part of a multi-hierarchy certificate chain. Thereby, a low number of cross-signed root certificates acts as the common anchor of trust, provided to ITS-Ss during manufacturing. Manufacturers of ITS-Ss, e.g., inside vehicles or road side units (RSUs), also equip their devices with their individual AAC alongside with PSCs.

AACs are used to secure PSCs, while PSCs are used to sign sent messages. The used PSC is changed frequently to avoid vehicle tracking. To enable realtime secured communication, participating ITS-S have to exchange their corresponding AACs as well as PSCs [3,8,32]. Otherwise, receivers cannot verify messages, which leads to so called cryptographic packet loss, i.e., dropping of messages.

Both ETSI ITS and WAVE do not use dedicated messages for certificate distribution. Instead, sporadic piggybacking of such data on higher level messages, e.g., cyclically sent CAMs or BSMs, is used. Explicit and implicit requests are used for PSCs dissemination as studied in [10]. In contrast, only explicit requests are used for AACs. This is done to keep the amount of transmissions of the certificate chain low, as thereby the AAC is emitted together with the currently used PSC. The overhead caused by including a certificate into the so called security envelope of a message is quite significant, almost doubling the size of the whole message [8,11]. Hence, inclusion of PSC and AAC into the security envelope increases a message's size by a factor of almost three. As many ITS-Ss share the same AAC, e.g., all cars from the same manufacturer, exchange of this information can be expected to happen with a much lower frequency then those of PSCs being individual to each ITS-S.

To the best of our knowledge, no detailed study on AAC, or the general case of a multi-hierarchy certificate chain, distribution within current VANET approaches has been published so far. Closest related work proposes a centralized distribution scheme for all CA certificates in VANETs [27], an approach not used in current VANET standards [5,8].

Instead of studying hierarchical CA schemes, prior work focused on decentralized CAs within the VANET itself [26,30]. However, such schemes do not provide the high level of security provided by infrastructure based CAs [26].

An illustration of a message sequence exchange between two ITS-Ss A and B causing an AAC request is given in Fig. 1 [8]. Mechanisms within WAVE are very similar. For a more compact presentation, we stick to ETSI ITS notation.

Due to the various inclusion rules of PSCs into CAMs it is also possible that the first message from B received at A contains the PSC, e.g., due to cyclic

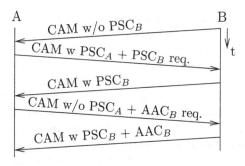

Fig. 1. Typical message sequence within ETSI ITS leading to an AAC request.

inclusion of PSCs into CAMs. However, in both cases an AAC request can only happen after station A has already received the PSC of B (called PSC_B in Fig. 1). This feature is used in the improvement suggested in Sect. 4.4.

An interesting finding is that requesting of AACs shows similarities to multi-hop forwarding in position-based routing (e.g., so called GeoNetworking in ETSI ITS). In both cases an ITS-S (security: responder/GeoNetworking: forwarder) has to be selected from a (possible) multitude of ITS-Ss possessing the data, which should be delivered to another ITS-S (security: requester/GeoNetworking: data sink). To minimize channel load, multiple delivery of the data to its destination should to be avoided.

In position-based routing mainly two mechanisms exist to select a packet forwarder. These are sender based and receiver based selection. A popular approach for selection of the packet forwarder by its sender is called greedy forwarding [31]. Thereby, the sender tries to maximize a specific metric, typically the covered distance, by selecting a particular forwarder. Moreover, different mechanisms using distributed receiver based forwarder selection, from the set of possible forwarders, have been studied [14,19,20,22,31]. An important concept is the so called contention-based forwarding (CBF) scheme [20]. It has been shown that CBF outperforms its greedy forwarding counterpart in many scenarios. An overview of this field is provided in [16,31].

We assume a single, static and active attacker, e.g., using an RSU. Its location is unknown to the legitimate ITS-Ss. Furthermore, the attacker does not possess valid cryptographic material to sign VANET messages.

3   Problem Statement

Two major issues are caused by on demand certificate chain dissemination in VANETs, as briefly outlined in Sect. 1. These are discussed in Sects. 3.1 and 3.2.

3.1   Normal VANET Operation

We assume normal VANET operation without presence of an attacker in this section. Requesting an AAC leads to a peak in channel utilization, as every receiver using the AAC includes its certificate chain in its next CAM. AACs are shared between many cars, e.g., such from the same manufacturer. In order to limit the amount of AAC requests in general, long term buffering of such certificates is discussed in Sect. 4.1.

The AAC distribution problem shows some similarities to packet forwarding within position-based routing protocols, as outlined in Sect. 2. Therefore, Sects. 4.2 and 4.3 study possibilities to reuse concepts from GeoNetworking protocols. The key difference between forwarding and an AAC response is that for AAC requests the initial sender is identical to the (end-)receiver. In contrast, for forwarding the initial sender wants to deliver a packet to another ITS-S.

In general, maximum message size within VANETs is strictly restricted, e.g., to 650 bytes in ETSI ITS [1]. This is caused by the lack of message fragmentation support in current VANETs. Moreover, higher layer functionality does not know when the network layer security entity is about to include certificate(s) in a message inside its so called security envelope [8]. Thus, always the maximum size of the security envelope has to be reserved, which significantly limits the size of higher level data sets. For example, 356 bytes (security envelope meta data + PSC + AAC [8]) have to be reserved for the security envelope within ETSI ITS, which is more than 50% of the maximum message size. Limiting the amount of included certificates to one can limit the maximum size of the security envelope. Hence, an approach for such a limitation without introduction of extra authentication delay is developed in Sect. 4.4. It uses buffering of received but unverified PSCs and is shown to work well in combination with the responder selection approach from Sect. 4.2.

3.2   DOS Attack on AAC Distribution

Two different possibilities to attack the AAC distribution mechanism explained above are discussed in the following. The attacker can either directly send out malicious AAC requests (direct attack) or he can trigger other vehicles to do so (indirect attack). Thereby, the direct attack yield more channel load, while the indirect attack yield a larger covered area by a single attack node.

Direct Attack. To request emission of a stations certificate chain an unsecured explicit AAC request is used in current ETSI ITS and WAVE systems. This is similar to the unsecured explicit PSCs request scheme looked at in [10] and standardized in [8]. Thereby, the current design of the security system requires the usage of unsecured messages to trigger AAC and PSC distribution. The main reason for this is the legitimate possibility of two (or even more) ITS-Ss meeting without any prior knowledge of each others certificate chains, except of the commonly known root certificate(s).

In such a case there is no possibility for performing a secured request for the certificate chain of another ITS-S without sending the certificate chain of its own ITS-S. Thus, an attacker without access to legitimate certificates can still misuse the AAC request mechanism to significantly increase channel load as follows.

The attacker sends CAMs (or BSMs), which contain a varying random value as the signer identifier and identifiers of valid AACs in the so called *request unknown certificates* header field of the security envelope. The signature gets filled by a random value, too. Receivers cannot verify the attacker's messages, as they do not possess a PSC for the used signer identifier (with high probability). Thus, the invalid signature will go unnoticed. The attacker can obtain the required valid AAC identifiers from received CAMs of legitimate ITS-Ss due to cyclic inclusion of PSCs containing their corresponding AAC identifier [8]. Up to six AACs can be requested in each CAM sent by the attacker.

In order to maximize the increase in channel load caused by the attack, the attacker selects the AACs used by the biggest share of ITS-Ss in its current surrounding. Thereby, he maximizes the number of ITS-Ss responding to his own CAMs by transmitting their certificate chain together with their next CAM. Using the maximum legitimate CAM generation rate (10 Hz [8]), the attacker can be assumed to be able to cause all successfully targeted ITS-Ss to include their certificate chain in each of their sent CAMs. Thereby, the channel load caused by these stations gets increased threefold.

In the worst case, all ITS-Ss in the attackers communication range only use six different AACs. Thus, he can target all these ITS-Ss. Hence, it can be expected that the channel load is increased by a factor of more than three. In case the wireless channel does not provide enough spare capacity to allow for transmission of the increased data volume, message sending by the ITS-Ss will be massively delayed (by CSMA-CA waiting times). Moreover, the probability of collisions on the wireless channel is increased significantly. Thus, the attacker has performed a successful denial of service attack against ITS-Ss.

Furthermore, as the attacker does not provide a valid PSC in its CAMs but only a random hash value, he also causes all vehicles with in its communication range to always include their PSC within every single CAM. This attack on the unsecured implicit certificate request scheme is described in detail in [10]. Thereby, it was shown that channel usage of all targeted stations can be more than doubled. Additionally, the area of effect of the attack is not limited to the broadcast area of the attacker. Instead, the increase in channel usage will only vanish at about two times the communication range of the attacker [10].

Section 5 provides an evaluation of the outlined attack alongside with the influence of efficiency increasing mechanisms proposed in the next section.

Indirect Attack. In contrast to the direct attack from the section before, an attacker can also cause other ITS-Ss to send superficial AAC requests. This vulnerability is caused by the difference between the eight byte AAC-ID used within the PSC to identify the issuing AA and the three byte certificate ID used for requesting an unknown certificate [5,8]. Thereby, the three byte ID is obtained by simple shortening from the eight byte ID.

To perform the attack, the attacker generates a PSC holding a faked AAC-ID as its signer identifier, with only its lower three bytes equal to the ones of a freely selectable valid AAC-ID. Thereby, the signature of the PSC just contains random data, as the attacker cannot obtain a valid PSC from the AA, i.e., he cannot have the AA sign his PSC. A receiver of such a faked PSC will look up the issuing AAC in the set of prior received AACs in order validate the PSC. This look-up will fail and the receiver will create an AAC request. Thereby, the shortened three bye AAC-ID will be equal to the one of a valid AAC. Thus, the request will cause other ITS-Ss, which use the requested AAC, to transmit their certificate chain. The invalid signature of the PSC is never checked, as this would require knowledge of the AAC which is never received.

The indirect attack only causes requests for one dedicated AAC per attacker message. Thus, the attacker needs to send out six messages to cause the channel load increase achievable from a single malicious message in the direct attack case, which can request six AACs at once. However, the area in which the channel load increase can be caused is significantly increased by the indirect attack. The bogus requests reach all ITS-Ss, which themselves can be reached by the ITS-Ss within the attacker's communication range. In contrast, the direct attack's requests reach only ITS-Ss within the attackers own communication range.

4   Efficient AA-Certificate Distribution

To enable verification of PSCs, AA certificates (AACs) are used. The impact of the distribution of such AACs on VANET system performance is outlined in Sect. 3 providing the general problem statement. Multiple approaches to overcome the stated performance issues are discussed in Sects. 4.1 to 4.4.

4.1   Long Term AA Certificate Buffering

In contrast to PSCs, the same AAC will be used by a multitude of ITS-Ss, e.g., by all vehicles from the same manufacturer running its own authorization authority. Moreover, the lifetime of AACs can be expected to be much longer than the one of PSCs, as there is no requirement for pseudonymity of AACs.

Thus, the exchange rate of AACs can be expected to be significantly limited by permanently buffering received AACs in the HSM (hardware security module containing the secure storage of cryptographic material) of an ITS-S after its verification using stored root certificates. Otherwise, an ITS-S has to request all AACs anew each time it starts up. Hence, in areas with many vehicle upstarts, e.g., parking spaces, there will always be a high amount of AAC requests.

Current VANET standards do not specify how long a receiver should keep a received certificate. Clearly, there is a trade off between additional memory space requirements inside the HSM and the decrease in channel load by sparing AAC emissions. However, the overall number of AACs can be expected to be limited and the impact on channel load by AAC emission can be significant, at least for the currently standardized approach as shown in Sect. 5.2.

4.2   Requester Selection of Responder

One possibility to avoid multiple AAC deliveries after an AAC request is to let the requester especially choose an ITS-S who should respond to the request. In GeoNetworking forwarder selection by the sender is often realized via a greedy forwarding approach. Thus, we call such kind of requester selection of the responder to an AAC request *greedy responding.*

This approach can be simply implemented within the current ETSI ITS framework. The requester just adds the ID of the PSC (of the asked ITS-S) alongside with the ID of the AAC in the so called "request unrecognized certificates" header field of the security envelope. According to [8], this ID would be the so called HashedID3 of the corresponding certificate. It is determined by taking the lowest three bytes of the SHA-256 hash value of the certificate. This approach would mean that an ITS-S would only respond to an AAC request in case also its own PSC gets requested within the same request.

The impact of the DOS weakness from Sect. 3.2 is limited by a limited maximum length of the request list. E.g., at most six IDs are used within ETSI ITS. Therefore, only the next messages of five ITS-Ss can be enlarged by the attack. Without presence of an attacker, only one ITS-S will respond to the request instead of a possible multitude of them.

However, effectiveness of requester based selection faces a major drawback. AAC requests typically occur when the environment of a vehicle is changing. Therefore, the requester may not be aware of all vehicles within its (new) communication area. Hence, responder selection may be sub-optimal as some available responder candidates for the selection process may be unknown to the requester or stations known to the requester left its communication range.

Possible selection mechanisms based on positions or sending times of known ITS-S in the requester's surrounding are discussed in the following sections. Clearly, such mechanisms are only required in case the set of possible responders to an AAC request has more than a single member.

Position Based Selection. The requester chooses the AAC provider in a way to maximize probability for a successful bidirectional communication (request and response). Thereby, different strategies can be used, which are a

- simple strategy just using the position of possible responders, and
- advanced strategies using an environment model of the requester ITS-S.

Required data like position, speed and heading of ITS-Ss is contained in cyclically distributed messages (CAMs/BSMs). For the simple strategy, a requester minimizes the distance between both ITS-Ss. Thereby, it tries to maximize chances that the chosen ITS-S really receives the request and also its reply is successfully delivered to the requester. This strategy assumes that the probability of two ITS-Ss exchanging data successfully increases with decreasing distance between these ITS-Ss. This strategy is used in the evaluation in Sect. 5.2. A similar approach from packet forwarding is to try to cover the maximum possible distance towards the (final) receiver by each forwarding hop.

Advanced strategies could use a model describing the communication conditions within the requester ITS-S's environment. An approach to generate such a model, which is among other inputs based on digital maps, is described in [15]. However, real time maintenance of such models is still a challenge due to high computational requirements.

Clearly, this approach does not guarantee to answer the request in minimal possible time. Time to delivery of the AAC ($t_{delivery}$) is determined by both CAM generation intervals at requester ($\Delta t_{CAM,requester}$) and responder ($\Delta t_{CAM,responder}$) due to the used piggybacking strategy for AAC distribution.

$$t_{delivery} \leq \Delta t_{CAM,requester} + \Delta t_{CAM,responder}$$

Thus, it can take up to two seconds until the AAC request gets answered. Due to high mobility of ITS-Ss in VANETs, it is quite likely that the responder is no longer the closest possible responder when it transmits the AAC to the requester. Therefore, this method has to be regarded as sub-optimal. However, it provides the benefit of simplicity. In order to reduce the chance of a long time span until AAC delivery, the following strategy uses the next expected sending time as the main criteria to select the responder.

Sending Time Based Selection. An AAC requester can try to minimize the time span Δt until the requested AAC is delivered. In systems using fixed message sending intervals, e.g., WAVE, the receiver can directly calculate the next sending time of all stations from whom he received messages based on the contained sending time stamps (within the security envelope). However, for CAMs in ETSI ITS message generation rate varies [7].

The CAM generation interval of an ITS-S is determined from vehicle dynamics, e.g., speed or turn rate, which are contained in CAMs. Moreover, the current generation interval is part of every CAM. Assuming that vehicle dynamics are quite constant in the short time span between emission of two CAMs, a receiver can determine a hypothesis about the next CAM sending time.

Position and Time Based Selection. Advanced strategies could combine position and time information to improve AAC distribution in comparison to simple strategies like the ones proposed before.

An approach could use trajectory prediction to obtain an hypothesis about the future position of a possible responder at the point in time it is to send its next message. Afterwards, the position-based selection algorithms proposed in Sect. 4.2 can be used with the position hypothesis as the input instead of the last received position. However, to obtain the parameters of the trajectory model, the requester has to analyze message content which could not be verified in advance, e.g., the speed of other ITS-S inside the CAM content. Thus, an attacker can try to send malicious messages to the message parser.

Another approach to combine time and position information is to use a weighting function. Thereby, each possible responder i is assigned a weight r_w, which characterizes its feasibility as a responder.

$$r_w = w_1 \cdot d_i + w_2 \cdot \Delta t_i$$

The individual weighting factors w_1 and w_2 can determined offline via simulation based evaluation of different scenarios leading to AAC requests. As both criteria d_i and Δt_i should be small to ensure successful rapid AAC delivery, low values of r_w show better responder feasibility than high ones. Thus, the ITS-S with lowest assigned value of r_w should be selected.

Adaptation the weights to current communication conditions is probability hard to realize, as AAC dissemination will not occur frequently in practice.

A more detailed analysis on advanced multi criteria based responder selection is subject to future work.

Attacking Requester Selection. An attacker can try to deny an ITS-S from obtaining an AAC by sending messages to the requester, which will always make him the target of the AAC request. For example, the attacker can claim to be very close to the requester. In case simple position-based responder selection is applied, the attacker will be the target of the request with high probability. After receiving the request, the attacker simply drops it. Thus, the ITS-S does not receive the AAC it wants to know about until it selects another responder.

However, to carry out the attack, the attacker has to claim its availability as a responder in advance to the request. Thus, the attacker would need to know that a targeted ITS-S does not know about a certain AAC which it needs to know about. This is clearly an internal status of the ITS-S, which is not known to other ITS-Ss until the request has been transmitted. Hence, the feasibility of the outlined attack to be carried out in practice can be expected to be very low.

4.3   Decentralized Responder Selection

Decentralized receiver based selection of a forwarder in GeoNetworking, e.g., via contention-based forwarding (CBF), was shown to provide a more system robustness in comparison to greedy forwarding approaches [19]. In analogy to CBF we call our approach *contention-based responding (CBR)*. To request an AAC one just sends out the request, e.g., as in [8]. However, the number of responses to the request is limited by decentralized coordination among possible responders.

After reception of an AAC request, all proper receivers start a timer. The AAC is only included after a timeout has happened. In case inclusion of the AAC by another ITS-S is detected before own AAC inclusion, the timer is canceled and the AAC is not included. Appropriate selection of the required timeout values is discussed in Sect. 4.3.

This approach includes all possible responders into the responder selection process. Thus, the problem of incomplete knowledge about an ITS-S's environment, as outlined in Sect. 4.2 for the greedy approach, can be overcome.

Position and Timeout Based Responding. The initial proposals of CBF in [19,20] suggest to use position and time based selection of forwarders. As initial sender and (final) target of the AAC request are identical, the selection criteria of CBF has to be changed to obtain a suitable CBR concept.

The CBF timeout function is modified to obtain the CBR timeout function

$$t = \begin{cases} t_{CAM,i} \cdot \left(1 - \frac{d_i}{d_{max}}\right) & 0 \le d_i < d_{max} \\ \infty & \text{otherwise} \end{cases}. \tag{1}$$

Additionally, as in CBF an ITS-S, which monitors that another ITS-S answered the request, cancels its own timeout. Thus, it does not include the AAC itself.

The intended effect of Eq. 1 is illustrated in Fig. 2. Thereby, the most left vehicle has just sent out an AAC request. The time until the next message is to be sent by the individual vehicles $t_{CAM,i}$ is illustrated via the filled part of (right) cycles next to the vehicles. The left cycle illustrates the effect of applying Eq. 1 to calculate the timeout until responding with an AAC being included in the security envelope. The initial sender of the request has no such timeout.

Fig. 2. Response times for CBR and pure timeout based responding.

One can see that the right vehicle is the first one to send a message after the AAC request, but it is not going to include the AAC into this message as the timeout will happen after sending the message.

As this approach minimizes the distance between requester and responder d_i, the set of vehicles receiving the response can be assumed to be similar to the set of vehicles which received the request. Thus, the amount of unnecessary extra responses caused by the hidden station problem should be low.

However, as many vehicles share the same AAC, it is pretty likely that the AAC requester will receive more than one CAM with the same AAC being part of their corresponding certificate chains. All these messages have to be discarded, as they cannot be validated. This is called cryptographic packet loss in [18]. The strategy proposed in the next Sect. 4.3 tries to minimize such packet loss at the cost of increased probability for duplicate responses.

Pure Timeout Based Responding. A simpler variant for decentralized responder selection is given by using only a responding timeout and discarding the location information used in the above outlined approach from Sect. 4.3.

The straight forward timeout period is given by the time until the next message is sent. Like in the concept proposed in the section before, an ITS-S cancels its timer when it receives a response from another station.

This concept minimizes the time span until the request is answered. Thus, probability of cryptographic packet loss by discarding CAMs from other ITS-Ss also using the requested AAC is minimized, too.

However, as the distance between requester and responder is discarded, the set of vehicles receiving the first response can differ significantly from the set of vehicles which received the request. Thus, the probability of duplicate replies is much higher for this strategy than for the one proposed in Sect. 4.3.

Moreover, the responder could leave the communication range of the requester before sending the response. In the worst case, all other responders still receive the response. Hence, they cancel their own responses. Thus, the requester does not receive any response. To avoid this scenario, a responder can keep track of its current average communication range and check whether the position of the requester is within this range before sending the response. Otherwise, it should not send the response. This improvement can be used for the strategy from Sect. 4.2, too.

The pure timeout based concept is also illustrated in Fig. 2 (right timeout). In contrast to CBR, the most right vehicle will send the requested AAC to the requester and the vehicle in the middle will suppress its own AAC transmission.

4.4 Pseudonym Certificate Buffering

An ITS-S whose AAC was requested has to include its certificate chain, containing AAC and current PSC, in the security envelope of its next message [8]. However, a request for an AAC can only happen in case the sender had already received the station's PSC using the requested AAC before (see also Fig. 1).

In order to remove the need for a transmission of PSC_B alongside with its corresponding AAC_B, station A could store PSC_B in a buffer for later verification before requesting AAC_B. This means that station B just has to send a message (e.g., CAM) containing a single certificate shortening the message by more than 33% or about 133 bytes [8].

However, the mechanism is somehow more complicated when the scenario is extended to multiple communicating vehicles. Thereby, multiple possible senders of an AAC exist. In this case, an ITS-S receiving an AAC request for its own used AAC cannot know whether itself caused this request by a prior CAM. The request could also be caused by a CAM of another ITS-S using the same AAC. Thus, the receiver cannot know whether the request's sender knows about its PSC. This can be changed by also applying the greedy requester selection algorithm from Sect. 4.2 before, because this request scheme explicitly asks for AAC delivery from an ITS-S whose PSC is already known.

The combination of these two mechanisms is especially powerful. It enables to remove sending of certificate chains (containing PSC and AAC in a single message) completely from current standards. ITS-Ss only have to send either their PSC or their used AAC in the security envelope of CAMs, while there is no longer the requirement to send both of them at once. Thus, the worst case length of the security envelope can be reduced significantly by the size of a full certificate. The overall size of a message handed over the access layer is typically limited, e.g., in ETSI ITS to about 650 bytes [1]. Hence, a shortened worst case size of the security envelope leaves more message length to higher level protocols.

In contrast, in the CBR algorithm the AAC sender cannot know whether he caused the AAC request. Thus, combination of this approach is not possible with PSC buffering as it is outlined above. Therefore, the emission of a certificate chain, which contains PSC as well as AAC, is required for CBR for the responder to the request. Hence, CBR cannot limit the worst case size of a CAM security envelope as greedy responding together with PSC buffering can do.

Thus, there is a trade off between greedy responding and CBR. Thereby, CBR can be expected to provide the AAC with higher probability to the requester, as it can be assumed to be less susceptible to packet loss than its counterpart. However, greedy responding together with PSC buffering will yield less channel usage and a system design advantage. Hence, in detail evaluation of both strategies is required to show which one provides better VANET system performance.

To limit the need for storage space for unauthorized certificates, one can remove them from the buffer after a timeout somewhat larger then the maximum sending interval of CAMs distributing AACs. Moreover, the buffer can be maintained in a FIFO manner to limit its size to a well defined maximum. This kind of strategy is also proposed in [10] for PSCs and has been shown to perform well.

5   Evaluation

To evaluate the impact of different AAC distribution mechanisms a simulation environment is used. Its details as well as the used traffic patterns are described in Sect. 5.1. Afterwards, the obtained results are discussed in Sect. 5.2.

5.1   Simulation Environment

The used simulation environment uses a combination of two dedicated simulators, which are SUMO for microscopic traffic simulation [9] and ns-3 for wireless network simulation [28]. Within ns-3 the ezCar2X framework is used to provide standard compatible ETSI ITS protocol functionality. An in detail description of the simulator can be found in [29].

Simulations use the so called core zone concept [4, 24]. Thereby, a considered traffic area is a subset of the full simulated road network to avoid edge effects.

The used traffic scenario for all simulation is the well known freeway model. Thereby, three lanes are used for each direction, i.e., there are six lanes in total. Parametrization of traffic shape is done as suggested in [4]. Due to quite high vehicle speed, all ITS-Ss use 10 Hz CAM generation rate [7].

Channel simulation uses a two ray ground model with parameters from the freeway channel model derived by real measurements in [17].

5.2 Evaluation Results

Evaluation results were obtained by using the framework from Sect. 5.1. The impact of the DOS attack from Sect. 3.2 is discussed first. Secondly, the impact on system performance without presence of an attacker is described.

DOS Attack. The amount of requested AACs per CAM of the attacker is limited by the maximum length of the certificate request vector in the security envelope, as mentioned in Sect. 3.2. Currently, the maximum length is six elements [8]. Thus, in order to calculate the average amount of targetable vehicles in Germany we determine the market share of the six highest volume OEMs. This is done by using statistical data available from reference [25].

Thereby, we find that the accumulated market share of highest volume OEMs (VW, Mercedes, Audi, BMW, Opel, Ford) is 61.06%. Thus, on average an attacker can assume to successfully cause 61.06% of all vehicles within his communication range to significantly increase their channel usage.

The attack increases the average message size of CAMs by a factor of i over the ordinary CAM size (without presence of an attacker). Regarding cyclic inclusion of PSCs into CAMs an upper bound on the achievable increase can be calculated by

$$i \leq \frac{s_{CAM,PSC+AAC}}{\overline{s}_{CAM}}. \tag{2}$$

Thereby, the size of a CAM with certificate chain is given by $s_{CAM,PSC+AAC}$ (=404 bytes) and the one of an average CAM by $\overline{s}_{CAM}$.

An upper bound on i can be obtained as follows. $\overline{s}_{CAM}$ is 108.5 bytes for 10 Hz CAM emission frequency and minimal 1 Hz PSC inclusion frequency. Thus, $i = 3.72$ is the upper bound on achievable increase in average message size. The bound is to be matched in case no implicit or explicit PSC requests happen in the VANET, which makes PSC inclusion happen more frequently. This increases average CAM size $\overline{s}_{CAM}$. Hence, i is smaller than the given bound. To obtain the given values corresponding standards [7,8] have been used.

The amount of PSC requests greatly depends on the traffic scenario, as such requests happen when the surrounding of ITS-Ss change. Thus, the achievable value of i depends on the traffic scenario, too.

The increase in average CAM size can be expected to increase the channel load. Clearly, the channel load cannot supersede its maximum determined by the maximum channel capacity. Thus, in case of an already high channel load the attack will cause the channel to saturate leading to significant system performance degradation. Thereby, mainly two effects can be seen, which are

1. reduced CAM generation rate on the facility layer enforced by decentralized congestion control (DCC), and
2. forced reduction of message emission frequency by denied channel access due to the used CSMA-CA mode on the access layer.

Both mechanisms reduce cooperative awareness among ITS-S by reduced update frequency of information about other ITS-Ss within their surrounding. Thus, data quality available for ADAS will decrease.

To simulate the attacker, we position an RSU in the center of our simulated area. It always sends out messages without PSC containing six AAC requests for the most commonly used AACs of ITS-S within its surrounding. Moreover, the attacker ignores DCC rules to send out his requests frequently even in case of already high channel load.

Table 1 gives achievable sizes of i within communication distance of the attacker. The vehicle interval for the displayed measurement results is three vehicles per second. This yields $\overline{s}_{CAM} = 134.3$ bytes, due to an average of 3.064 PSC emissions per second. Additionally, for the first experiment all ITS-S were equipped with only six different AACs (column "worst"). For the second case, AACs were distributed according to OEM sales figures from [25]. The attacker always requests the six most common AACs at once.

The average communication distance in the used traffic scenario is about 300 m. Thus, the increase in message size caused by the attack works for ITS-Ss at a distance of up to 300 m form the attacker's position. Moreover, results from Table 1 show that practically achievable increases are lower than their corresponding bounds. This is caused by the fact that, in the reference scenario without an attacker already a significant amount of PSC inclusions take place.

Channel busy ratio (CHBR) is an important metric for channel load. Measured values for CHBR in dependence on the distance from the attacker are given in Figs. 3(a) and (b). Two displayed scenarios use the worst case in which all receivers include their certificate chain in their next transmitted CAM. Additionally, the corresponding scenarios, in which all ITS-Ss using the six most common AACs respond, are given. Vehicle density is varied by using two different intervals between vehicle insertion into the simulation (9 s and 2 s).

As a reference scenario, the pure attack on PSC distribution from [10], which is always part of the attack on AAC distribution as outlined in Sect. 3.2, is given in Figs. 3(a) and (b). It serves as a lower bound for the channel busy ratio increase. CHBR without an attacker is constant and equal to the one given for a distance of 650 m in Fig. 3(a) (or 950 m in Fig. 3(b)) to the attacker.

One can see from Fig. 3(a) that the increase in channel load drops to zero at about 600 m (=2·300 m) distance to the attacker, i.e., double of the attacker's communication distance. The channel busy ratios for the DOS attack are higher than the ones for peak channel busy ratios on case of normal AAC requests (see Fig. 4), due to the extra PSC distribution attack.

Comparison of Figs. 3(a) and (b) shows that the area of impact of the indirect attack is significantly larger than the one of the direct attack. Channel load is constantly very high within the communication radius of the attacker, as all ITS-Ss within this area are equally affected by the attack. The decrease in CHBR starts at about 300 m distance from the attacker (ends at about 900 m (=3·300 m)) and from this on is similar to the decrease experienced in the direct attack scenario in the area of 0 to 600 m distance from the attacker.

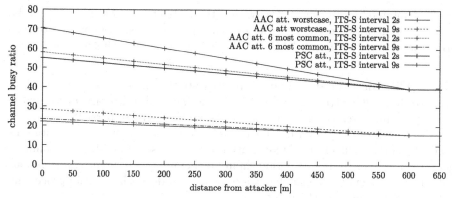

(a) CHBR in dependence of distance from an attacker using the direct DOS attack.

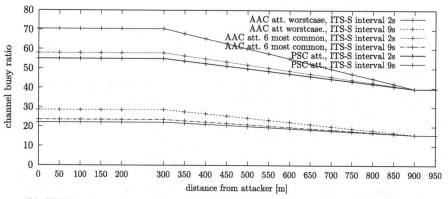

(b) CHBR in dependence of distance from an attacker using the indirect DOS attack.

Fig. 3. CHBRs in dependence of distance from an attacker.

From comparison of the results from Table 1 and Fig. 3(a), one can see that the channel load does not increase as much as the messages size does. This is due to saturation effects of the wireless channel, caused by the used CSMA-CA mechanism. Thus, ITS-Ss are (temporarily) denied from accessing the channel while the attack is present. Hence, the attacker can reduce frequency of message exchange and thereby decrease data quality (e.g., lower update rate) available for VANET applications.

Evaluation of countermeasures (AAC distribution according to Sect. 4) shows that they can all efficiently avoid both DOS attacks. For all strategies, the increase in average message size and channel load is hardly noticeable even in case of frequently repeated AAC requests. The maximum observed amount of responders for CBR was just two. For the other AAC delivery schemes only one node sent its AAC as expected. Thus, the massive amount of certificate chain emissions happening for the standardized approach can clearly be avoided by the proposed schemes.

The obtained results show clearly, that the DOS attack from Sect. 3.2 can be carried out and severely affects the usability of VANETs. Moreover, proposed strategies for more efficient AAC distribution can overcome this weakness.

Normal Traffic Scenario. In order to evaluate the impact on channel load we use two different metrics. The first one is the increase in average message size (see Eq. 2) and the second one is the time span the increase persists.

The length of the period in which AAC responses from other ITS-S are sent depends on their current CAM generation rate. In case all ITS-S use a common generation rate of 10 Hz, the period should be about 100 ms. Some transmissions will probably occur with a small extra delay, due to delays in internal processing within ITS-Ss and from channel access.

Four different cases have been studied in detail for AAC requests in respect to channel load. Thereby, the requester requests

1. one AAC and all other ITS-Ss answer the request (worst case),
2. the maximum of six different AACs being answered on average by 61.06% of receivers,
3. one AAC which is equal to the most common on and thus the request is answered on average by 21.31% of receiving ITS-Ss, and
4. one randomly picked AAC, which is answered on average by 8.6% of receiving ITS-Ss (most right column in Table 1).

Thereby, the numbers were obtained from figures in [25].

Table 1 gives theoretical bounds as well as simulation results for both values at the location of the ITS-S sending the AAC request. The requesting ITS-S is inserted as an RSU into the simulation at its center after the remaining traffic flow has been already build up. Unfortunately, no reference scenarios have been suggested in prior work to simulate AAC requests.

Table 1. Message size increase after AAC request.

	Worst	6 AACs	1 AAC (most popular)	1 ACC (average)
Bound	3.72	2.66	1.58	1.23
Measured	3.01	2.23	1.43	1.17

Single AAC requests can be expected to be the most common case in practice. For them, values in Table 1 show that average message size increase is significant.

The average channel load, during the time responders send their certificate chains, is given in Fig. 4. As can be expected, Fig. 4 shows that the channel busy ratio increases alongside with increasing traffic density (i.e., decreasing vehicle interval). Additionally, an increase in the number of responders clearly increases the channel busy ratio. This shows that one can limit the channel busy ratio

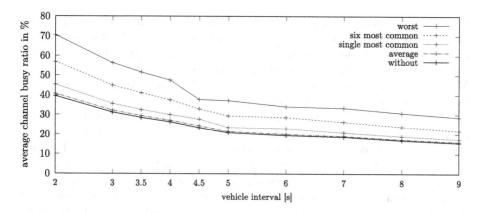

Fig. 4. Channel busy ratios after an AAC request at the position of the requester.

increase after an AAC request by limiting the number of responders, as done by the methods discussed in Sects. 4.2 and 4.3.

The amount of channel busy ratio increase decreases with higher distances to the vehicle which sends the AAC request. Thereby, the distribution is like given in Fig. 3(a). However, the increase last only for limited time, in contrast to the DOS scenario in Sect. 5.2 for which the increase is permanent.

Response times of the different efficient response mechanisms from Sects. 4.2 and 4.3 are given in Fig. 5. Moreover, performance of the standardized approach from [8] is illustrated. Both purely time based schemes limit responder selection to ITS-Ss within 300 m distance to the requester.

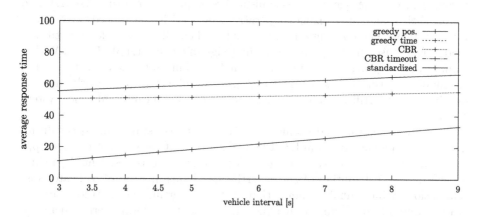

Fig. 5. Response times for AAC requests targeting the most common single AAC.

The time based response mechanisms outperform their position based counterparts, as one can see from Fig. 5. Furthermore, both schemes reach performance of the standardized approach. Moreover, the purely position based greedy responding schemes performs worst. The CBR scheme using time and position information cannot reach the performance of purely time based schemes. In detail analysis shows that many responses are delayed by the location dependent time-out leading to a significant delay of an actually carried out AAC transmission. Moreover, CAMs of ITS-Ss which skipped sending the AAC are discarded by the requester, as they cannot be verified due to the missing AAC.

In contrast to the position-based routing problem, no serious drawback of the requester based selection scheme in comparison to responder based selection was obtained. This is caused by the contrasting goals of cooperation between routing and AAC distribution. For AAC distribution the target of the caused reaction from the addressed responder(s) is the sender itself. In contrast, for packet forwarding the target is a distant node out of direct communication range of the sender. Moreover, forwarding can trigger message sending on its own, while AAC dissemination relies on piggybacking to higher level messages, e.g., CAMs.

Additionally, the time based response mechanisms yield minimal cryptographic packet loss. In the ideal case, no other ITS-S using the same AAC unknown to the requester transmits before the one distributing the AAC. Thus, the requester does not have to disregard further messages due to missing AACs.

Our evaluation shows that both proposed response time based AAC distribution schemes perform well. However, only the requester based selection scheme allows to avoid the transmission of certificate chains in one message completely. As this property can be very beneficial for the design of VANET protocols, the scheme from Sect. 4.2 should be used for AAC distribution in future VANETs.

6   Conclusions and Future Work

Strong and efficient security mechanisms are required for future VANETs, to enable their usage for realizing cooperative safety critical advanced driver assistance systems. Thereby, digital signatures together with a multi-level certificate hierarchy are used in the security system design of current ETSI ITS and WAVE standards. Our provided analysis shows that in addition to the dissemination of pseudonym certificates, which is a well studied subject in prior work, also the distribution of certificate authority certificates can significantly influence system performance.

The given analysis and evaluation of the currently standardized certificate dissemination algorithm from ETSI ITS [8] shows that the straight forward approach taken so far can lead to significant performance issues. This is mainly caused by the distribution of entire certificate chains, instead of dedicated dissemination of individual authorization authority certificates (AACs). Furthermore, the standardized approach allows an attacker to perform a serious denial of service (DOS) attack on VANETs. Thereby, the impact range massively exceeds the transmission distance of the attacker. Multiple proposals for minimizing the number of required AAC emissions are discussed.

In general, the frequency of AAC requests can be greatly limited by long term buffering of received AACs. Thereby, repeated distribution can be avoided altogether. Furthermore, requester or responder based responder selection schemes for AAC dissemination can limit the number of AAC emissions following an AAC request. Thereby, the identified DOS attack vulnerability can be avoided by design. Moreover, buffering of PSCs leading to an AAC request together with greedy responding completely removes the requirement for distribution of certificate chains. This design improvement allows to reduce the worst case size of the security envelope, and hence the security overhead, by more then a third.

Therefore, the proposed greedy response scheme, based on predicted message sending time of possible responders, is regarded as a promising approach for future usage in VANETs.

Future work can look at the influence of different traffic conditions on the performance of the suggested AAC dissemination algorithm. Thereby, the impact of variable rate CAM emission on prediction of response times from possible responders at a requester can be studied in low and medium velocity traffic scenarios.

References

1. Intelligent Transport Systems (ITS); Decentralized Congestion Control Mechanisms for Intelligent Transport Systems operating in the 5 GHz range; Access layer Part, V1.1.1, July 2011
2. Memorandum of Understanding for OEMs within the CAR 2 CAR Communication Consortium on Deployment Strategy for cooperative ITS in Europe, V4.0102, June 2011
3. Intelligent Transport Systems (ITS); Security; ITS communications security architecture and security management, V1.1.1 (2012)
4. Intelligent Transport Systems (ITS); STDMA recommended parameters and settings for cooperative ITS; Access Layer Part, V1.1.1 (2012)
5. IEEE Standard for Wireless Access in Vehicular Environments - Security Services for Applications and Management Messages, P1609.2-2013, April 2013
6. Intelligent Transport Systems (ITS); Security; Security header and certificate formats, V1.1.1, April 2013
7. Intelligent Transport Systems (ITS); Vehicular Communications; Basic Set of Applications; Part 2: Specification of Cooperative Awareness Basic Service, V1.3.2, November 2014
8. Intelligent Transport Systems (ITS); Security; Security header and certificate formats, V1.2.1, June 2015
9. Behrisch, M., Bieker, L., Erdmann, J., Krajzewicz, D.: SUMO - simulation of urban mobility: an overview. In: The Third International Conference on Advances in System Simulation, pp. 63–68, October 2011
10. Bittl, S., Aydinli, B., Roscher, K.: Effective certificate distribution in ETSI ITS VANETs using implicit and explicit requests. In: Kassab, M., Berbineau, M., Vinel, A., Jonsson, M., Garcia, F., Soler, J. (eds.) Nets4Cars/Nets4Trains/Nets4Aircraft 2015. LNCS, vol. 9066, pp. 72–83. Springer, Cham (2015). doi:10.1007/978-3-319-17765-6_7
11. Bittl, S., Gonzalez, A.A., Spähn, M., Heidrich, W.: Performance comparison of data serialization schemes for ETSI ITS car-to-X communication systems. Int. J. Adv. Telecommun. 8, 48–58 (2015)

12. Bittl, S., Roscher, K.: Efficient authorization authority certificate distribution in VANETs. In: 2nd International Conference on Information Systems Security and Privacy, pp. 85–96, February 2016
13. Bittl, S., Roscher, K., Gonzalez, A.A.: Security overhead and its impact in VANETs. In: 8th IFIP Wireless Mobile Networking Conference, pp. 192–199, October 2015
14. Blum, B., He, T., Son, S.: IGF: a state-free robust communication protocol for wireless sensor networks. Technical report CS-2003-11. Department of Computer Science, University of Virginia (2003)
15. Boban, M.: Realistic and efficient channel modeling for vehicular networks. Ph.D. thesis. Department of Electrical and Computer Engineering, Carnegie Mellon University, December 2012
16. Campolo, C., Molinaro, A., Scopigno, R. (eds.): Vehicular Ad Hoc Networks - Standards, Solutions, and Research. Springer, Heidelberg (2015)
17. Cheng, L., Henty, B.E., Stancil, D.D., Bai, F., Mudalige, P.: Mobile vehicle-to-vehicle narrow-band channel measurement and characterization of the 5.9 GHz dedicated short range communication (DSRC) frquency band. IEEE J. Sel. Areas Commun. $25(8)$, 1501–1516 (2007)
18. Feiri, M., Petit, J., Kargl, F.: Evaluation of congestion-based certificate omission in VANETs. In: IEEE Vehicular Networking Conference, pp. 101–108, November 2012
19. Füßler, H., Hartenstein, H., Martin, M., Effelsberg, W., Widmer, J.: Contention-based forwarding for street scenarios. In: 1st International Workshop in Intelligent Transportation, pp. 155–160, March 2004
20. Füßler, H., Widmer, J., Käsemann, M., Mauve, M., Hartenstein, H.: Contention-based forwarding for mobile ad hoc networks. Elsevier's Ad Hoc Netw. $1(4)$, 351–369 (2003)
21. Harding, J., Powell, G.R., Yoon, R.F., J., Doyle, C., Sade, D., Lukuc, M., Simons, J., Wang, J.: Vehicle-to-vehicle communications: readiness of V2V technology for application. Technical report DOT HS 812 014, National Highway Traffic Safety Administration, Washington, DC, August 2014
22. Heissenbüttel, M., Braun, T., Bernoulli, T., Wälchli, M.: BLR: beacon-less routing algorithm for mobile ad-hoc networks. Elsevier's Comput. Commun. J. (Special Issue) $27(11)$, 1076–1086 (2004)
23. Kargl, F., Schoch, E., Wiedersheim, B., Leinmüller, T.: Secure and efficient beaconing for vehicular networks. In: Fifth ACM International Workshop on Vehicular Inter-NETworking, pp. 82–83 (2008)
24. Kloiber, B., Strang, T., de Ponte-Mueller, F., Rico Garcia, C., Roeckl, M.: An approach for performance analysis of ETSI ITS-G5A MAC for safety applications. In: The 10th International Conference on Intelligent Transport Systems Telecommunications, November 2010
25. Kraftfahrt-Bundesamt: Neuzulassungen von Personenkraftwagen im August 2014 nach Marken und Modellreihen (2014). http://www.kba.de/DE/Statistik/Fahrzeuge/Neuzulassungen/MonatlicheNeuzulassungen/monatl_neuzulassungen_node.html
26. Masdari, M., Barbin, J.P.: Distributed certificate management in mobile ad hoc networks. Int. J. Appl. Inf. Syst. $1(1)$, 33–40 (2012)
27. Morogan, M.S., Muftic, S.: Certificate management in ad hoc networks. In: Symposium on Applications and the Internet Workshops, pp. 337–341, January 2003

28. Riley, G.F., Henderson, T.R.: The ns-3 network simulator. In: Wehrle, K., Günes, M., Gross, J. (eds.) Modeling and Tools for Network Simulation, pp. 15–34. Springer, Berlin Heidelberg (2010)
29. Roscher, K., Bittl, S., Gonzalez, A.A., Myrtus, M., Jiru, J.: ezCar2X: rapid-prototyping of communication technologies and cooperative its applications on real targets and inside simulation environments. In: 11th Conference Wireless Communication and Information, pp. 51–62, October 2014
30. Sen, J., Chandra, M.G., Balamuradlidhar, P., Harihara, S.G.: A scheme of certificate authority for ad hoc networks. In: 18th International Workshop on Database and Expert Systems Applications, pp. 615–619, September 2007
31. Sommer, C., Dressler, F.: Vehiclular Networking. Cambridge University Press, Cambridge (2015)
32. Task Force PKI, WG Security C2C-CC: C2C-CC PKI Memo. Technical report 1.7, Car2Car Communication Consortium, May 2012

A Snow-Ball Algorithm for Automating Privacy Policy Configuration in Social Media

Ammar Abuelgasim[1]([✉]) and Anne V.D.M. Kayem[2]

[1] Department of Computer Science, University of Cape Town,
Rondebosch 7701, Cape Town, South Africa
aabuelgasim@cs.uct.ac.za
[2] Internet Technologies and Systems, Hasso-Plattner Institute,
Prof.-Dr.-Helmert-Str. 2-3, Potsdam 14482, Germany
anne@mykayem.org
https://www.cs.uct.ac.za

Abstract. Recommender systems offer an effective method of alleviating privacy policy usability issues on Social Media Platforms. However, matching usability with privacy preservation is a challenging problem. In this paper, we first present a comparative analysis to demonstrate that supporting recommender systems with the Random Forest Algorithm (RFA) instead of the J48 decision tree algorithm results in an extra improvement of 5.7% in classification accuracy and that when feature vectors are extended, added classification accuracies of 15%–25% on average are achieved. This improvement comes at the cost of performance, from the usability perspective, due to the high requirement of manual user input. We address this issue with a "Snow-Ball" algorithm that reduces the user input requirement by 81.8%–87.5% and works by employing privacy policy correlation graphs. Our results indicate that the accuracy levels are similar to those of the RFA with manual user input.

Keywords: Privacy policies · Recommendation systems · Social Media

1 Introduction

Social Media Platforms (SMPs) have revolutionized the way that users interact and communicate online, by introducing new and innovative ways for self-expression, information sharing, and relationship formation. Popular SMPs nowadays attract a large number of users as attested by Facebook which has 1.49 billion monthly active users, of which 968 million users access Facebook daily [5]. Likewise, Twitter has drawn over 316 million users since its creation [24].

Users of SMPs disclose large volumes of information during their daily interactions. For instance, everyday about 350 million photos are shared on Facebook [7], and 500 million tweets are sent on Twitter [24]. The majority of this information is sensitive in nature as Gross et al. [12] have pointed out.

ⓒ Springer International Publishing AG 2017
O. Camp et al. (Eds.): ICISSP 2016, CCIS 691, pp. 108–129, 2017.
DOI: 10.1007/978-3-319-54433-5_7

The ease with which such sensitive information can be accessed, and by a large number of people, exposes SMPs' users to many privacy and security risks. Examples of such privacy and security risks include identity theft, financial fraud, cyberstalking, cyberbullying, insurance and employment discrimination, embarrassment and losing face with friends [2,7,8]. As a result, in order to protect users against privacy violations, most SMPs have implemented privacy policies. Privacy policies are essentially a set of rules that enable users to control who can access their disclosed information. For example, SMPs like Google+ and Facebook have fine grained privacy policies that allow users to control access to individual profile attributes such as birthdate, and address, as well as to user-generated content such as posts, photos, and videos. However, it has been shown that numerous users fail to configure their privacy policies either due to lack of awareness of the existence of these policies, or because the policies are complex and time consuming to understand and configure correctly [15,16].

Consequently, various automated approaches have been proposed to assist users with privacy policy configuration [4,6,10,19,21,22]. These approaches are however, limited to either configuring privacy policies for profile attributes, or configuring privacy policies for user-generated content. This is problematic, because both profile attributes and user-generated content can contain sensitive information. For instance, users have been documented to have put their real cell phone numbers on their profiles, and also disclosing their physical whereabouts in status updates [9,11,13,23]. Therefore, protecting profile attributes without user-generated content (and vice-versa), is not a good privacy protection solution for SMPs. Furthermore, most of the proposed approaches require substantial manual user input, which is a time consuming process.

In order to address the aforementioned problems, Abuelgasim et al. [1] introduced an automated privacy policy recommender system. This recommender system consists of two main components namely, a Profile Attributes Protector (PAP), which is responsible for recommending privacy policies for profile attributes; and a User Content Protector (UCP) which handles recommending privacy policies for user-generated content. In this paper, we further improve upon the Abuelgasim et al. approach by first presenting a comparative analysis to demonstrate that supporting the Abuelgasim recommender system with a Random Forest Algorithm instead of the J48 decision tree algorithm result in a classification accuracy improvement of 5.7% extra on average. We note however, that when feature vectors are extended we achieve classification accuracies of 15%–25% extra on average, but observe that the system is inefficient from the usability perspective due to the high requirement of manual user input. We address this issue by introducing a "Snow-Ball" algorithm for training/testing the profile attributes' classifiers, so that classifications are handled with minimal manual user input. The "Snow-Ball" algorithm reduces the user input requirement by 81.8%–87.5% and works primarily by employing privacy policy correlation graphs. Our results demonstrate that the levels of accuracy achieved with the "Snow-Ball" algorithm are similar to what we achieve using the RFA with manual user input.

The rest of the paper is structured as follows, in Sect. 2 we provide an overview of the related work on automated privacy policy specification in SMPs. We describe the Abuelgasim et al. [1] privacy policy recommender system in Sect. 3 and briefly discuss the results of the recommender's prototype implementation in Sect. 4. Section 5 presents the extensions that we have introduced to the Abuelgasim recommender system as well as results of experiments on the system. Finally, we conclude in Sect. 6 with a summary and offer some ideas for future work.

2 Related Work

Several studies have proposed helping SMPs' users with privacy policy configuration, by automating the process of privacy policy configuration. Fang and LeFevre [6] pioneered this area with a mechanism for configuring privacy policies. Their privacy policy configuration mechanism follows an active learning approach, whereby for each profile attribute, the user is prompted to label a subset of his/her friends by stating whether or not the friends are allowed to access that profile attribute. Next, the wizard uses this subset of friends to train a classifier that predicts which of the user's remaining friends are allowed (or not allowed) to access that particular profile attribute. While this approach facilitates setting fine-grained privacy policies, users are required to provide considerable input to enable the system run efficiently. In fact, for every profile attribute (and one can have up to 27 attributes) the user is required to manually label a group of friends, in order to train the attribute's classifier. A further caveat of this solution is that it does not handle privacy policies for user-generated content, since the classifiers are trained to predict privacy policies for profile attributes only.

Shehab et al. [21] proposed a solution similar to the one of [6], in which the user is required to label a selected subset of his/her friends as trusted or not trusted to access a particular profile object. This subset is then used to train a classifier that predicts which of the remaining friends are trusted (or not trusted) to access that particular object. In contrast to [6]'s scheme, the Shehab et al. scheme introduces an interesting concept, where the resulting classifier is merged with other neighbouring users' classifiers to enhance the classifier's performance. However, the Shehab et al. scheme also requires substantial user input, because the user has to manually label a group of his/her friends for every profile object.

Ghazinour et al. [9,10] introduced a tool for recommending privacy policies called 'YourPrivacyProtector'. YourPrivacyProtector uses K-Nearest Neighbours algorithm to find the closest 3 profiles to the user's, and then it uses the privacy policies of the neighbour users to suggest to the user whether to disclose a particular profile attribute or not. This tool however only provides coarse-grained privacy policy suggestions. Furthermore, this approach cannot support privacy policies for user-generated content. Unlike profile attributes, users might generate different types of content. For instance, Bob's status updates are usually very different form Alice's status updates. Thus, it is not feasible to rely on other users content's policies for providing suggestions. Alsalibi and Zakaria [4] criticise the approach of [6], arguing that it incapable of providing recommendations for user's who do not have friends yet. Therefore, Alsalibi and Zakaria proposed a collaborative filtering privacy recommender system. In order to recommend privacy policies to a particular target user; this system first identifies a group of similar users (to the target), and then it uses the most frequently used privacy policies within this group, to make privacy policy recommendation to the target user. However, this system also fails to handle privacy policies for user-generated content for the same reason as that of Ghazinour et al.

Sinha et al. [22] were the first to identify that none of the existing approaches, caters for user-generated content. Therefore, Sinha et al. propose an automated tool to help users configure privacy policies for text-based content. Sinha et al. used the Maximum Entropy classification algorithm (MaxEnt) to predict and recommend privacy policies for text-based content. However, despite being able to protect users' text-based content, this tool does not provide any protection for the profile attributes.

Along the same lines, Sánchez and Viejo [19] proposed an automated mechanism to inform SMPs' users about the privacy risks inherent to their unstructured text-based content, to enable users to make more informed privacy policy choices. The proposed mechanism adopts an information theoretic approach, and it works by comparing the text-based content's "sensitivity" against the content owner's "privacy requirements" for all types of users in the SMP. However, this approach only warns users about potential privacy conflicts within their generated content, it does not suggest privacy policies directly to the users.

We note that existing schemes offer automated privacy policy configuration for either profile attributes or user generated content but not both. This is problematic, because as mentioned before, protecting one without the other can lead to privacy violations. Furthermore, requiring users to provide considerable content to support privacy policy configuration offers the advantage of high accuracy, but has the downside of being cumbersome to use for the average user. In the following section we discuss the details of the recommender system proposed by Abuelgasim et al. [1] for addressing these issues.

3   The Privacy Policy Recommender System

The privacy policy recommender system introduced in [1] is designed as 'server-side' solution, with the understanding that it would be maintained by the SMP provider. This privacy policy recommender system (henceforth, the recommender) consists of two independent components, that work in parallel to protect the users' sensitive information.

The first component, the Profile Attributes Protector (PAP), utilizes privacy policies that existing experienced SMP users have specified for their profile attributes, to suggest to new target users[1], how to configure privacy policies for

---

[1] In the recommender systems' literature, the user that receives the recommendations (i.e. suggestions) is usually referred to as the "target user".

their profile attributes. The second component, which is the User Content Protector (UCP), utilizes the target user's privacy policy history, to suggest suitable privacy policies for content that the target user might share in the future.

More specifically, and as can be seen in the recommender overview depicted in Fig. 1 below; the PAP component extracts certain data from the profiles of experienced users, and then it uses this extracted data to train several Decision Tree classifiers. These classifiers then output privacy policy suggestions for the target user. The UCP component works in a similar fashion, first, it extracts certain data from the target user's privacy policy history, then it (i.e. the UCP) uses this data to train a Naïve Bayes classifier, and in-turn, this classifier outputs privacy policy suggestions for user generated content.

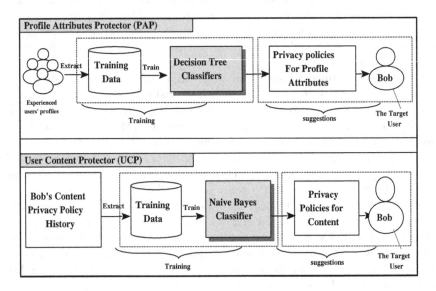

Fig. 1. An overview of the privacy policy recommender system [1].

In the following subsections, we describe both the PAP and UCP components in more detail. However, it is helpful to first construct a formal SMP notation, so that, it can be the foundation, upon which we ground our subsequent discussion.

3.1   Notation

We model an SMP as an undirected graph $G = (V, E)$, where V is the set of users represented by nodes in the graph, and E is the set of social relationships between the users, represented by edges in the graph. Every user $u \in V$ creates and maintains a profile P_u, which is a personal page (or space) that serves as a digital representation of the user. The user's profile consists of a fixed set of attributes $A_u = \{a_{u1}, a_{u2}, \ldots, a_{un}\}$ and a collection of pieces of user-generated content $C_u = \{c_{u1}, c_{u2}, \ldots, c_{uk}\}$. Profile attributes A_u describe the profile owner (i.e. the user). These profile attributes include demographic information such as: age, gender, political views/interests. User-generated content C_u is the materials created by users during SMP's interactions. Examples of user-generated content include: status updates, notes, posts, photos, and so on.

We assume that the SMP users can specify privacy policies, to control access to their profile attributes and content. A privacy policy is a user-defined rule in the form $<item, l>$, where *item* can be any profile attribute $a_j \in A_u$ or any piece of content $c_j \in C_u$, while $l \subseteq V$ represents the audience, that is, the set of users allowed to access the *item*. Users are provided with a finite set of audiences $L = \{l_1, l_2, \ldots, l_k\}$ to choose from.

Now that we have built our SMP notation; we proceed with describing the recommender's components in a more detailed way, starting with a detailed description of the PAP component in the next subsection.

3.2   Profile Attributes Protector (PAP)

The Profile Attributes Protector (PAP) is the component responsible for suggesting privacy policies for all the profile attributes in the target user's profile. However, in order to easily understand the inner-workings of the PAP; we first describe how it suggests privacy policies for individual profile attributes.

The process by which PAP suggests privacy policies for an individual profile attribute, say $a_i \in A$ consists of three main phases. The first phase is the *data collection phase*. In this phase, we collect data from the profiles of existing SMP users[2]. Particularly, from every profile, we extract the user's demographic information, and the privacy policy of the a_i attribute. Then we store the collected information in a dataset D, in which every record is of the form $(\boldsymbol{F}, l_j)$, where $\boldsymbol{F} = \langle f_1, f_2, \ldots, f_m \rangle$ are the user's demographics, representing the features, and l_j is attribute a_i's privacy policy, and it represents the class label.

The second phase is the *classifier training phase*. We train a Decision Tree classifier to predict the privacy policies of the a_i attribute. We specifically chose Decision Tree algorithms, because they are capable of handling classification of categorical, noisy, and incomplete data such as our training data D [17].

The third and final phase is the *suggestion phase*. When a target user registers on the SMP, we extract demographical information from his/her newly created profile, and pass it to attribute a_i's classifier, which in-turn predicts a privacy policy for the a_i attribute. This privacy policy is then simply suggested to the target user. In Fig. 2, we depict the process of suggesting privacy policies for individual profile attributes, that we have described above.

So far we showed how PAP suggest privacy policies for a single profile attribute, in order to suggest privacy policies for *all* the attributes in the target user's profile; we build a series of training datasets $\{D_1, D_2, \ldots, D_{|A|}\}$, one for each profile attribute $a_i \in A$. Next, we use these training datasets, to train a series of classifiers $CL = \{cl_1, cl_2, \ldots, cl_{|A|}\}$. Such that, each classifier $cl_i \in CL$

---

[2] Since the recommender is designed to be a server-side solution, we expect that it will have direct access to users' profiles' data.

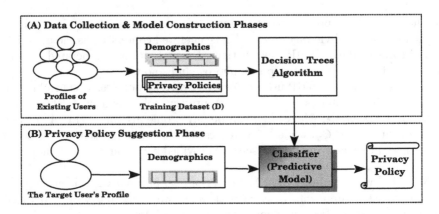

Fig. 2. The process of suggesting privacy policies for an individual attribute in the target user's profile [1].

predicts the privacy policies for an attribute $a_i \in A$, $\forall i \in \{1, 2, \ldots, |A|\}$. Finally, each time a target user registers at the SMP. We pass his/her demographics to every classifier $cl_i \in CL$, to predict (and hence suggest) the privacy policies for each attribute in the target user's profile.

3.3   User Content Protector (UCP)

The User Content Protector (UCP) handles enforcing privacy on the target user's generated content. The process by which the UCP suggests privacy policies for content generated by a particular target user, say $u_t \in V$ is as follows.

The first phase is the *data collection phase*, in this phase we collect the privacy policy history of the target user's content, and arrange it into a dataset Ω, where every record is in the form (c_i, l_j), where c_i is a piece of content generated by the target user u_t, and l_j is the privacy policy that u_t has specified for c_i.

The second phase is the *preprocessing phase*, in this phase we transform every piece of content $c_i \in \Omega$ to a vector of features that characterize c_i, thereby transforming Ω to a dataset of labelled feature vectors $\hat{\Omega}$, in which every record is in the form ($\boldsymbol{c_i}$, l_j), where, $\boldsymbol{c_i} = \langle f_{i1}, f_{i2}, \ldots, f_{im} \rangle$ is c_i's feature vector.

The third phase is *classifier training phase*. Here, we train a Naïve Bayes classifier to predict privacy policies for the target user's content. We opted to use the Naïve Bayes algorithm, because it is quick to test and train, which is a necessity when it comes to predicting privacy policies for user-generated content.

The fourth and the final phase is the *suggestion phase*, this phase is triggered when the target user u_t generates any new piece of content c_{new}. We first pre-process c_{new} to transform it into a vector of features. We then, pass this feature vector to u_t's classifier, which in-turn predicts c_{new}'s privacy policy. Then we simply suggest the predicted policy to u_t. Figure 3 below, we depict the process of suggesting privacy policies for user-generated content.

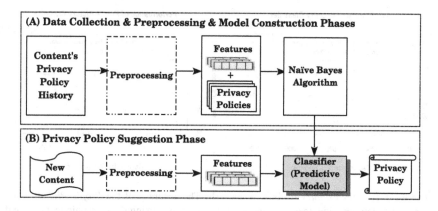

Fig. 3. Suggesting privacy policies for user-generated content [1].

Next, we briefly present an overview of the results obtained from the proof-of-concept prototype of the Abuelgasim recommender system in [1].

4   Recommender System: Prototype Implementation

In order to implement the Abuelgasim privacy policy recommender system prototype, we carried-out several experiments which were primarily focused on building the classifiers that predict privacy policies for our target users. For implementing the PAP component, we began by obtaining training data from two different sources. First, we simulated five datasets of different sizes[3]. Second, we obtained a "real" dataset from another similar study [4]. This real dataset is divided into ten datasets; such that, each one of these datasets contains a percentage of records from the real dataset.

The simulated datasets consist of 8 profile attributes, and are structured as tables of 16 columns. Such that, the first 8 columns correspond to profile attributes, and the following 8 columns correspond to the attributes' privacy policies. The real datasets on the other hand, consist of 11 profile attributes; however, we only have the actual values of three attributes; therefore, they are structured as tables of 14 columns, where, the first 3 columns corresponds to three available profile attributes, while the following 11 columns corresponds to the privacy policies of all the 11 profile attributes.

Next, we applied the J48 algorithm (i.e. implementation of the C4.5 decision tree learning algorithm) on each of our simulated and real datasets; to train a classifier for each profile attribute in these datasets. We then performed a 10-fold cross-validation test, and recorded the accuracy of each model (that is the percentage of the records for which the classifier was successful). Cross-validation results show that the classifiers trained on simulated datasets achieved a high

---

[3] For more information about the simulated datasets, and the simulation model used to generated them, please refer to [1].

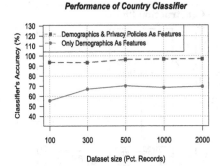

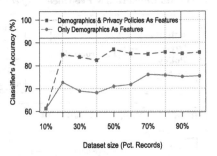

(a) The accuracy of the *Country* attribute, when trained using demographic features, and extended features.

(b) The accuracy of the *Profile Pic.* attribute, when trained using demographic features, and extended features.

Fig. 4. The performance of two selected profile attribute's classifiers when trained on both real and simulated datasets, while using demographic and extended features. The accuracy of each classifier is plotted against the size of the dataset used for training it.

accuracy percentage that ranges from 60% to 80%. While those trained on real datasets achieved accuracy ranging between 60% to 70%, which is a bit lower than the classifiers trained on the simulated datasets.

We enhance the classifiers' accuracy, by extending the features used in training these classifiers. Particularly, instead of using only demographics as features, this time we used a combination of demographics and the privacy policies of other profile attributes. We then, retrained our classifiers on the new datasets, and measured their accuracy using the aforementioned methodologies. The results showed an average of 15% to 25% improvement in the accuracy of classifiers trained on simulated datasets, and a similar average of 17% improvement in the accuracy of classifiers trained on real datasets, as illustrated in Fig. 4, which shows the accuracy of two selected profile attribute classifiers, plotted against the size of their training datasets.

Next, in order to implement the UCP component, we began by collecting the data necessary for building the UCP classifier. Particularly, we used Facebook's graph Application Programming Interface (API) to download posts (i.e. user-generated content) from one of the author's Facebook accounts and manually labelled each post with a suitable privacy policy. Then, in order to transform the data Ω, from a 'corpus' of text, to a dataset of labelled feature vectors $\hat{\Omega}$, we used 'text classification' pre-processing methods. Specifically, we normalised each content (i.e. post) $c_i \in \Omega$ by lower-casing letters and removing diacritical marks. Then, we stemmed the data using the Lovins Stemming Algorithm implemented by Weka [14]. Afterwards, we break-down our text corpus Ω into small units called terms or words. We experimented with both word and n-gram tokenization. Lastly, we vectorised Ω such that, each content $c_i \in \Omega$ is represented

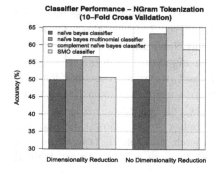
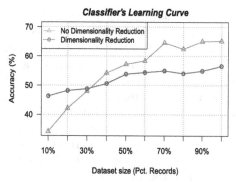

(a) The accuracy of the UCP content's classifier when the training data is preprocessed using 3-gram tokenisation and $tf\text{-}idf$ vectorisation.

(b) The learning curve of the UCP classifier (i.e. the classifier accuracy plotted against the percentage of records from $\hat{\Omega}_{TV}$ that were used to train it).

Fig. 5. The accuracy of the best-performing UCP content classifier.

as a k-dimensional vector $<c_{i1}, c_{i2}, \ldots, c_{ik}>$, where c_{ij} is a value associated with a term j in c_i. To calculate each c_i, we experimented with both the binary approach and the $tf\text{-}idf$ approach. This resulted in several pre-processed datasets $\hat{\Omega}$, such that, each combination of pre-processing steps, resulted in a different pre-processed dataset.

Before building the UCP classifier, we first divided each preprocessed dataset $\hat{\Omega}$ into: a training & validation dataset $\hat{\Omega}_{TV}$ (contains 70% of the records in $\hat{\Omega}$); and a *test* dataset $\hat{\Omega}_{Te}$ (contains the remaining 30%), as advised by [20].

Next, in order to build the UCP content classifier; we applied each of the naïve bayes, multinomial naïve bayes, complement Naïve Bayes, and SMO algorithms on each of our training & validation datasets $\hat{\Omega}_{TV}$. Afterwards, we performed a 10-fold cross-validation test to measure the accuracy of each resulting classifier.

Results showed that the highest accuracy was achieved by the classifier trained using complement Naïve Bayes; on a dataset pre-processed using a combination of normalisation, stemming, 3-gram tokenisation, stop-words removal, and $tf\text{-}idf$ vectorisation, as evident in Fig. 5a. We then further validated this classifier on our 'untouched' testing data set $\hat{\Omega}_{Te}$. The results showed that the classifier's performance was stable, achieving an accuracy around 64.2%.

Now that we have comprehensively introduced the recommender system proposed in [1] we move on to the improvements that this paper introduces to the recommender.

5   Enhancing the Profile Attributes' Classifiers Accuracy

In an effort to further enhance the accuracy of the PAP classifiers, we performed extended experiments, in which we experimented with training the PAP classifiers using all of the decision tree learning algorithms provided by Weka [14], instead of solely relying on the J48 algorithm. We namely used each of the BFTree, DecisionStump, FT, J48, J48graft, LADTree, LMT, NBTree, Random-Forest, RandomTree, REPTree, SimpleCart, and Naive Bayes algorithms.

Next, we applied each of our classification algorithm (a total of 13 algorithms), on each of our real and simulated dataset, to train a classifier for each profile attribute within these datasets. Afterwards, we performed a 10-fold cross validation test, and recorded the accuracy of each classifier.

The results can be seen in Figs. 6a and b below, which show the "learning curves" of two "selected" attribute classifiers; such that, one is trained on real datasets, and the other is trained on simulated datasets, while both are trained using each of the 13 algorithms.

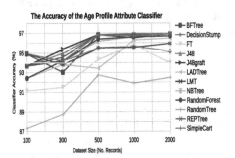
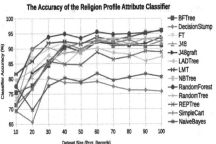

(a) The accuracy of the *Age* classifier as its being trained on different *real* dataset, using different decision tree algorithms.

(b) The accuracy of the *Religion* classifier as its being trained on different *simulated* dataset, using different decision tree algos.

Fig. 6. The performance of a "selected" profile attribute classifiers, when trained on different real/simulated datasets of different sizes, while using a wide range of decision tree learning algorithms.

As can be seen in Figs. 6a and b above, there is hardly a unanimous agreement on which classification algorithm is the best performing algorithm, as different classification algorithms have different performances on different profile attributes and training datasets. Therefore, in order to get a clearer picture of which algorithms are superior; we took the average accuracy of each algorithm across all training datasets, and then averaged it across all profile attributes. Then we plotted each algorithm against its average of average accuracies, as can be show in Fig. 7 below.

As can be seen in Fig. 7a below, for simulated datasets, the best performing algorithms are the BFTree, J48, J48graft, LMT, RandomForest, REPTree, and SimpleCart algorithms, with a slight advance for the J48 algorithm. On the other hand and as illustrated in Fig. 7b, for real datasets, the best performing algorithms are the BFTree, J48, J48graft, LMT, and Random Forest algorithms, with a clear dominance for the Random Forest algorithm, with an average of 5.7% performance increase over the J48 algorithm.

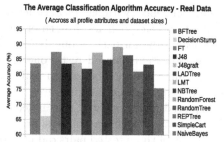

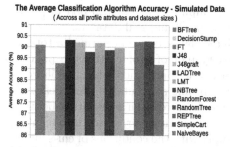

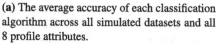

(a) The average accuracy of each classification algorithm across all simulated datasets and all 8 profile attributes.

(b) The average accuracy of each classification algorithm across all real datasets and all 11 profile attributes.

Fig. 7. The average accuracy of each classification algorithms under experiment, across all datasets and profile attributes.

Based on the above, we opted to use the Random Forest algorithm as the main classification algorithm for training the PAP attribute classifiers. This is not only because the Random Forest Algorithm performed well on both real and simulated datasets; but also because the Random Forest Algorithm is the best performing algorithm on real datasets, which we think are a better representation of reality than the simulated datasets.

5.1   Attribute Privacy Policy Relationships

Abuelgasim et al. [1] noted that, extending the feature vector used to train the profile attribute classifiers, by incorporating the privacy policies of other profile attribute can dramatically enhance the accuracy of these classifiers. For Instance, training the *Age* classifier on a features vector consisting of users demographics and privacy policies of other attributes like gender, language, and so on; results in a classifier with higher accuracy, than simply training the *Age* classifier on a features vector consisting of demographics only.

In reality however, this is inefficient, because in order for target users to get privacy policy recommendations for one profile attribute, say $a_i \in A$; the target users must input (i.e. provide) the privacy policies of all the remaining profile attributes $\in \{A - \{a_i\}\}$, to a_i's classifier. This input constitutes a considerable overhead, and is almost equivalent to configuring privacy policies manually. Understanding the positive effect of extending feature vectors, on the accuracy of the profile attributes' classifiers; is key to improving the PAP component. Therefore, in the following sub-section, we investigate exactly this phenomenon.

The intuitive justification of the performance increase that the profile attribute classifiers experience, when we use a combination of demographic and privacy policies as features; would be the existence of some form of correlation or association between the privacy policies of different profile attributes. Therefore, in order to test this hypothesis; we performed a Pearson's chi-squared test of independence, with significance level (i.e. alpha) 0.01, on each pair of profile attribute privacy policies in both of our simulated and real datasets.

Specifically, for each of our five simulated datasets, we performed a total of 28 Pearson's chi-squared tests, one for every pair of profile attribute policies. Furthermore, for each of our ten real datasets, we performed a total of 55 Pearson's chi-squared test, one for every pair of profile attribute policies. Pearson's chi-squared results showed that indeed there is correlation/association between the majority of profile attributes' privacy policies. However, it worth to mention that some of these tested pairs did not comply with the conditions of chi-squared test, Therefore, we should approach these results with caution. Next, since test results support the hypothesis of the existence of correlation/association between our profile attributes' privacy policies we proceeded with quantifying this correlation/association.

In order to measure and quantify the correlation/association between the profile attributes' privacy policies; we used Cramér's V measure on each pair of profile attribute policies, in a similar way to what we did with chi-squared. Cramér's V is a measure of association between two categorical variables [3]. Cramér's V is based on Pearson's chi-square statistic, and it (i.e. Cramér's V) given by Eq. 1 below.

$$V = \sqrt{\frac{\chi^2}{N * (min(k - 1, r - 1))}} \tag{1}$$

where χ^2 is chi-squared statistic, N is the grand total of observations, k and r are the number of columns and rows respectively, such that, $V \in [0, 1]$.

We calculated Cramér's V for each pair of profile attribute privacy policies in all our real and simulated datasets. Such that, for each dataset, every pair of profile attribute policies, has a numeric value in [0, 1] quantifying the correlation/association between them.

As can be seen in Fig. 8 below —which shows the correlation between privacy policies of different attribute— there are many strong correlations between

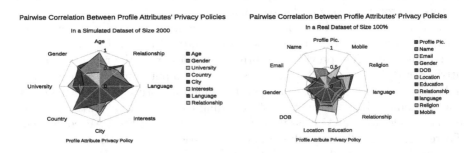

(a) The correlation between attributes' privacy policies in a real dataset.

(b) The correlation between attributes' privacy policies in asimulated dataset.

Fig. 8. The correlation between profile attributes' privacy policies in two "selected" real and simulated datasets.

profile attributes' privacy policies. For instance, Fig. 8a we can see a strong correlation between the privacy policies of each of the (age, country), (gender, language), and (city, relationship) profile attributes. Similarly, Fig. 8b shows a strong association between the privacy policies of each of the (Location, Education), (Email, Mobile), and (Religion, Education) attributes. In addition to some medium associations between the privacy policies of each of the (Profile Pic., Gender), (DoB, Relationship), and (Name, Gender) attributes.

However, in general, the observations show that the associations/correlations between profile attributes' privacy policies in real datasets are a bit lower than those in their simulated counterparts.

5.2   Privacy Policy Correlations

In the previous sections, we showed that extending feature vectors by adding privacy policies of other attributes, does indeed yield high accuracy; but we also showed that it is inefficient in terms of massive increase in user input associated with extending feature vectors.

This highlights the pressing need for an efficient method for incorporating privacy policies in the feature vectors. Such that, we still get high accuracy, and at the same time, the target users would have to input only a few privacy policies, as opposed to inputting the privacy policies of all other attributes. The remainder of this section paves the way for introducing such a method.

In the current architecture of the recommender, we have a total n profile attributes $A = \{a_1, a_2, \ldots, a_n\}$, and n classifiers $CL = \{cl_1, cl_2, \ldots, cl_n\}$. Each classifier $cl_i \in CL$ takes this feature vector $F = \langle F_*, L_* \rangle$ as an input, and predicts the privacy policies of attribute $a_i \in A$ as an output. Such that, $F_* = \{f_1, f_2, \ldots, f_m\}$ are the demographics, and $L_* = \{l_1, l_2, \ldots, l_{n-1}\}$ are the privacy policies of attributes $\in \{A - \{a_i\}\}$.

However, we also know from our recent experiments, that many correlations exist amongst the privacy policies of profile attributes (denoted as L). This means that, for many $(a_k, a_j) \in A$, knowing the privacy policy of attribute a_k (i.e. l_k), can help us predict the privacy policy of attribute a_j (i.e. l_j) and vice-versa. Therefore, we could devise a method for utilizing these correlations/associations to incorporate privacy policies $L*$ in the feature vectors F in a more realistic and efficient way, that maximizes accuracy, and minimizes user input.

In order to get a clearer idea about our proposed method, lets create the Correlation Graph (CG), which is an undirected weighted graph $G = (V, E, W, \alpha)$, where V represents profile attributes, E represents correlations between profile attributes' privacy policies, W represents the strength of the correlation in E as measured by the Cramer's V measure, and finally, α is a numeric value $\in [0, 1]$. An edge $e = (a_i, a_j) \in E$ exists between attributes a_i, $a_j \in V$ if and only if the correlation between their privacy policies is greater than α. Figure 9 below, shows such a graph. It shows a real correlation graph of two simulated and real datasets of size 100 and 2000 respectively.

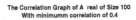

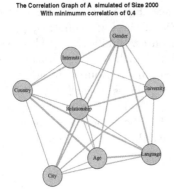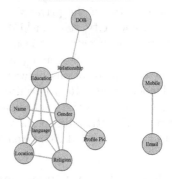

(a) The correlation graph of a simulated dataset of size 2000, with $\alpha = 0.4$.   (b) The correlation graph of a real of size 100, with $\alpha = 0.4$.

Fig. 9. The correlation graph of two datasets, one real and one simulated (the edges weights are proportionate to their thickness).

For the next step, we compute the Correlation Maximum Spanning Tree (CMSP) within the CG[4]. We chose maximum spanning trees, because we are looking for spanning trees that have the strongest correlations between its nodes. Figure 10, shows the CMSPs of the CGs shown in Fig. 9 above.

Unlike the CGs, the CMSTs capture the correlation/association relationships between the privacy policies of profile attributes in a clean, clear, and intuitive way. For instance, by observing Fig. 10a we can see that if we somehow knew the privacy policy of the root (i.e. *gender*); it can help us predict the privacy policy of the *city* and *language* attributes due to the correlation between them. Then, if we correctly predicted the privacy policies of the *city* and *language* attributes; we could in-turn use them to help us predict the privacy policies of the *country* and *relationship* attributes and so on. One can quickly notice the "snow-balling" pattern that develops from simply knowing the privacy policy of the root attribute of the CMST.

Our method leverages the associations within CMSTs, to add privacy policies to the feature vectors in an accumulative "snow-balling" fashion. Specifically for the classifier training phase, we begin by adding the privacy policies of the root l_r (or roots, if the CG has more than one CMST) to the feature vector F, then use F to train the classifiers of the root's children. Next, we add the privacy policies of the root's children $\{l_{r1}, l_{r2}, \ldots, l_{rh}\}$ to F and use it to train the classifiers of root's children's children and so on until we train the classifiers of all nodes in the CMST.

For the classifier testing phase, when a new target user registers, we immediately add his/her demographic information to his/her feature vec-

---

[4] This can be done by slightly changing any known algorithm for finding minimum spanning trees such as Kruskal's algorithm.

The Maximum Spanning Tree Graph of A simulated of Size 2000
With minimumm correlation of 0.4

The Maximum Spanning Tree Graph of A real of Size 100
With minimumm correlation of 0.4

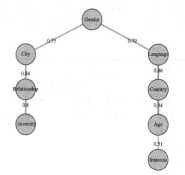

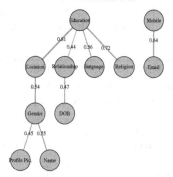

(a) The CMSP of a simulated dataset of size 2000, where $\alpha = 0.4$.

(b) The CMSP of a real of size 100, where $\alpha = 0.4$.

Fig. 10. The CMSTs of the CGs in Figs. 9a and b.

tor F_t. Next, we ask the target user to provide us with the privacy policy of the root attribute l_r, and then add it (i.e. l_r) to F_t. Afterwards, we pass F_t to the classifiers of the root's children. These classifiers will in-turn predict the privacy policies of the root's children $\{l_{r1}, l_{r2}, \ldots, l_{rh}\}$. Next, we add the privacy policies of the root's children $\{l_{r1}, l_{r2}, \ldots, l_{rh}\}$ to F_t. Then, we pass F_t to the classifiers of the root's children's children, and so on, until we get a privacy policy prediction for all attributes in the CMST. Finally, we recommend the predicted privacy policies to the target user.

This way, target users would only provide privacy policies of the root (or roots, if the CG has more than one CMST), to bootstrap a "snow-balling" process, that will provide him/her with privacy policy recommendations for all of his/her profile attributes. In the following two section, we introduce two algorithms that formally define the method that we have discussed above.

5.3   The "Snow-Ball" Algorithm

In this section, we define an algorithm for efficiently incorporating privacy policies in feature vectors, during the classifier training phase. The algorithm leverages on the correlations between profile attributes in order to train profile attribute classifiers in an accumulative "snow-balling" fashion. The algorithm, which we term, the "Snow-Ball" training algorithm is shown in Algorithm 1 below.

Lines 1–5 in Algorithm 1 above, initialize the variables that are going to be used throughout the algorithm. Specifically, line 1, loads the raw data (i.e. *Data*), which is a table who's rows are users, and columns are the profile attributes (i.e. demographic information) and privacy policies of these attributes. Line 2, initializes the training data T by including demographic information form $Data$. Line 3, defines an empty classifier set CL. Line 4, builds the CG $Cgraph$ from the raw data. Line 5, finds all the CMSTs in $Cgraph$ an puts them in $CMStrees$.

Algorithm 1. The "Snow-Ball" Training Algorithm.

1: $Data \leftarrow \text{GETRAWDATA}(\,)$ ▷ Loading the raw data
2: $T \leftarrow \text{GETPRIVACYPOLICIES}(Data)$ ▷ The initial set of traning features
3: $CL \leftarrow \emptyset$ ▷ The initial set of attribute classifiers
4: $Cgraph \leftarrow \text{BUILDCORRELATIONGRAPH}(Data)$
5: $CMStrees \leftarrow \text{GETCORRELATIONTREES}(Cgraph)$
6:
7: **for** $< \ t \in CMStrees \ >$ **do**
8:      $r_t \leftarrow \text{ROOTOF}(t)$
9:      $policy_{r_t} \leftarrow \text{PRIVACYPOLICYOF}(r_t)$
10:      $T \leftarrow T \cup \{policy_{r_t}\}$ ▷ Adding the privacy policy of the r_t attribute, to T
11: **end for**
12: **for** $< \ L = 1; L \le max(\{t.length() : \forall t \in CMStrees\}); L\text{++} \ >$ **do**
13:      **for** $< \ t \in CMStrees \ >$ **do**
14:          **if** $t.NodesAtLevel(L) \ne \emptyset$ **then**
15:              **for** $< \ a \in t.NodesAtLevel(L) \ >$ **do**
16:                  $T \leftarrow T \cup \text{PRIVACYPOLICYOF}(a)$
17:                  $cl_a \leftarrow \text{TRAINCLASSIFIER}(F, a)$ ▷ Training a's classifier
18:                  $CL \leftarrow CL \cup \{cl_a\}$
19:              **end for**
20:          **end if**
21:      **end for**
22: **end for**
23: $\text{STORE}(CL)$ ▷ Store the trained profile attributes classifiers
24: $\text{STORE}(CMStrees)$ ▷ Store the set of correlation maximum spanning trees

---

Lines 7–11, loop through $CMStrees$, and for every CMST $\in CMStrees$, find it's root attribute (i.e. the node with the highest weighted-degree), and then add the privacy policies of that root attribute to F. Such that, our training data T will consist of demographic information, in addition to the privacy policies of the root attribute of every CMST $\in CMStrees$.

Lines 12–22, actually trains the profile attributes' classifiers. For each level (not counting level 0) L, it goes through the CMSTs $\in CMStrees$. For every CMST $t \in CMStrees$, if it has nodes the level L, then for every node a at level L it does the following. First, it adds the privacy policies of node a to T. Second, it uses T to train a classifier for node a. Third, it adds node a's classifier (i.e. cl_a) to the set of profile attributes classifiers CL.

Next we extend the "Snow-ball" algorithm to efficiently incorporate privacy policies in feature vectors, during the classifier testing phase. This algorithm, which we term, the "Snow-Ball" testing algorithm, is very similar to Algorithm 1 in the sense that both rely on the correlations between profile attributes, and that both work in a "snow-balling" fashion.

However, the "Snow-Ball" testing algorithm shown in Algorithm 2 below, is concerned with using an existing set of profile attribute classifiers, in order to get privacy policy recommendations.

Algorithm 2. The "Snow-Ball" Testing Algorithm.

1: $Pr \leftarrow \emptyset$ ▷ The initial set of predicted privacy policies
2: $F \leftarrow \{f_i : f_i$ is a demographic feature$\}$ ▷ The initial features' vector
3: $CL \leftarrow$ GETSTOREDCLASSIFIERS( )
4: $CMStrees \leftarrow$ GETSTOREDCORRELATIONTREES( )
5: **for** $< t \in CMStrees >$ **do**
6:     $r_t \leftarrow$ ROOTOF(t)
7:     $policy_{r_t} \leftarrow$ (Ask the target user to provide r_t's privacy policy)
8:     $F \leftarrow F \cup \{policy_{r_t}\}$ ▷ Adding the privacy policy of the r_t attribute, to F
9: **end for**
10:
11: **for** $< L = 1; L \leq max(\{t.lengh() : \forall t \in CMStrees\}); L++ >$ **do**
12:     **for** $< t \in CMStrees >$ **do**
13:        **if** $t.NodesAtLevel(L) \neq \emptyset$ **then**
14:           **for** $< a \in t.NodesAtLevel(L) >$ **do**
15:              $cl_a \leftarrow$ GETCLASSIFIEROF(a, CL) ▷ Getting node a's classifier
16:              $r_a \leftarrow cl_a.Predict(F)$ ▷ Preductubg node a's privacy policy
17:              $F \leftarrow F \cup \{r_a\}$
18:              $Pr \leftarrow Pr \cup \{r_a\}$
19:           **end for**
20:        **end if**
21:     **end for**
22: **end for**
23: RECOMMEND(Pr) ▷ Recommend Pr to the target user

Lines 1–4 in Algorithm 2 above, initialize the variables that are going to be used throughout the algorithm. Specifically, line 1, initializes the set of predicted privacy policies, Pr to an empty set, $\emptyset$. Line 2, initializes the target user's feature vector F with the target users demographics. Line 3, gets the set of attribute classifier CL stored by Algorithm 1. Line 4, gets the $CMStrees$ stored by Algorithm 1.

Lines 5–9, loop through $CMStrees$, and for every CMST $t \in CMStrees$, find it's root attribute r_t, and ask the target user to provide the privacy policy of the root $policy_{r_t}$. Then, adds $policy_{r_t}$ to F. Such that, the feature vector F will consist of the target user's demographics, and the privacy policies of the root attribute of every CMST $\in CMStrees$.

Lines 11–21, actually get the privacy policy predictions. For each level (not counting level 0) L, it goes through the CMSTs $\in CMStrees$. For every CMST $t \in CMStrees$, if t has nodes the level L, then for every node a at level L it does the following. First, it gets the classifier of node a (i.e. cl_a) from CL. Second, it passes F to cl_a to predict the privacy policy of node a (i.e. r_a). Third, it adds $r_a$to both F and CL.

This algorithm (with the help of Algorithm 1) greatly minimize user input, as users are required to only input the privacy policies of the root attributes. Normally CGs contain few CMSTs, for instance, at $\alpha = 0.4$, most of the real datasets had only two CMSTs, which means that users need to input the privacy policies of only 2 profile attributes (the CMSTs' roots), as opposed to 10 ($n-1$).

5.4   Experiments and Results

In order to test the validity and plausibility of our proposed method; we implemented the "Snow-Ball" training algorithm (described in Algorithm 1 above), and applied it on both of our simulated and real datasets, to accumulatively train the profile attribute classifiers of these datasets.

To accomplish this task we used several open-source software packages and libraries such as, R, which is a well-known statistical analysis package [18], "GraphStream", which is a Java-based graph manipulation and visualization library, and Weka's Java Application Programming Interface (API) [14].

We began by using R to build the CGs, find the CMST(s) within each CG, and store the resulting CMSTs in the standard GML format. Afterwards, we used the GraphStream library to read the previously stored CMSTs, and perform manipulations on these CMSTs, such as, finding subtrees, and traversing the CMSTs. Lastly, we used Weka's java API to manipulate the training datasets, and to train the profile attribute classifiers.

Next, after training our classifiers using the "Snow-Ball" training algorithm, we performed a 10-fold cross-validation test to measure the accuracy these classifier. So that, we could compare their accuracy with the accuracy of the classifiers trained using the other approaches.

The results of our experiments can be observed in Fig. 11 below, which shows the accuracy of the classifiers of two "selected" profile attribute (one real, one

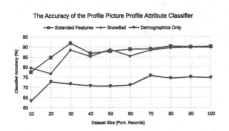
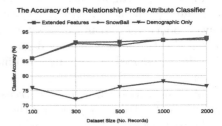

(a) The accuracy of the *Profile Pic.* classifier when using extended features, demographics features, and the "Snow-ball" method.

(b) The accuracy of the *Relationship* classifier when using extended features, demographics features, and the "Snow-ball" method.

Fig. 11. The performance of the classifiers of two "selected" profile attributes, when they are trained using the "Snow-Ball" algorithm, when trained using demographic features, extended features (i.e. demographic and privacy policies), in addition to the "Snow-Ball" method.

simulated), when they are trained using the "Snow-Ball" algorithm, compared to their accuracy (i.e. classifiers) when they are trained using demographic features, and extended features (i.e. demographics and privacy policies).

As we can see in Figs. 11a and b above, the accuracy of the classifiers trained using the "Snow-Ball" algorithm, is very close to the accuracy of the classifiers trained using extended features for both simulated and real datasets. But at the same time, the "Snow-Ball" algorithm requires only a fraction of the input that extended features require. For instance, in simulated datasets, users need to input the privacy policies of one root attribute (i.e. gender) instead of 8 attributes, which forms an 87.5% decrease in user input. Similarly, in real datasets, users need to input the privacy policies of two root attribute (i.e. education and mobile) instead of 11 attributes, which amounts to 81.8% decrease in user input. This shows that the "Snow-Ball" algorithm is not only capable of achieving accuracy comparable to that of extended features, but it does so with far less user input.

However, it also important to note the fact that these results might be a little bit optimistic. Because, in order for us to get a real idea of the performance of the "Snow-Ball" approach; we need to test the classifiers on a separate testing set as described in the "Snow-Ball" testing Algorithm 2, not just rely on cross validation. Doing so would in theory, yield lower performance, due to the inherited error form previous levels of the CMST.

6   Conclusions

In this paper some improvements in the privacy policy recommender system proposed in [1]. The improvements focused specifically on the PAP component of the recommender system. First, we conducted extended experiments, in which we trained the PAP profile attributes classifiers using a wide array of classification algorithms. Results showed that Random Forests had the best performance out of all the tested algorithms, especially when applied to real datasets.

Second, we introduced a "Snow-Ball" algorithm for training/testing the PAP profile attributes classifiers. Furthermore, we tested the validity of the proposed "Snow-Ball" algorithm, by implementing and applying it on both of our real and simulated datasets. The results showed that the "Snow-Ball" algorithm achieved high accuracy that comparable to that of the extended features approach, and at the same it requires only a small fraction of the input that the extended features approach requires.

We are aware of the fact that improvements did not include the UCP component of the recommender system; that is why for future works we plan to work on improving the accuracy of the UCP content classifiers, and studying how the UCP will "generalise" to other content-types such as photos for instance.

Acknowledgements. The authors gratefully acknowledge funding for this research provided by the National Research Foundation (NRF) of South Africa, and the Norwegian National Research Council.

References

1. Abuelgasim, A., Kayem, A.: An approach to personalized privacy policy recommendation on online social networks. In: Proceedings of the 2nd International Conference for Information Systems Security and Privacy (ICISSP), pp. 126–137. SCITEPRESS, February 2016
2. Acquisti, A., Carrara, E., Stutzman, F., Callas, J., Schimmer, K., Nadjm, M., Gorge, M., Ellison, N., King, P., Gross, R., Golder, S.: Security issues and recommendations for online social networks. Technical report 1, European Network and Information Security Agency (2007)
3. Acock, A.C., Stavig, G.R.: A measure of association for nonparametric statistics. Soc. Forces **57**(4), 1381–1386 (1979). http://www.jstor.org/stable/2577276
4. Alsalibi, B., Zakaria, N.: CFPRS: collaborative filtering privacy recommender system for online social networks. J. Eng. Res. Appl. **3**(5), 1850–1858 (2013)
5. Facebook Inc.: Statistics, September 2015. https://newsroom.fb.com/company-info/
6. Fang, L., LeFevre, K.: Privacy wizards for social networking sites. In: Proceedings of the 19th International Conference on World Wide Web, WWW 2010, pp. 351–360. ACM, New York (2010)
7. Fire, M., Goldschmidt, R., Elovici, Y.: Online social networks: threats and solutions. IEEE Commun. Surv. Tutor. **16**(4), 2019–2036 (2014)
8. Gao, H., Hu, J., Huang, T., Wang, J., Chen, Y.: Security issues in online social networks. IEEE Internet Comput. **15**(4), 56–63 (2011)
9. Ghazinour, K., Matwin, S., Sokolova, M.: Monitoring and recommending privacy settings in social networks. In: Proceedings of the Joint EDBT/ICDT 2013 Workshops, EDBT 2013, pp. 164–168. ACM, New York (2013)
10. Ghazinour, K., Matwin, S., Sokolova, M.: YourPrivacyProtector: a recommender system for privacy settings in social networks. Int. J. Secur. **2**(4), 11–25 (2013)
11. Gross, R., Acquisti, A.: Information revelation and privacy in online social networks. In: Proceedings of the 2005 ACM Workshop on Privacy in the Electronic Society, WPES 2005, pp. 71–80. ACM, New York (2005)
12. Gross, R., Stutzman, F., Acquisti, A.: Silent listeners: the evolution of privacy and disclosure on Facebook. J. Priv. Confid. **4**(2), 7–41 (2013)
13. Gundecha, P., Barbier, G., Liu, H.: Exploiting vulnerability to secure user privacy on a social networking site. In: Proceedings of the 17th ACM SIGKDD International Conference on Knowledge Discovery and Data Mining, KDD 2011, pp. 511–519, USA (2011). http://doi.acm.org/10.1145/2020408.2020489
14. Hall, M., Frank, E., Holmes, G., Pfahringer, B., Reutemann, P., Witten, I.H.: The Weka data mining software: an update. SIGKDD Explor. Newsl. **11**(1), 10–18 (2009). http://doi.acm.org/10.1145/1656274.1656278, http://www.cs.waikato.ac.nz/ml/weka/
15. Liu, Y., Gummadi, K.P., Krishnamurthy, B., Mislove, A.: Analyzing Facebook privacy settings: user expectations vs. reality. In: Proceedings of the 2011 ACM SIGCOMM Conference on Internet Measurement Conference. IMC 2011, pp. 61–70. ACM, New York (2011)
16. Madejski, M., Johnson, M., Bellovin, S.: A study of privacy settings errors in an online social network. In: 2012 IEEE International Conference on Pervasive Computing and Communications Workshops (PERCOM Workshops), pp. 340–345. IEEE, March 2012

17. Mitchell, T.M.: Decision tree learning. In: Tucker, C.L.B. (ed.) Machine Learning. Chapter 3, 1st edn, pp. 52–80. McGraw-Hill Inc., New York (1997)
18. Core Team, R.: R: a language and environment for statistical computing. R foundation for statistical computing, Vienna (2016). https://www.R-project.org/
19. Sánchez, D., Viejo, A.: Privacy risk assessment of textual publications in social networks. In: Proceedings of the International Conference on Agents and Artificial Intelligence, pp. 236–241 (2015)
20. Sebastiani, F.: Machine learning in automated text categorization. ACM Comput. Surv. **34**(1), 1–47 (2002)
21. Shehab, M., Cheek, G., Touati, H., Squicciarini, A.C., Cheng, P.C.: Learning based access control in online social networks. In: Proceedings of the 19th International Conference on World Wide Web, WWW 2010, pp. 1179–1180. ACM, New York (2010)
22. Sinha, A., Li, Y., Bauer, L.: What you want is not what you get: predicting sharing policies for text-based content on Facebook. In: Proceedings of the 2013 ACM Workshop on Artificial Intelligence and Security - AISec 2013, pp. 13–24. ACM, New York (2013)
23. Toch, E., Sadeh, N.M., Hong, J.: Generating default privacy policies for online social networks. In: CHI 2010 Extended Abstracts on Human Factors in Computing Systems, CHI EA 2010, pp. 4243–4248. ACM, New York (2010)
24. Twitter: Statistics, September 2015. https://about.twitter.com/company

The Evolution of Third-Party Web Tracking

Tim Wambach[✉] and Katharina Bräunlich[✉]

University Koblenz-Landau, Universitätsstr. 1, 56070 Koblenz, Germany
{wambach,braeunlich}@uni-koblenz.de

Abstract. Web tracking is ubiquitous and its current state is well known and researched. However, previous work in this field does not provide an overview of the tracking evolution over time. In our work, we use archived websites between the years 2000 and 2015 to measure the influence of tracking providers on the world wide web. With network graphs for each year, we show a significant growth of web tracking in a relatively short time. In the year 2005, about 10% of the websites were covered by the most popular three web trackers. This has grown up to 73% in the year 2015. In a 10 year period, one company managed to spread its tracker coverage to track more than 80% of our internet usage. This poses a still underestimated risk for both our security and privacy.

Keywords: Web tracking · Tracker · Privacy · Data leakage · Data protection · Web Archive · Security · Retrospective analysis · History of web tracking

1 Introduction

Nowadays web tracking is ubiquitous on the internet. In [10] Libert analyzed one million websites and found out that nearly nine of ten websites leak information to third parties. The implications of third party tracking on privacy are outlined in [11].

A disadvantage associated with web tracking is the potential loss of privacy for end users, as for example illustrated in [13]. Collecting data about web surfing behavior can be used for business, marketing, or other purposes. From our point of view, the implications for organizations and enterprises are still underestimated. For example, consider an employee working in a development department that uses the web to gain further information about products they are working on. The browsing history would usually be kept undisclosed, but [5] shows how an adversary on the web can reconstruct 62–73% of a typical user's browsing history. Information about current development within a company could be revealed by their web activities. The usage of company wide web proxies that aggregate requests does not solve the issue. Hiding internal IP address information or removing HTTP referrers do not prevent web tracking, because a wide range of different technologies exists that implement web tracking by other means.

O. Camp et al. (Eds.): ICISSP 2016, CCIS 691, pp. 130–147, 2017.
DOI: 10.1007/978-3-319-54433-5_8

Monitoring internet routers might be possible for internet providers or intelligence services, but they should not be able to analyze the content of TLS *(Transport Layer Security)* encrypted requests. This does not apply to web tracking mechanisms that create a separate (encrypted or unencrypted) request to the tracking provider and inform them about activities. This could also include very detailed usage information about something like mouse movement.

Web tracking must also be considered if privacy protection of end users on the web is a concern. Network layer anonymization (e.g. using a TOR network [20]) is not effective if the browser assists in tracking users. It is well known that cookies can be used to track users. However, a strong cookie policy might not be an effective protection: [8] shows how other browser technologies can be used as cookie replacements or circumvent cookie detection and deletion. How these so-called evercookies are used to facilitate web tracking is shown in [14].

This makes web tracking a possible threat the privacy of not only end users but also companies. However, web tracking as a privacy threat and a potential data leakage seams to be underestimated in IT security research. One reason could be that there is a wide range of tracking and advertising providers. Due to the number of different tracking providers, one might think they will not be able to grasp the whole picture of a specific company or person. Another reason for this underestimation might be the novelty of this threat. Ten years ago, third-party web tracking was relatively rare but is now growing to be a serious problem. Currently, there exists no overview on how web tracking has grown over the last 10–16 (cf. Sect. 6). Our goal is to analyze how third-party web tracking has changed over the last 16 years.

A common assumption is that the diversity of tracking providers makes it impossible for a single tracker to gain the whole picture of a specific person (as explained above). It is based on the fact that 10 years ago, third-party web tracking was relatively rare compared to today. In this paper we show that few providers currently track the majority of users visiting the most popular websites. This is the first analysis that covers a more than 5 year range and (graphically) demonstrates how this tracking network has grown over the last decade.

This is an extended and revised version of [22] with an increased quantity of analyzed websites (from 10,000 to 30,000) and further analysis. It is structured as follows: our methodology is explained in Sect. 2. The required software implementations are described in Sect. 3. However, the results in Sect. 4 show a remarkable increase in external connections that can mostly be linked to web tracking – a trend that was already partly shown in other work. The paper closes with a conclusion in Sect. 7.

2 Methodology

The questions this paper strives to answer are: How many trackers have existed historically, how the number of trackers has changed throughout the last years, how trackers have been distributed, and how their distribution has changed over time.

Section 2.1 provides a general overview of web tracking mechanisms. Section 2.2 explains how we detect trackers on websites. This method differs from privacy enhancing technologies but fits our special requirements for such a retrospective analysis. For such an analysis, we need a large amount of website snapshots over the past years. We use website snapshots from *archive.org* and perform an analysis of web tracking on them – further explained in Sect. 2.3.

2.1 Tracker Mechanism

At the beginning of the World Wide Web, website analytics were performed by an analysis of the web server log files. The website operator collected information about the IP addresses of the visitors, possible locations and most requested websites. An analysis, performed by the web server's owner, can be classified as first-party analysis.

Embedding resources is a common technique for web tracking. HTML allows embedding content from local and remote servers. During the parsing and interpretation process, the browser automatically loads content from any location specified in the HTML code. The server notices a resource request from the visitor's browser. A picture (so-called web bug) embedded in a web site allows a third-party to track visitors over different domains. Such a request contains the user's IP address and additional meta information (e.g. HTTP header). Additionally, cookies can facilitate the recognition of visitors.

JavaScript, developed in 1995 and first provided in 1996 by Netscape Navigator 2.0 and Internet Explorer 3.0, introduced the possibility to execute scripts on the client side. This technique can also be used to perform web tracking to gain fine-grained usage information. Data collected on the client-side can afterwards be sent to the server. The *Same-Origin Policy* implemented in browsers since 1996 lead to a separation of data from different websites. To achieve cross domain tracking, a shared third party tracking provider is required.

In active web tracking, the browser is part of the tracking mechanism. Tracking from a third-party that is supported by the browser in any way (e.g. creating remote connections, performing scripts, etc.) is known as active third-party web tracking. Today, different techniques are used to track visitors across domains. Unlike the passive type of web tracking, like the use of browser fingerprinting [1,4], the active part can be detected. [13] explains how modern web tracking works.

2.2 Tracker Detection

Most currently available tracker recognition techniques are focused on detecting trackers on existing and active websites. For example by blacklisting known tracker patterns (e.g. Ghostery [6]) or by behavioral analysis (e.g. TrackingObserver [21]).

[17] presents a classification framework and shows five different classes of typical tracker behavior. However, we cannot use existing tracking recognition tools to find tracking mechanisms from *archive.org* websites due to the fact that

the web server of the tracker might not exist anymore or might show different behavior as in the past. If a visited website (A) includes an image or script that causes the browser to open a connection to the tracking domain (B), (B) might set a cookie for tracking purposes. This active part – setting a cookie – is not preserved by *archive.org*. But what we can see in the archived data of (A) is the fact that there is an active part (e.g. image, script, etc.) that causes a request by the browser to open a connection to (B).

Embedding content is not necessarily associated with tracking. Examples include embedding a video player or third-party requests caused by the server infrastructure (Content Delivery Network). By creating a new connection from the browser to another domain, a transmission of source/location information (IP address) is caused and may also reveal further protocol specific information like HTTP referrers. [4] shows how this kind of information can be used for passive web tracking. From our point of view today, disclosing IP address information must be classified as personal data transfer that can be used for tracking purposes. In this paper, tracking is defined as a connection to an external (third party) host, that is not part of the visited/requested website. It cannot be proven whether the third party uses personal data for tracking purposes or not. However, it is clear that the data could be used to track users.

The results are similar to the ones generated by the Firefox add-on Lightbeam [12] that also provides a graphical overview about third party connections. Due to the fact that we need the ability to block connections not directed to *archive.org*, further development was necessary. In Sect. 3 we describe how a development framework (PyQt) was modified to obtain all external requests that occur during a web request. As soon as a website is fully parsed, all network requests are saved in a list and can be processed further.

2.3   Retrospective Analysis

Founded in 1996, *archive.org* became well known as an internet library by preserving the state of popular websites. If not prohibited by the website owner, *archive.org* stores the current state of public internet websites several times a year [3,15]. Information about new popular websites are donated by the *Alexa.org* database. This information will be used for a retrospective analysis of the websites with a focus on third-party connections.

We can now obtain all requests for a given *archive.org* website. We also need to restrict our analysis to a set of websites. We decided to use the 30,000 most popular websites according to the *Alexa.org* database (as of March 2016). Unfortunately, *Alexa.org* was not able to provide a list of the most visited websites for the years before 2007. Other databases, like Netcraft or *archive.org*, were not able to provide it either. Therefore, our analysis is based on the most popular 30,000 websites today (as of March 2016).

The *archive.org* JSON API[1] allows us to check how many snapshots are available and where they can be found. For each of the 30,000 websites and for

---

[1] JSON API for *archive.org* services and metadata, https://archive.org/help/json.php.

each year between the years 2000 and 2015, we request a snapshot overview from *archive.org*. The result is a list of snapshots that can be processed. This processing results in up to 16 lists of resources (for each year) that the browser loads after visiting the website in the archive. Finally, we perform an analysis of what kind of third party connections were used historically and how this changed in the last years.

As explained in Sect. 2.2, an ideal analysis of web tracking cannot be performed due to the fact that active parts (web servers) sometimes do not exist anymore or do not exhibit the same behavior. Furthermore, redirections to content on other websites cannot be followed if they are not preserved by *archive.org*. For example if an advertising spot was sold by the website owner and filled with different content for each request. This could generate much more external requests if visited multiple times.

3   Implementation

For our analysis, it is necessary to identify external connections from an archived website. A static analysis, like using regular expression to find external resources within HTML source code, has been shown to be insufficient. A reason for this is code obfuscation that looks like this:

```
var src = (document.location.protocol ==='https:' ?'https:/' :
'http:/') +'/imagesrv.adition.com/js/srp.js';
document.write('<scr' +'ipt type="text/javascript"src="' +
src + '"charset="utf-8"></scr' + 'ipt>');
```

In this code, the address of the tracker (*adition.com*) is obfuscated in a simple form, but good enough to defeat an automatic URL search in the source code.

Thus, a more dynamic analysis of websites is required. PyQt is a library that connects the Qt C++ cross-platform application framework with the interpreted language Python. Qt is a toolkit that includes a web browser widget that supports all modern web techniques (JavaScript, CSS, AJAX etc.) according to their whitepaper [16]. When this browser widget is parsing a website, there are various points where resources (images, scripts, etc.) are requested. We identified the `PyQt4.QtNetwork.QNetworkAccessManager` class where all network-based requests come together. If a resource must be loaded, the method `createRequest` is called and contains the full address (URL) of the resource. We overwrote this class, so that:

- all requests on the network are stored permanently, and
- requests not directed to *archive.org* are blocked using an empty dummy request.

A dummy request allows the library to continue the parsing process of the website without this requested/blocked resource – so this approach can unfortunately not reveal requests resulting from resources (e.g. scripts) that are not available any

Table 1. Overview of the request types – A stands for http(s)://web.archive.org.

Type	Request	Counted	Blocked
I	`A/web/<(time <= year)>/<int domain>/<res>`	No	No
II	`A/web/<(time > year)>/<int domain>/<res>`	No	Yes
III	`A/web/<(time <= year)>/<ext domain>/<res>`	Yes	No
IV	`A/web/<(time > year)>/<ext domain>/<res>`	Yes	Yes
V	`<int domain>/<res>`	No	Yes
VI	`<ext domain>/<res>`	Yes	Yes

more. How this `createRequest` method was changed is explained in detail in Algorithm 1.

Using this modified library, we obtain a list of all connections that are created by the browser during the parsing process. If the requested resource is available on *archive.org*, it is loaded and processed. All upcoming `JavaSript` alerts are accepted. All other requests outside the archive are blocked. It must be clarified that only the main website (landing page) was initially requested – the browser does not try to "click" on hyperlinks if it is not forced to do so by the content. However, we assume that most trackers will be loaded by the main page.

In [9], third-party domains are identified by their DNS record. Due to the fact that we do not have DNS records from the last 16 years, this method cannot be applied here. Therefore, we define a tracker as a loading process from an external domain. We define an external domain as a host, where the second-level domain (SLD) differs from the requested. For example, if "example.com" is requested, "web.example.com" and "example.net" count as internal resources, while "notexample.com" counts as external. A public available suffix list[2] is used to identify the top-level domain. In Table 1 we provide an overview of request types and how they are handled. Each external domain is counted once. For external domains, we also take the top level domain into account, so that "facebook.com" and "facebook.net" are different resources. According to the *archive.org* Frequently Asked Questions website[3] the Wayback Machine will grab the closest available date for missing links. This could lead to processing resources with content which is newer and different from the one in the requested year. Therefore, in case an *archive.org*-link leads to a resource that is younger than the requested one, we block the connection (case II and IV).

For graphical representation, we use networkx [7]. All data was obtained in March 2016.

---

[2] Public Suffix List https://publicsuffix.org/list/public_suffix_list.dat.

[3] Internet Archive Frequently Asked Questions https://archive.org/about/faqs.php.

Input: Request $rURL$ from content parser while processing a website $wURL$
from archive.org: called for each ressource on a website.

```
/*                                                    */
/* Overwritten createRequest() in
   QNetworkAccessManager                              */
/*                                                    */
```
if $sld(rURL) \neq sld(wURL)$ **then**
$\quad | \quad ressourceList[] \leftarrow host(rURL)$;   /* count 3rd parties only.
$\quad | \quad$ */
end
$websiteYear \leftarrow parseArchiveYear(wURL)$;
if $host(rURL) = $ *.archive.org **then**
$\quad | \quad requestYear \leftarrow parseArchiveYear(rURL)$;
$\quad | \quad$ **if** $requestYear \leq websiteYear)$ **then**
$\quad | \quad | \quad$ **return** $parent.createRequest(rURL)$;   /* accept */
$\quad | \quad$ **end**
end
return $parent.createRequest(null)$;   /* block */

Algorithm 1. Operation of the modified NetworkManager class.

4   Results

For our analysis, we determined how many years of history of the Alexa Top
30,000 domains we can find on *archive.org*. For 2,615 domains, no history is
available – website owners are able to block[4] being archived. For 7,041 domains,
archive.org only provides a 1–5 year history. For the following analysis, a history
of ≥ 10 years must be available, which includes 12,547 domains. How the snapshots are distributed over the 10–16 years is not relevant for our analysis. For
3,558 domains, we have the full 16 year history. For less than 100 cases per year
(554 overall), the archived websites failed to load and we removed these websites
completely from the analysis. In conclusion, we identified 11,568 domains with
at least a 10 year history for further analysis.

Table 2 shows an overview of the results of websites with at least 10 years of
history. The second column (column #) shows the number of analyzed websites
that were available for a particular year. The columns x_{min} and x_{max} show the
minimum and maximum number of external requests from a single website. $\bar{x}_{med}$
is the median, $x_{Q0.25}$ is the first and $x_{Q0.75}$ the third quartile. Column $\bar{x}$ is the
sample mean, σ is the standard deviation, and $\sigma^2 = Var(x)$. For comparison
this analysis was also done for websites where a full 16 year history is available
only an can be found in Table 5. The results show only little deviation.

---

[4] Removing Documents From the Wayback Machine, https://archive.org/about/
exclude.php.

Table 2. Statistical report of external requests on websites for the years 2000 to 2015 with at least 10 years history.

Year	#	x_{min}	$x_{Q0.25}$	$\bar{x}_{med}$	$x_{Q0.75}$	x_{max}	$\bar{x}$	σ	$Var(x)$
2000	6506	0	0	0	2	18	0.61	1.31	1.72
2001	7743	0	0	0	2	24	0.77	1.55	2.39
2002	8316	0	0	0	2	33	0.81	1.56	2.43
2003	8925	0	0	0	2	34	0.85	1.62	2.61
2004	9785	0	0	0	2	36	0.99	1.89	3.56
2005	10320	0	0	0	2	44	1.13	2.00	4.00
2006	10819	0	0	1	5	49	1.45	2.27	5.17
2007	11015	0	0	1	7	44	1.92	2.54	6.44
2008	11346	0	0	1	7	35	2.09	2.57	6.58
2009	10901	0	0	2	8	38	2.53	2.86	8.20
2010	10966	0	0	2	8	46	3.06	3.25	10.58
2011	11210	0	0	3	13	44	3.91	3.90	15.24
2012	11176	0	0	4	16	44	4.63	4.33	18.76
2013	11176	0	0	4	17	44	5.44	4.92	24.20
2014	10862	0	0	5	19	60	6.27	5.30	28.11
2015	10738	0	0	5	22	57	6.61	5.50	30.28

During the years 2000 to 2005, the number of analyzed websites is below 11,000 and therefore hard to compare with the rest. As of the year 2005, the number of analyzed websites is between 10,300 and 11,300. Therefore, the best range for a comparison is between 2005 and 2015. Within this range the number of web inclusions increased more than five fold. The median in 2015 shows that half of the websites include at least 5 different external resources. The fact that in the year 2005 50% have no inclusions and 75% only two inclusions lead us to the question how these external resources are distributed.

4.1   Most Used Trackers

In this section, we show which domains are most prominently included throughout our 16 years of analysis. For each year, we analyzed how often a domain showed up in our results. The 15 most used domains can be seen in Table 4. For the year 2000, the most included domain was *doubleclick.net* which is still a popular web tracking domain. But in our 6,506 analyzed websites it only occurred 276 times. In comparison: the most included domain in 2015 was *google-analytics.com* with 5,940 occurrences on 10,738 analyzed domains.

It needs to be noted that domains are not grouped by company. For example, *Akamai Technologies* is still in the top 15 of the year 2015 with 715 occurrences, but currently known under the domain *akamaihd.net*.

As explained in the previous section, the range most suitable for comparison are the years 2005 to 2015. In 2005, *doubleclick.net* is the most included domain but only present in about 4% of the websites. In the year 2015, *google-analytics.com* is the most included domain with 5,940 occurrences. On more than every second website, the visitor is tracked by *Google Analytics*. Due to the fact that since 2007, *doubleclick.net* is part of *Google Inc.*, at least 3 of these top 5 included domains have been part of a *Google Inc.* service for the last years. It is still unclear how data from Google services like *googleapis.com* are connected to other Google services.

A further analysis of the drop in requests (Table 4) between 2013 and 2014 of *Google Analytics* showed that 557 websites which removed *Google-Analytics* in 2013 added *doubleclick.net* in 2014.

4.2   Distribution

In this section we use a graph to visually represent at the distribution of trackers. Figures 1, 2, 3, 4, 5, 6, 7, 8, 9, 10, 11, 12, 13, 14, 15 and 16 show undirected graphs where every edge stands for at least one load process from an external domain. The top 5 from Sect. 4.1 are marked with the corresponding letter as explained in Table 4. For the sake of clarity, nodes are not plotted, only their edges, therefore nodes without any connections are not visible. The position of each domain (node) is the same for all graphs.

For 2005, nearly the same amount of websites were analyzed (10,320) as for 2015 (10,738). Thus, the differences between these graphs are mostly additional requests. In Figs. 18, 19, 20, 21, 22 and 23 the top 5 most included domains of each year are labeled – the legend can be found in Table 4. In Figs. 21 and 22 (2010 and 2012) we can see a monopolization: while we had a more equal distribution in earlier years, the graph from 2010 shows fewer nodes with significantly more connections than the others. Especially *google-analytics.com* (K) is in the top 5 since 2006 and its growing influence on the web can be easily grasped.

Fig. 1. Year 2000.   **Fig. 2.** Year 2001.   **Fig. 3.** Year 2002.

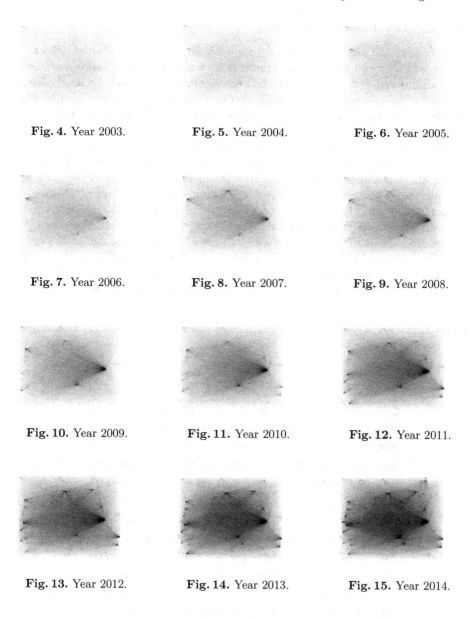

Fig. 4. Year 2003.   **Fig. 5.** Year 2004.   **Fig. 6.** Year 2005.

Fig. 7. Year 2006.   **Fig. 8.** Year 2007.   **Fig. 9.** Year 2008.

Fig. 10. Year 2009.   **Fig. 11.** Year 2010.   **Fig. 12.** Year 2011.

Fig. 13. Year 2012.   **Fig. 14.** Year 2013.   **Fig. 15.** Year 2014.

Fig. 16. Year 2015.

4.3   Top Level Domain Analysis

Table 3 shows the amount of analyzed websites for five most prevalent top-level domains (TLD) and the average connection count. The distribution matches with existing reports[5] (from 2015) which states that *.com* is used for nearly 50% of all websites, followed by *.ru* (5.2%), *.net* (4.7%), *.org* (4.4%), and *.de* (3.1%). The data is not representative for the whole World Wide Web. However, it gives a good estimate for a complete picture.

An interesting fact is that *.org* domains, originally intended for non-profit organisations, seem to have less third-part connections than the other TLDs. A deeper analysis showed that the top 10 most included thirds party domains in 2015 are nearly the same for *.com*, *.net*, and *.org* (with GA at the first position). For *.ru*, *yandex.ru* is the most referenced domain in 2015 with 314 inclusions and *google-analytics.com* is on second place with 266 inclusions. For *.de*, the most referenced domain in 2015 is *ioam.de* with 145 inclusions and *google-analytics.com* is second place with 138. From 2002 to 2011, *ivwbox.de* had been the most included domain for German websites and, from 2011 to 2014, had still been in the top 3. Since 2015 only few (4) connections to this domain be found.

Table 3. Statistical overview about the amount (#) and mean value ($\bar{x}$) for the five most occured top level domains.

Year	com		net		ru		org		de	
	#	$\bar{x}$	#	$\bar{x}$	#	$\bar{x}$	#	$\bar{x}$	#	$\bar{x}$
2000	3506	0.66	174	1.26	171	2.74	221	0.24	274	0.45
2001	4192	0.81	238	1.33	254	2.96	252	0.43	299	0.68
2002	4479	0.83	284	1.36	287	3.17	277	0.39	303	0.72
2003	4816	0.84	320	1.31	315	3.34	288	0.43	309	0.85
2004	5339	0.99	362	1.48	337	3.44	309	0.48	325	1.07
2005	5603	1.16	377	1.79	369	3.36	337	0.62	339	1.16
2006	5800	1.54	405	2.1	398	3.91	352	0.87	351	1.52
2007	5937	2.02	412	2.59	416	4.22	357	1.53	355	1.98
2008	6249	2.21	434	2.6	410	4.4	369	1.46	345	2.09
2009	5950	2.75	418	3.02	405	4.76	355	1.97	342	2.3
2010	5936	3.39	415	3.49	403	5.14	354	2.23	345	2.87
2011	6119	4.33	422	4.37	411	6.11	364	3.05	348	3.49
2012	6064	5.13	427	4.7	413	6.67	369	3.39	352	4.02
2013	6105	5.94	420	5.51	413	7.5	361	3.98	353	5.07
2014	5940	6.73	417	6.54	408	8.38	353	4.76	343	6.2
2015	5889	7.1	410	6.56	410	8.46	353	5.24	342	6.58

---

[5] http://w3techs.com/technologies/overview/top_level_domain/all.

5 Top Tracker Coverage

An important question is how many trackers cover how many popular websites' users and can thus track a large number of users. In Fig. 17, we show how many of all analyzed websites are covered (y-axis) by the top n trackers, with n being on the x-axis. For instance, in 2015 about 73% of all analyzed websites are covered by the top three of the most included third party trackers from 2015: according to Table 4 these are *google-analytics.com*, *doubleclick.net*, and *facebook.net*. In 2005, only 10% of the websites are covered by the top three from 2005 (*google-syndication.com*, *doubleclick.net*, and *rambler.ru*).

This kind of analysis could also be interesting if domains of a specific company are grouped together. For example, to analyze the coverage of *Google*-hosts. For this analysis they are simply identified by "google" in their hostname – other services that are today (as of 2015) part of the google company (like *doubleclick.net* since 2007 or youtube.com since 2006) are not considered. The results for this analysis are that in the year 2005 only 5% of the websites were covered by *Google*. This figure rapidly increased for the following years (2006–2015): 19%, 36%, 49%, 57%, 65%, 72%, 78%, 80%, 81%, 82%. This means that *Google* increased their coverage from 5% to 82% in the last 10 years.

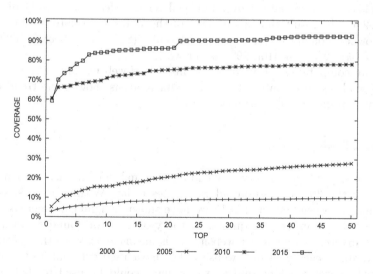

Fig. 17. Coverage the most included third parties.

The same analysis can be done for *Facebook* (identified by "facebook" or "fbcdn" in the hostname) for the years 2009–2015: 0.7%, 7%, 20%, 27%, 29%, 29%, 29%.

6   Related Work

Using data from *archive.org* in connection with the Alexa top 10,000 was also applied in [19] for an analysis of web application vulnerabilities. Analysis of archived data in general is also performed by the LAWA project (Longitudinal Analytics of Web Archive data) [18].

In [9], a long-term study over 5 epochs between October 2005 and September 2008 was performed. The results showed a steadily decreasing number of entities where a handful of companies are able to track user movement across almost all of the popular websites. Our results also show that *Google-Analytics* and *Doubleclick* are the most widely used trackers. [2] shows an analysis of the Alexa Top 10,000 regarding tracking mechanisms and social media plugins but is limited to October 2012.

The top one million websites (as of May 2014) are analyzed for third party connections in [10]. In this work the amount of domains contacted on average is 9.47, so about 3 connections higher than the measured 6.27 (for 2014) in our work. This can be explained by additional reload effects as already discussed in Sect. 2.3. The result that about 78% of the websites initiate a request to a *Google*-owned domain matches with our results (81%) from Sect. 5. The same for *Facebook*: 32.42% in [10], 29% in our work.

A fully comparable overview of the history of web tracking is missing and existing analysis cover only a few years. Our analysis showed the trend of less diversity identified in [9] continues.

7   Conclusion

In our work, we showed how embedding external content has seen a usage increase in the 30,000 most popular websites today. Within the best comparable range between 2005 and 2015 we have shown a significant increase (more than five fold) of external requests. In the year 2015 we found an average of around 6 external requests per website. This means at least 6 other hosts were informed about each visit of a website. The most used external hosts could be connected to web tracking and so the request could be used to deduce even more information about a user, e.g. an analysis of user behavior. We presented an impression of the distribution and diversity in our graphs.

As our methodology is based on evaluation of archived websites there are limitations for such a retrospective analysis. However, our results are in accordance with "real-internet" results provided by Libert as explained in Sect. 6.

Our top tracker coverage analysis showed that the diversity of web tracking and content providers, that we assumed in the beginning, does not exist. This leads to security issues: if a globally acting company has an insight in about 80% of visited websites of a specific user, it is clear that information disclosure of e.g. corporate information cannot be prevented. The usage of further services like search, mail, calendar, or translation services contributes to the problem. From our point of view, information security officers should be more sensitive about privacy and web tracking for two reasons: for employee privacy and for an effective protection of corporate secrets. The consequences of such a centralization of tracking, which allows the formation of an increasingly complete picture about a specific person, are difficult to predict.

We showed that a reason for the underestimation of third-party web tracking consequences could be due to the fact that it did not exist 10 years ago. From a security point of view, considering web tracking and the usage of PET (Privacy-Enhancing Technologies) should be a part of every corporate security policy. With our analysis we have proven that this is today more important than 10 years ago.

Further research about security implications of web tracking is required. Additionally, a more detailed analysis of differences between countries (as partially done in Sect. 4.3) could also be interesting. Grouping the hosts of providers together (as in Sect. 5) is also possible future work.

Acknowledgement. This study has been made possible by the participation of the interdisciplinary project "Transformations of Privacy" (http://www.strukturwandeldesprivaten.de/) funded by VolkswagenStiftung (https://www.volkswagenstiftung.de/en.html).

Appendix

A   TOP 15 Most Included Domains

Table 4. Top 15 of the most included external domains. Top 5 of each year with a gray cell background.

		'00	'01	'02	'03	'04	'05	'06	'07	'08	'09	'10	'11	'12	'13	'14	'15
A	doubleclick.net	276	345	339	287	306	346	406	643	851	1868	1738	1567	1223	1890	2978	2707
B	rambler.ru	113	152	184	215	246	264	296	317	312	312	296	286	254	213	178	157
C	hitbox.com	81	93	88	111	95	134	152	154	119	63	30	16	4	1		
D	akamai.net	65	160	149	142	130	143	154	135	103	78	72	69	66	76	50	40
E	imgis.com	61	18														
	bfast.com	57	68	41	34	24	17	9									
F	spylog.com	52	148	135	127	125	113	127	113	84	88	62	51	38	34	23	16
	extreme-dm.com	47	59	63	81	95	106	113	78	67	52	36	31	32	25	17	13
	flycast.com	46	36														
	linkexchange.com	46	37	25	23	6	1	1	1	1							
G	list.ru	45	110	150	174	192	195	225	227	199	162	133	106	90	70	51	42
	register.com	43	66	46	36	29	21	5	2	3							
	thecounter.com	42	57	21	18	18	12	2	2	2	1						
	akamaitech.net	41	32	15	14	8	7	7	7	6	3	4	1				
	linksynergy.com	29	41	32	32	27	35	32	27	23	14	13	12	10	10	8	2
	webtrendslive.com	12	72	46	40	54	77	89	102	106	105	96	116	114	93	70	51
	216.21.232.20	15	60	40	32	31	17										
	209.10.130.68	15	57														
I	imrworldwide.com	28	55	68	97	149	166	199	222	265	266	285	428	424	380	293	240
	qksrv.net		41	72	74	53	13	7	4	1	2	2	1	1			
	hotlog.ru			67	102	129	110	101	80	65	41	34	31	25	21	16	12
	fastclick.net	2	10	59	57	70	63	61	66	58	56	61	45	43	35	20	16
	advertising.com	11	14	54	59	85	62	65	102	121	108	120	108	98	80	55	51
	nedstatbasic.net	17	30	53	73	65	53	16	8	6	3	3	1	1	1		
	oingo.com		6	49	76	74	41	24									
	facetz.net			47	70	96	82	68	50	45	26	20	17	18	14	10	9
H	googlesyndication.com			32		259	523	813	995	977	946	924	970	902	858	865	966
L	2o7.net			15	24	84	152	225	318	351	337	414	444	406	378	294	224
	yadro.ru			12	43	72	119	200	255	288	311	331	349	347	345	331	314
	falkag.net				2	35	101	132	46	12							
M	google.com	5	10	15	26	38	96	161	1587	466	604	736	1241	2115	2212	2397	2231
K	google-analytics.com						13	1404	3157	4567	5394	6072	6666	7040	6881	6087	5940
	statcounter.com				3	14	69	132	125	122	111	91	81	77	75	64	64
	gemius.pl		4	14	37	56	67	106	172	177	175	260	343	359	375	365	336
	atdmt.com		10	11	31	47	68	108	141	159	149	163	175	136	119	72	40
	scanalert.com				4	22	40	66	128	192	188	176	141	125	105	70	54
N	quantserve.com								90	376	689	793	851	861	816	687	589
	googleadservices.com							13	38	136	321	643	1058	1306	1530	1572	1392
	tacoda.net						2	66	82	133	106	89	72	37	15	17	10
P	ajax.googleapis.com									20	222	623	1199	1711	2076	2170	2153
	addthis.com		1						20	115	220	317	369	432	451	474	446
	revsci.net						4	48	48	120	167	208	235	244	222	172	189
O	facebook.com										67	580	1638	1826	1604	1403	1083
	scorecardresearch.com										86	448	777	988	1124	1196	1190
Q	facebook.net											161	851	1611	1952	2137	2400
	fbcdn.net									1	52	121	777	497	1136	655	251
	twitter.com										34	137	636	1116	1440	1598	1547
	googletagservices.com												17	317	836	1353	1681
	fonts.googleapis.com											5	61	308	773	1464	2023
	googleusercontent.com											2	41	182	537	522	29
	gstatic.com									1	11	33	88	262	357	1081	1239
	googletagmanager.com														327	979	1782
	akamaihd.net												6	17	90	435	715

B   Network Graph from 2000, 2006, 2007, 2010, 2012, and 2015

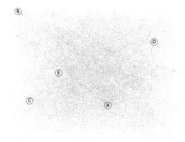

Fig. 18. Year 2000.

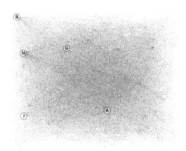

Fig. 19. Year 2005.

Fig. 20. Year 2007.

Fig. 21. Year 2010.

Fig. 22. Year 2012.

Fig. 23. Year 2015.

C   Full 16 Year History Report

Table 5. Statistical report of external requests on websites for the years 2000 to 2015 with a full 16 years history.

Year	#	x_{min}	$x_{Q0.25}$	$\bar{x}_{med}$	$x_{Q0.75}$	x_{max}	$\bar{x}$	σ	$Var(x)$
2000	3369	0	0	0	2	18	0.69	1.45	2.11
2001	3369	0	0	0	2	21	0.85	1.64	2.69
2002	3369	0	0	0	2	22	0.88	1.62	2.63
2003	3369	0	0	0	2	17	0.87	1.56	2.44
2004	3369	0	0	0	2	18	0.99	1.68	2.81
2005	3369	0	0	0	5	33	1.11	1.84	3.40
2006	3369	0	0	1	5	49	1.42	2.16	4.67
2007	3369	0	0	1	7	44	1.91	2.37	5.62
2008	3369	0	0	1	7	33	2.05	2.44	5.95
2009	3369	0	0	2	8	35	2.51	2.76	7.60
2010	3369	0	0	2	8	23	3.00	3.04	9.25
2011	3369	0	0	3	13	26	3.91	3.80	14.46
2012	3369	0	0	4	16	25	4.65	4.30	18.50
2013	3369	0	0	4	17	39	5.52	4.97	24.70
2014	3369	0	0	5	19	49	6.32	5.40	29.11
2015	3369	0	0	5	19	46	6.61	5.44	29.56

References

1. Boda, K., Földes, Á.M., Gulyás, G.G., Imre, S.: User tracking on the web via cross-browser fingerprinting. In: Laud, P. (ed.) NordSec 2011. LNCS, vol. 7161, pp. 31–46. Springer, Heidelberg (2012). doi:10.1007/978-3-642-29615-4_4
2. Chaabane, A., Kaafar, M.A., Boreli, R.: Big friend is watching you: analyzing online social networks tracking capabilities. In: Proceedings of the 2012 ACM Workshop on Online Social Networks, WOSN 2012, pp. 7–12, USA (2012). http://doi.acm.org/10.1145/2342549.2342552
3. Day, M.: The long-term preservation of web content. In: Web Archiving, pp. 177–199. Springer, Heidelberg (2006). doi:10.1007/978-3-540-46332-0_8
4. Eckersley, P.: How unique is your web browser? In: Atallah, M.J., Hopper, N.J. (eds.) PETS 2010. LNCS, vol. 6205, pp. 1–18. Springer, Heidelberg (2010). doi:10.1007/978-3-642-14527-8_1
5. Englehardt, S., Reisman, D., Eubank, C., Zimmerman, P., Mayer, J., Narayanan, A., Felten, E.W.: Cookies that give you away: the surveillance implications of web tracking. In: Proceedings of the 24th International Conference on World Wide Web, WWW 2015, Florence, pp. 289–299, 18–22 May 2015. http://doi.acm.org/10.1145/2736277.2741679

6. Ghostery, I.: Ghostery - home page (2015). https://www.ghostery.com/
7. Hagberg, A.A., Schult, D.A., Swart, P.J.: Exploring network structure, dynamics, and function using NetworkX. In: Proceedings of the 7th Python in Science Conference (SciPy 2008), Pasadena, pp. 11–15, August 2008
8. Kamkar, S.: Evercookie - virtually irrevocable persistent cookies (2010). http://samy.pl/evercookie/
9. Krishnamurthy, B., Wills, C.E.: Privacy diffusion on the web: a longitudinal perspective. In: Proceedings of the World Wide Web Conference, p. 09 (2009)
10. Libert, T.: Exposing the hidden web: an analysis of third-party HTTP requests on 1 million websites. CoRR abs/1511.00619 (2015). http://arxiv.org/abs/1511.00619
11. Libert, T.: Privacy implications of health information seeking on the web. Commun. ACM 58(3), 68–77 (2015). http://doi.acm.org/10.1145/2658983
12. Lightbeam: Lightbeam addon for Firefox (2015). https://addons.mozilla.org/en-US/firefox/addon/lightbeam/
13. Mayer, J.R., Mitchell, J.C.: Third-party web tracking: policy and technology. In: Proceedings of the 2012 IEEE Symposium on Security and Privacy, SP 2012, pp. 413–427. IEEE Computer Society, Washington, DC (2012). doi:10.1109/SP.2012.47
14. Mcdonald, A.M., Cranor, L.F., Mcdonald, A.M., Cranor, L.F.: A survey of the use of adobe flash local shared objects to respawn HTTP cookies (2011)
15. Olston, C., Najork, M.: Web crawling. Found. Trends Inf. Retr. 4(3), 175–246 (2010). doi:10.1561/1500000017
16. Riverbank: PyQt Whitepaper (2013). http://www.riverbankcomputing.com/
17. Roesner, F., Kohno, T., Wetherall, D.: Detecting and defending against third-party tracking on the web. In: Proceedings of the 9th USENIX Conference on Networked Systems Design and Implementation, NSDI 2012, p. 12. USENIX Association, Berkeley (2012). http://dl.acm.org/citation.cfm?id=2228298.2228315
18. Spaniol, M., Weikum, G.: Tracking entities in web archives: the lawa project (2012)
19. Stamm, S., Sterne, B., Markham, G.: Reining in the web with content security policy. In: Proceedings of the 19th International Conference on World Wide Web, WWW 2010, USA, pp. 921–930 (2010). http://doi.acm.org/10.1145/1772690.1772784
20. TorProject: Tor: an anonymous Internet communication system (2015). http://www.torproject.org/
21. TrackingObserver: A browser-based web tracking detection platform (2012). http://trackingobserver.cs.washington.edu/
22. Wambach, T., Bräunlich, K.: Retrospective analysis of third-party web tracking. In: ICISSP 2016 - Proceedings of the 2nd International Conference on Information Systems Security and Privacy, Rome, 19–21 February 2016

SEYARN: Enhancing Security of YARN Clusters Based on Health Check Service

Wenting Li, Qingni Shen$^{(\boxtimes)}$, Chuntao Dong, Yahui Yang, and Zhonghai Wu

School of Software and Microelectronics,
MoE Key Lab of Network and Software Assurance, Peking University, Beijing, China
{wentingli,chuntaodong}@pku.edu.cn,
{qingnishen,yhyang,zhwu}@ss.pku.edu.cn

Abstract. Hadoop serves as an essential tool in the rise of big data, it has insufficient security model. The internal attacks can bypass current Hadoop security mechanism, and compromised Hadoop components can be used to threaten overall Hadoop. This paper studies the vulnerabilities of Health Check Service in Hadoop/YARN and the threat of denial-of-service to a YARN cluster with multi-tenancy. We use theoretical analysis and numerical simulations to demonstrate the effectiveness of this DDoS attack based on health check service (DDHCS). Our experiments show that DDHCS is capable of causing significant impacts on the performance of a YARN cluster in terms of high attack broadness (averagely 85.6%), high attack strength (more than 80%). In addition, we developed a security enhancement for YARN, named SEYARN. We have implemented the SEYARN model, and demonstrated that SEYARN fixes the above vulnerabilities with extending 95% accuracy and minimal run-time overhead, and effectively resists related attacks.

Keywords: DDoS · Hadoop · YARN · Security

1   Introduction

Hadoop is a framework that allows for the distributed processing of large data sets across clusters of computers using simple programming models. At present, Apache Hadoop has matured and developed to a data platform for not just processing humongous amount of data in batch but also with the advent of YARN, it supports for managing computing resources in clusters and scheduling user applications. Now, Hadoop/YARN supports many diverse workloads such as interactive queries over large data with Hive on Tez, real-time data processing with Apache Storm, in-memory data store like Spark and the list goes on.

For Hadoop's initial purpose, it was always assumed that clusters would consist of cooperating, trusted machines used by trusted users in a trusted environment. Initially, there was no security model – Hadoop didn't authenticate users or services, and there was no data privacy [13, 20]. There is a rising concern that Hadoop in its present form may not be able to maintain the same security level in a public cloud as it does in a protected environment. In the past few years, Hypervisor vulnerabilities have been

© Springer International Publishing AG 2017
O. Camp et al. (Eds.): ICISSP 2016, CCIS 691, pp. 148–168, 2017.
DOI: 10.1007/978-3-319-54433-5_9

reported. These internal cloud attacks can bypass Hadoop security mechanisms to compromise the safety of data and computing in Hadoop.

A distributed denial-of-service (DDoS) is where the attack source is more than one– and often thousands–of unique IP addresses, it is an attempt to make a machine or network resource unavailable to its intended users, such as to temporarily or indefinitely interrupt or suspend services of a host connected to the Internet. The first DDoS attack incident [4] was reported in 1999 by the Computer Incident Advisory Capability (CIAC). Since then, most of the DDoS attacks continue to grow in frequency, sophistication and bandwidth [9, 15].

Previous work has demonstrated the threat and stealthiness of DDoS attack in cloud environment [5, 6, 22]. As a solution, [1, 11, 19] have successfully demonstrated how to mitigate DDoS attack with cloud techniques. There also have been numerous suggestions on how to detect DDoS attack. For example, using MapReduce for DDoS Forensics [12], a hybrid statistical model to detect DDoS attack [7, 18]. Unlike in cloud environment, DDoS attacks in BigData based on Hadoop/YARN environment are more aggressive and destructive, but the security issues seemly have not received sufficient attention.

One problem with the Hadoop/YARN system is that by assigning the tasks to many nodes, it is possible for malicious users submitting attack program to affect the entire cluster. In this paper, we study the vulnerabilities of Health Check Service in YARN. These vulnerabilities encountered in YARN motivate a new type of DDoS attacks, which we call DDoS attack based on health check service (DDHCS). Our work innovatively exposes health check service in YARN as a possible vulnerability to adversarial attacks, hence it opens new avenue to improving the security of YARN.

In summary, this paper makes the following contribution:

- We present three vulnerabilities of Health Check Service in YARN, including (i) Resource-Manager (RM) is lack of Job Validation; (ii) It is easy for a user to make a job failed, which will make the node transform into unhealthy state; (iii) RM will add the unhealthy nodes to the exclude list, which means the decrease of service nodes in the cluster.
- We design a DDHCS attack model, we use theoretical analysis and numerical simulations to demonstrate the effectiveness of this attack for different scenarios. Moreover, we empirically show that DDHCS is capable of causing significant impacts on the performance of a YARN cluster in terms of high attack broadness (averagely 85.6%), high attack strength (more than 80%) and obviously resource utilization degradation.
- We developed and implemented a security enhancement for YARN (SEYARN), including Code comparison, Parameter check and Map-tracing for preventing malicious users to submit failed jobs. And we increase User blacklist mechanism according to user log history. In addition, we demonstrated that SEYARN fixed the above vulnerabilities and effectively resists related attacks.

The rest of this paper is organized as follows. Section 2 discusses the background. Section 3 describes the vulnerabilities we found in YARN. Section 4 presents DDHCS attack model. Section 5 demonstrates implementation of our attack model and evaluates attack effect by MapReduce job. Section 6 describes the details of SEYARN implementation. Section 7 concludes the paper and discusses some future work.

2   Background

Health Check Service is a YARN service-level health test that checks the health of the node it is executing on. ResourceManager (RM) using health check service to manage NodeManagers (NM). If any health check fails, the NM marks the node as unhealthy and communicates this to the RM, which then stops assigning containers (resource representation) to the node. Before we introduce health check service, we should know about RM component, NM States and triggering conditions.

2.1   YARN-ResourceManager

Hadoop has evolved into a new generation—Hadoop 2, in which the classic MapReduce module is upgraded into a new computing platform, called YARN (or MRv2) [24].

YARN uses RM to replace classic JobTracker, and uses ApplicationMaster (AM) to replace classic TaskTracker [17]. The RM runs as a daemon on a dedicated machine, and acts as the central authority arbitrating resources among various competing applications in the cluster. The AM is "head" of a job, managing all life-cycle aspects including dynamically increasing and decreasing resources consumption, managing the flow of execution, handling faults and computation skew, and performing other local optimizations.

The NM is YARN's per-node agent, and takes care of the individual compute nodes in a Hadoop cluster. This includes keeping up-to date with the RM, overseeing containers' life-cycle management [10], monitoring resource usage of individual containers, tracking node-health, log's management and auxiliary services which may be exploited by different YARN applications.

There are three components connecting RM to NM, which co-manage the life-cycle of NM, as shown in Fig. 1. They are NMLivelinessMonitor, NodesListManager and ResourceTrackerService. We discuss the three services as follows.

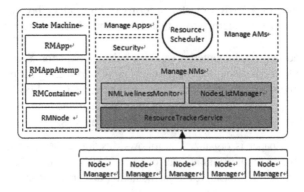

Fig. 1. ResourceManager architecture.

NMLivelinessMonitor keeps track of each NM's last one heartbeat time. Any DataNode that doesn't have any heartbeat within a configured interval of time, by default 10 min, is deemed dead and expired by the RM. All the containers currently running on an expired DataNode are marked as dead and no new containers are scheduling on it.

NodesListManager manages a collection of included and excluded DataNodes. It is responsible for reading the host configuration files to seed the initial list of DataNodes. The files are specified as *"yarn.resourcemanager.nodes.include-path"* and *"yarn.resourceman-ager.nodes.exclude-path"*. It also keeps track of DataNodes that are decommissioned as time progresses.

ResourceTrackerService responds to RPCs from all the DataNodes. It is responsible for registration of new DataNode, rejecting requests from any invalid/decommissioned DataNodes, obtain node-heartbeats and forward them over to the Yarn Scheduler.

2.2 Node States

In YARN, an object is abstracted as a state machine when it is composed of several states and events triggering transfer of these states. There are four types of state machines inside RM—RMApp, RMAppAttempt, RMContainer and RMNode. We focus on RMNode state machine.

RMNode state machine is the data structure used to maintain a node lifecycle in the RM, and its implementation is RMNodeImpl class. The class maintains a node state machine, and records the possible node states and events that may lead to the state transform [23].

As shown in Fig. 2 and Table 1, each node has six basic states (NodeState) and eight kinds of events that lead to the transfer of the six states (RMNodeEventType), the role of RMNodeImpl is waiting to receive events of RMNodeEventType type from the other objects, and transfer the current state to another state, and trigger another behavior at the same time. In subsequent articles, we focus on the *unhealthy* state and *decommission* state:

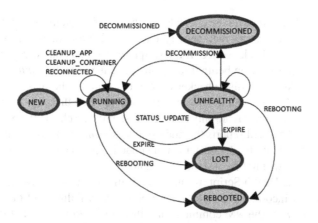

Fig. 2. Node state machine.

Table 1. Basic states and basic events of node.

States	Describe	Trigger events
NEW	The initial state of state machine	–
RUNNING	NM register to RM	STARTED
DECOMMISSION	A DataNode is added to exclude list	DECOMMISSION
UNHEALTHY	Health Check Service determines whether NM is unhealthy	STATUS_UPDATE
LOST	NM doesn't heartbeat within 10 min, is deemed dead	EXPIRE
REBOOTING	RM finds NM's heartbeat ID doesn't agree with its preservation, RM require it to restart	REBOOTING

UNHEALTHY: The administrator configures on each NM a health monitoring scripts, NM has a dedicated thread to execute the script periodically, to determine whether the NM is under *healthy* state. The NM communicates this *"unhealthy"* state to the RM via heartbeats. After that, RM won't assign a new task to the node until it turns to be *healthy* state.

DECOMMSSIONED: If a node is added to exclude list, the corresponding NM would be set for *decommission* state, thus the NM would not be able to communicate with the RM.

2.3   Health Check Service

The NM runs health check service to determine the health of the node it is executing on, in intervals of 10 min. If any health check fails, the NM marks the node as *unhealthy* and communicates this to the RM, which then stops assigning containers to the node. Communication of the node status is done as part of the heartbeat between the NM and the RM.

This service determines the health status of the nodes through two strategies, one is Health Script, administrators may specify their own health check script that will be invoked by the health check service. If the script exits with a non-zero exit code, times out or results in an exception being thrown, the node is marked as *unhealthy*. Another one is Disk Checker. The disk checker checks the state of the disks that the NM is configured to use. The checks include permissions and free disk space. It also checks that the file system isn't in a read-only state. If a disk fails the check, the NM stops using that particular disk but still reports the node status as *healthy*. However, if a number of disks fail the check (25% by default), then the node is reported as *unhealthy* to the RM and new containers will not be assigned to the node.

We focus on the Health Script, we note that if the script cannot be executed due to permissions or an incorrect path, etc. then it counts as a failure and the node will be reported as *unhealthy*. The NM communicates this *"unhealthy"* state to the RM, which then adds it into exclude list. The NM will run this Health Script continuously, once the state is transformed into *"healthy"*, RM will remove it from the exclude list, and reassign

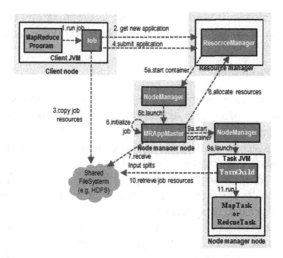

Fig. 3. YARN reject a MapReduce job.

containers to the node. The administrator can modify the configuration parameter in yarn-site.xml.

3   Vulnerability Analysis

3.1   Lack of Job Validation

The fundamental idea of MRv2 is to split up the two major functionalities of the JobTracker into separate daemons. The idea is to have a global RM and per-application AM. An application is a single job in the classical sense of Map-Reduce jobs.

Jobs are submitted to the RM via a public submission protocol and go through an admission control phase during which security credentials are validated and various operational and administrative checks are performed.

RMApp is the data structure used to maintain a job life-cycle in RM, and its implementation is RMAppImpl class. RMAppImpl holds the basic information about the job (i.e. Job ID, job name, queue name, start time) and the instance attempts.

We found that only the following situations will lead to *APP_REJECTED* (an event of RMApp state machine) event, as shown in Fig. 3:

(1) The client submit a job to RM via RPC function *ApplicationClientProto-col#submi-tApplication* may throw an exception, it happens when ResourceRequest over the minimum or maximum of the resources;

(2) Once the scheduler discovers that the job is illegal, (i.e. users submit to the inexistent queue or the queue reaches the upper limit of job numbers), it refuses to accept the job.

RM validates resource access permission, but lack of job validation about whether or not the job can finish. The only event that causes the job to enter the *finished* state is the normal exit from the AM container. We can submit a job to the cluster which is bound to fail, RM allocates resources for it and it's running on corresponding NM. However, RM doesn't check whether the job can be successfully completed.

3.2 Lack of Job Validation

The MapReduce enforces a strict structure: the computation task splits into map and reduce operations. Each instance of a map or reduce, called a computation unit, takes a list of key-value tuples. A MapReduce task consists of sequential phases of map and reduce operations. Once the map step is finished, the intermediate tuples are grouped by their key-components. This process of grouping is known as shuffling. All tuples belong to one group are processed by a reduce instance which expects to receive tuples sorted by their key-component [25]. Outputs of the reduce step can be used as inputs for the map step in the next phase, creating a chained MapReduce task.

Each Map/Reduce Task is just a concrete description of computing tasks, the real mission is done by TaskAttempt. The MRAppMaster executes the Mapper/Reducer task as a child process in a separate JVM, it can start multiple instances in order. If the first running instance failed, it starts another one instance to recalculate, until this data processing is completed or the number of attempts reaches the upper limit. By default, the maximum attempts are 4 times. The users can configure parameter in the job via mapreduce.map.maxattempts and mapreduce.reduce.maxattempts [20]. MRAppMaster may also start multiple instances simultaneously, so they will complete data processing. In MRApp-Master, the life-cycle of the TaskAttempt, Task and Job are described by a finite state machine, as shown in Fig. 4, where TaskAttempt is the actual task for the calculation, the other two components are only responsible for monitoring and management.

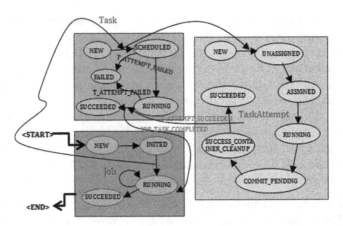

Fig. 4. The job/task state transition.

To our best knowledge, in some cases, the task never completes successfully even after multiple attempts. And it is easy to make the failed job, for instance, hardware failure, software bugs, process crashes and OOM (Out Of Memory). If there is no response from a NM in a certain amount of time, the MRAppMaster makes the task as failed. We summarize the five conditions result in task failed as follows:

(1) Map Task or Reduce Task fails. It means the problems of the MapReduce program itself which makes the task failed. There may be some errors in the user code.
(2) Time out. It may be due to network delay to read data out of time, or the task itself takes longer time than expected. In this case, the long-running tasks take up system resources and will reduce the performance of the cluster over time.
(3) The bottleneck of reading files. If the number of tasks performed by a job is very great, the common input file may become a bottleneck.
(4) Shuffle error. If the map task completes quickly, and all the data is ready to copy for shuffle, it will lead to overload of threads and memory usage of buffer in the shuffle process, which will cause a shortage of memory.
(5) The child process JVM quit suddenly. It may be caused by the bug of JVM, which makes the MapReduce code running failed.

We can easily make job failed using one of these items, for instance, we write program with an infinite loop, or we specify the timeout as 10 s, but submit a long-running job, which need at least 2 min.

3.3   Weak Exclude List Mechanism

As discussed in Sect. 2.3, NM runs health check service to determine the health of the node it is executing on. If the task failed more than 3 times in a node, the node is regarded under the *unhealthy* state. When a DataNode under *unhealthy* state, all the containers currently running on this DataNode are marked as dead and no new containers are scheduled on it. Explicitly point out the default failure times in the RMContainerRequestor class as follows:

```
maxTaskFailuresPerNode =  conf.getInt(MRJobConfig.
MAX_TASK_FAILURES_PER_TRACKER, 3);
```

NodesListManager maintains an exclude list - a file that resides on the RM and contains IP address of the DataNodes to be excluded. When NM reports its *unhealthy* state to RM via heartbeat, RM doesn't check why and how it becomes *unhealthy*, but adds it into exclude list directly.

Before that, RM calculates the proportion of the nodes in exclude list, which gets parameter information from MRJobConfig interface. When the node number of exclude list is less than a certain percentage (default is 33%), RM will add the node into exclude list, otherwise the *unhealthy* node won't be added to exclude list.

Finally, the failure handling of the containers themselves is completely left to the framework. The RM collects all container exit events from the NMs and propagates those to the corresponding AMs in a heartbeat response. AM already listens to these notifications and retries map or reduce tasks by requesting new containers from the RM.

4   SEYARN Threat Models

The adversary is the malicious insider in the cloud, aiming to subvert availability of the cluster. As discussed in Sect. 3, we discovered three vulnerabilities of YARN platform, we can use the health check service to submit easy failed jobs to add DataNodes to exclude list, which will cause service degradation and the reduction of active DataNodes.

Considering the scenario in Fig. 5, the normal users and malicious users can submit jobs to the YARN cluster. The jobs that normal users submitted can finish completely, while the jobs that malicious users submitted are the failed jobs, which will never complete. We use the running process of an application to analyze the attack process. The steps are detailed as follows:

(1) Distributed attackers and normal users submit applications to the RM via a public submission protocol and go through an admission control phase during which security credentials are validated and various operational and administrative checks are performed.

(2) Accepted applications are passed to the scheduler to run. Once the scheduler has enough resources, the application is moved from accepted to *running* state. Aside from internal bookkeeping, this involves allocating a container for the AM and spawning it on a node in the cluster.

(3) When RM starts the AM, it should register with the RM and periodically advertise its liveness and requirements via heartbeat. To obtain containers, AM issues resource requests to the RM.

(4) Once the RM allocates a container, AM can construct a container launch context (CLC) to launch the container on the corresponding NM. Monitoring the progress of work done inside the container is strictly the AM's responsibility.

(5) To launch the container, the NM copies all the necessary dependencies to local storage. Map tasks process each block of input (typically 128 MB) and produce intermediate results, which are key-value pairs. These are saved to disk. Reduce tasks fetch the list of intermediate results associated with each key and run it through the user's reduce function, which produces output.

(6) If the task fails to complete, the task will be tried for a number of times, saying 3 times; if all tries fail, this task will be treated as a failure, and AM will contact RM to set up another container (possibly in another node) for this task, until this task is completed or the MapReduce job is terminated.

(7) For each DataNode, which executes the failed task, its health check service will add one to its total number of failures. And if the DataNode has failed more than 3 times, the node will be marked as *unhealthy*. The NM reports this *unhealthy* state to the RM, which then adds it into exclude node lists.

(8) Once the AM is done with its work, it should unregister from the RM and exit cleanly.

Attackers repeat the procedure until the exclude list has 33% nodes of the total number, aiming at reducing the service availability and performance by exhausting the resources of the cluster (including memory, processing resources, and network bandwidth).

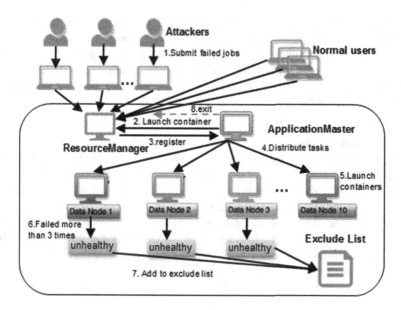

Fig. 5. DDHCS: DDoS attack based on health check service.

5   Evaluation

5.1   Experiment Setup

We set up our Hadoop cluster with 20 nodes. Each node runs a DataNode and a Node-Manager with an Intel Core i7 processor running at 3.4 GHz, 4096 MB of RAM, and run Hadoop 2.6.0, which is a distributed, scalable, and portable system. All experiments use the default configuration in Hadoop for HDFS and MapReduce except otherwise noted (e.g., the HDFS block size is 128 MB, max java heap size is 2 GB).

5.1.1   Attack Programs

Attack Setting. We consider a setting in which attackers and normal users are concurrent using the same YARN platform. It is well known that YARN in public clouds makes extensive use of multi-tenancy. We design three attack programs as follows:

WordCount_A: We use WordCount benchmark in Hadoop as our main intrusion program because it is widely used and represents many kinds of data-intensive jobs. We specify the timeout parameter as 10 ms (named as WordCount_A).

Since the input file we used is the full English Wikipedia archive with the total data size of 31 GB, the program can't finish within the time limit.

BeerAndDiaper: We write an infinite loop in this program and specify the timeout parameter as 10 ms, which will fail to complete within the time limit.

WordCount_N: We use an executable program, but as a normal user, we can modify the configuration file–*map-site.xml* in client. We change the value of *mapreduce.task.timeout* from 1000 (ms) to 10 (ms). We use the "*hadoop dfsadmin -refreshNodes*" command to reload the configuration file. We submit executable WordCount program (named as WordCount_N) with large input file, since it can't finish in 10 ms, it will be marked as failed.

5.1.2   Evaluation Index

First, we introduce the variable to be used as follows. N denotes the total number of living nodes that a Hadoop cluster currently has; m denotes the number of *unhealthy* nodes after DDHCS attack. Here for simplicity, we assume that all of the nodes in a cluster are identical. T_{start} denotes the start time of the job, T_{finish} denotes the end time, then we calculate the total completion times under normal circumstances as $T = T_{finish} - T_{start}$, we repeat the jobs for 20 times, recording the start time and finish time, so we can obtain the average time under normal circumstances as

$$\bar{T} = \frac{\sum_{i=1}^{n} T_i}{n} \tag{1}$$

Similarly, we calculate the average time under DDoS attack as:

$$\bar{T}' = \frac{\sum_{i=1}^{n} \bar{T}'}{n} \tag{2}$$

Wherein, T' denotes the total completion times under DDoS attack, calculated by

$$T' = T'_{finish} - T'_{start} \tag{3}$$

We can characterize the scale of the addressed DDHCS attacks in three dimensions: (i) attack broadness, which is defined as $b = m/N$; (ii) attack strength, denoted as s, which in the portion of resource occupied by the DDHCS attack in an infected node. For example, given attack broadness $b = 83.2\%$, and attack strength $s = 80\%$, a task will cost as $1/(1 - s)$ (here 5) times long as usual to complete, with the probability of b (here 83.2%). As shown in the follow, we can go through a mathematical derivation that attack strength is as follows:

$$s = \frac{\bar{T}' - \bar{T}}{\bar{T}'} \tag{4}$$

(iii) resource degradation, we compare the CPU, memory occupancy rate and network bandwidth usage with and without DDHCS attacks, which can read from the job logs.

5.2 Evaluations

To verify the attack effectiveness of our approach, we test three programs mentioned above for evaluating attack broadness, attack strength and resource degradation. In the following section, we describe the details of the experimental records.

5.2.1 Attack Broadness

As we discussed in Sect. 5.1, N denotes the total number of living nodes that a Hadoop cluster currently has; m denotes the number of unhealthy nodes after DDHCS attack. We use b = m/N to describe the attack broadness. We investigate a range of DDHCS intensities with three programs: WordCount_A, BeerAndDiaper and WordCount_N, running 100 times, 80 times, 60 times respectively. We can check the unhealthy nodes and decommission nodes in the cluster using the website http://www.master:8088/cluster/apps. We record the unhealthy nodes and decommission nodes after each DDHCS attack, as shown in Table 2.

Table 2. Summary of DDHCS Attack broadness.

Job type	Times	Total nodes	Unhealthy nodes	Decommission nodes	Exclude list nodes rate	Attack broadness
WordCount_A	100	20	18	6	30%	90%
	80	20	18	6	30%	90%
	60	20	16	5	25%	80%
BeerAndDiaper	100	20	17	6	30%	85%
	80	20	17	6	30%	85%
	60	20	16	5	25%	80%
WordCount_N	100	20	18	6	30%	90%
	80	20	17	5	25%	85%
	60	20	17	5	25%	85%

As we can see in Table 2, the experimental results are the same as our research results. The decommission nodes represent the nodes which are added to exclude list, it accounts for less than 33% of total nodes. The average attack broadness of these three programs are 86.7%, 83.3%, 86.7% respectively, we can see that the cluster becomes unable to provide the services to its legitimate user and hence the cluster performance will be greatly deteriorated.

5.2.2 Attack Strength

In this experiment, we run 4 benchmark applications to cover a wide range of data-intensive tasks: compute intensive (Grep), shuffle intensive (Index), database queries (Join), iterative (Randomwriter). We first run the 4 benchmark applications 20 times before the DDHCS attack to calculate the average running time, then we run three attack programs 100 times separately as three attack scenarios. After each attack scenarios we run each benchmark 20 times again to calculate the average running time after DDHCS attack.

Grep. Grep is a popular application for large scale data processing. It searches some regular expressions through input text files and outputs the lines which contain the matched expressions.

Inverted index. Inverted index is widely used in search area. We implement a job in Hadoop that builds an inverted index from given documents and generates a compressed bit vector posting list for each word.

Join. Join is one of the most common applications that experience the data skew problem.

Randomwriter. Randomwriter writes 10 GB data to each node randomly, it is memory intensive, CPU intensive and have high I/O consumption.

Table 3. Summary of the attack strength of 4 benchmark applications.

		Average running time				Attack strength			
		Grep	Inverted index	Join	Random writer	Grep	Inverted index	Join	Random writer
Normal		112.4 s	86.4 s	113.6 s	71.3 s	0%			
DDoS	Word-Count_A	726.7 s	444.6 s	745.2 s	563.7 s	84.5%	80.6%	84.8%	87.4%
	BeerAnd-Diaper	737.8 s	435.1 s	751.3 s	579.2 s	86.1%	80.1%	84.9%	87.8%
	Word-Count_N	733.1 s	453.3 s	749.5 s	553.8	84.7%	80.9%	84.8%	87.1%

Firstly, we run each benchmark 20 times with no DDHCS attack to summarize the average running time $\bar{T}$. Then we run 100 times of the three attack programs Word-Count_A, BeerAndDiaper, WordCount_N separately and record the running time of each legal benchmark application after each attack program. We summarize the average running time $\bar{T}''_{grep}$, $\bar{T}''_{inverted index}$, $\bar{T}''_{join}$, $\bar{T}''_{randomwrite}$ in Table 3, and analyze the attack strength. The result shows that under each type of DDHCS attack, the attack strength is more than 80 percent, and the cluster performance is more degraded.

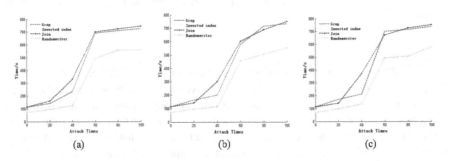

Fig. 6. Job running time under 3 attack scenarios: (a) under WordCount_A DDHCS attack (b) under BeerAndDiaper DDHCS attack (c) under WordCount_N DDHCS attack.

Figure 6 demonstrate the average running time of the 4 benchmark applications with the increase of DDHCS attacks. We can see that as the increase of the attack program running times, the average running time of each benchmark applications prolonged significantly, which means the cluster is unable to provide service and the average time to access user request is higher than normal (Figs. 7 and 8).

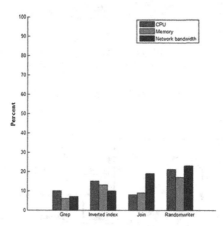

Fig. 7. Summary of the CPU, memory occupancy rate and network bandwidth usage before DDHCS attack.

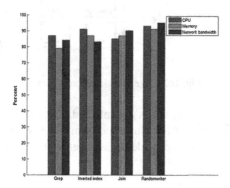

Fig. 8. Summary of the CPU, memory occupancy rate and network bandwidth usage after BeerAndDiaper DDHCS attack.

5.2.3   Resource Degradation

In order to demonstrate these results, we run additional experiments trying to compare the resources degradation. We simulated a scenario with BeerAndDiaper DDHCS attack. We run a range of attack program intensities: 20 times, 40 times, 60 times, 80 times and 100 times. The CPU, memory usage and network bandwidth usage before and after BeerAndDiaper DDHCS attack are illustrated in Figs. 9 and 10.

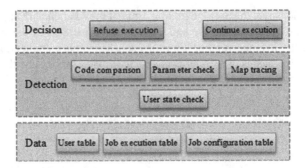

Fig. 9. The architecture of SEYARN.

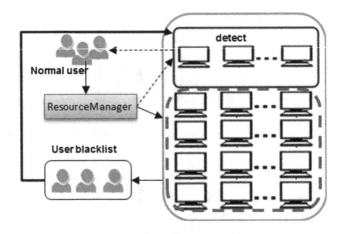

Fig. 10. User blacklist mechanism.

In this scenario, most of the nodes are infected, and resource consumption has a significant rise and hence the YARN cluster performance is greatly deteriorated, which makes YARN become unable to provide the services to its legitimate user.

6 Implementation

Recent work has proposed many methods to detect or prevent traditional DDoS attack, but these techniques are not suitable for Big Data platform [8, 15, 22]. According to the vulnerabilities of our study, it is mainly because of legal users submitting malicious programs to launch attacks against YARN, we can't make defense by predicting user behavior. An important method to prevent DDoS attacks against YARN is to enhance the cluster. This requires a heightened awareness of security issues and prevention techniques from all YARN users.

6.1   Strategy and Architecture

We proposed a safety inspection module to enhance YARN security, named SEYARN it has three layers including four kinds of strategy. We can see from the Fig. 9 the architecture of SEYARN, it includes one data layer which used to record the user information and job information, one detection layer, this layer uses one method to detect user state and three methods to detect job condition. After finishing the detection, the decision layer determines whether the job should be executed.

The four key technologies are User blacklist mechanism, Code comparison, Parameter check and Map-tracing. We deploy the SEYARN module on NameNode, certainly, we can deploy it on the DataNodes, since it implements safety inspection by network communication. We should say that it is easier to implement on NameNode since it has the default permission to access other data nodes.

Now, we will discuss the four methods briefly:

User Blacklist Mechanism. Just like the node excluded list mechanism, we could construct user blacklist. As shown in Fig. 10. When a user submitted jobs fail more than M times, the user is added into User blacklist. A user that matches an entry in the blacklists cannot distribute his jobs on the cluster until he proves to be clean. We use database to record the state of the user, we will describe it later. We can calculate the values of M by machine learning algorithm. In this part, we specify M as 10 for testing the module.

A user should not be blacklisted forever. A blacklisted user should be allowed to gain his/her rights back if it can be verified that the user's jobs are no longer failed. Periodically each job submitted by the user runs test on the nodes, if it can finish successfully, the values of user failure times is reduced by one. The user is removed from the User blacklist when his failure times are less than M.

Code Comparison. Malicious users usually submit the same attack programs many times within a short time. It has no time to modify the attack programs since the default heart beat time is 10 min in YARN. So we can check the source code, if the same user submits the same code more than N times, this job will be refused. We use MD5 hash algorithm in this part, certainly, we can use the existing program code similarity detection techniques, such as, attribute counting, structure metrics, LCS etc.

Parameter Check. We all know that MapReduce program has a fixed structure. The user writes code to fill in a MapReduce specification object with the names of the input and output files and optional tuning parameters. So we can check these parameters before the program execution. If we find that some of the parameters are too high or too low compared with the normal value, the MapReduce program is not allowed to execute. We can see the Table 4, we summarize part of the parameters and those default values that users can modify. For instance, the default execution time are 600000 ms, if the user specifies it as 10 ms, this job will be rejected. When you use SEYANR you can specify the maximum and minimum of each value.

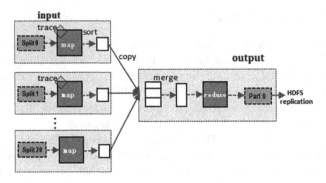

Fig. 11. MapReduce execution overview.

Table 4. Basic parameters of mapred-default.

Name	Value	Description
mapreduce.task.timeout	600000	The maximum amount of time (in milli seconds) reduce task spends in trying to connect to a task-tracker for getting map output
mapreduce.map.memory.mb	1024	The amount of memory to request from the scheduler for each map task
mapreduce.map.cpu.vcores	1	The number of virtual cores to request from the scheduler for each map task
mapreduce.map.maxattempts	4	The maximum number of attempts per map task. In other words, framework will try to execute a map task these many number of times before giving up on it
mapre-duce.reduce.memory.mb	1024	The amount of memory to request from the scheduler for each reduce task
mapreduce.reduce.cpu.vcores	1	The number of virtual cores to request from the scheduler for each reduce task
mapreduce.reduce.maxat-tempts	4	The maximum number of attempts per reduce task. In other words, framework will try to execute a reduce task these many number of times before giving up on it

Map-tracing. Novel visualizations and statistical views of the behavior of MapReduce programs enable users to trace the MapReduce program behavior through the program's stages. Also, most previous techniques for tracing have extracted distributed execution traces at the programming language level (e.g. using instrumented middleware or libraries to track requests [2, 3, 16]), we can learn from them and generate views at the higher-level MapReduce abstraction. Figure 11 shows the overall flow of a MapReduce operation, we mainly focus on the Map phase.

We observed that, for each phase, the logs faithfully repeat the observed distributions of task completion time, data read by each task, size and location of inputs, state of each task, probability of failures and recomputations, and fairness based evictions. So we trace K maps for each job by jobID, we capture the logs periodically and if the maps have some problems, such as, can't finish successfully, we will kill the job.

Finally, the DDoS attacks exist in multi-tenancy environment, so it is important for a user to learn the security and the resource usage patterns of other users sharing the cluster. It is necessary for rational planning the number of nodes that each user can use.

6.2   Feasible Confirmation

6.2.1   Process

We use SQLite3 database, it is a relational database management system contained in a C programming library. In contrast to many other database management systems, SQLite3 is not a client–server database engine. Rather, it is embedded into the end program. SQLite3 is arguably the most widely deployed database engine, as it is used today by several operating systems, and embedded systems, among others. We build three data tables, one of the tables records the user information, including userID, username, and two flags, one is forbidden flag which used to determine whether to forbid this user running jobs, and another is health_point flag, which used to add the user to blacklist after performing irregularities several times. Other two tables record the execution information and the configuration information of jobs, we can gather these information from the job logs.

Before we aggregate the jobs, we should modify the core-site.xml configuration file to enable the log history and log aggregation. Log aggregation collects each container's logs and moves these logs onto a file-system, for instance, HDFS, after the application completes. Then we can configure the "yarn.nodemanager.remote-app-log-dir" and "yarn.nodemanager.remote-app-log-dir-suffix" properties to determine where these logs are moved to. We can access the logs via the Application Timeline Server. The logs faithfully repeat the real-time running state of each task, we can gather all data we need from the logs.

Once users submit jobs, our SEYARN has the following steps:

(1) Get user state from user table. After log aggregation, we move the logs of the same user to each username direction. We determine the user state according to the logs and record it in the user table. For example, we determine m_1 as normal failed jobs of each user (they have failed label), m_2 as abnormal failed jobs of each user (they have killed label). m_2 has higher weight than m_1, e.g 3 times. We sum m_1 and m_2 to compare with M (discussed in Sect. 6.1) to determine user state.

(2) If the user is non-forbidden, we submit his jobs to the cluster to inspect. We extract the jar packet and decompile it to obtain the source code. Verify that the sources are not the same by using MD5 algorithm. We define that if the same user submits the identical code more than N times, this job will be refused.

(3) Then we compare the default value (as shown in Table 4) with the source code parameter. If we find the parameter is abnormal, we will kill the job.

(4) We provide real-time monitoring of the job. We capture the logs periodically with the jobID, if we find the first K map tasks have some problems, such as, can't finish successfully, we will kill the job.

(5) Once the job is done with the inspection, the job continues to run on the corresponding NM (Fig. 12).

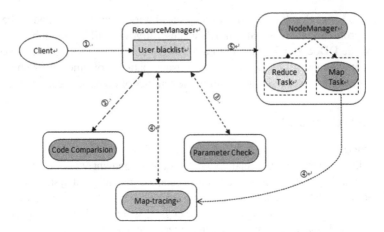

Fig. 12. The process of SEYARN.

6.2.2 Evaluation

To verify the viability of our approach, we test two attack programs mentioned in Sect. 5.1, those are WordCount_A and BeerAndDiaper. As we discussed above, when a user submitted jobs fail more than M times, the user is added into User blacklist. In addition, if the same user submits the same code more than N times, this job will be refused. Besides, if the first K maps have some problems, we will kill the job. For testing, in the following section, we determine M as 10, N as 10 and K as 5.

We run WordCount_A and BeerAndDiaper 5 times, 10 times and 20 times separately, we record the number of jobs which are killed, as shown in Table 5 denotes the number of killed jobs, total denotes the running times. We use v/total to calculate the accuracy of our SEYARN model.

Table 5. Summary of SEYARN accuracy.

Attack programs		Launch Inspection				Killed jobs	Average Accuracy
		User blacklist	Code comparison	Decompile	Map-tracing		
WordCount_A	5			✓		5	
	10	✓	✓	✓		10	98.3%
	20	✓	✓	✓		19	
BeerAndDiaper	5				✓	5	
	10	✓	✓		✓	9	96.7%
	20	✓	✓		✓	20	

As we can see in Table 5, our approach achieves higher than 95% accuracy that means our SEYARN model can defend DDHCS attack effectively. Since it is a simple engine, only needs little time to inspect jobs, it has little side effects to the cluster's performance.

7   Conclusion

In this paper, we studied the vulnerability of YARN and proposed a DDoS attack based on health check service (DDHCS). We designed DDHCS attack model by submitting abundant of failed jobs to demonstrate how many nodes in a YARN cluster can be invaded by malicious users. Our study shows that these vulnerabilities may be easily used by attackers and can cause significant impact on the performance of a YARN cluster. The highest 90% of the nodes deny of service and attack strength is more than 80%. Given this, we proposed a security enhancement for YARN, including Code comparison, Parameter check, Maptracing and User blacklist mechanism. In addition, we implemented SEYARN model on NameNode, our experiments showed that SEYARN fixed these three vulnerabilities with extending 95% accuracy.

Regarding future research, we will move forward to improve our SEYARN. We will use theoretical analysis and numerical simulations to define the parameters which predefined in this paper. Moreover, we will optimize our algorithm for code comparison with a higher level accuracy, increasing Syntactic analysis and lexical analysis. We hope to make a more complete SEYARN for resisting related attacks effectively.

Acknowledgements. The authors gratefully acknowledge the support of the National High Technology Research and Development Program ("863" Program) of China under Grant No. 2015AA016009, the National Natural Science Foundation of China under Grant No. 61232005, and the Science and Technology Program of Shen Zhen, China under Grant No. JSGG20140516162852628. Specially thanks to Ziyao Zhu and Wenjun Qian for the support of experiments.

References

1. Alarifi, S., Wolthusen, S.D.: Mitigation of cloud-internal denial of service attacks. In: IEEE 8th International Symposium on Service Oriented System Engineering (SOSE), pp. 478–483. IEEE (2014)
2. Barham, P., Donnelly, A., Isaacs, R.: Using magpie for request extraction and workload modelling. In: USENIX OSDI, vol. 6, pp. 259–272 (2004)
3. Chen, M.Y., Kiciman, E., Fratkin, E.: Pinpoint: problem determination in large, dynamic internet services. In: International Conference on Dependable Systems and Networks (DSN), pp. 595–604. IEEE (2002)
4. Criscuolo, P.J.: Distributed Denial of Service: Trin00, Tribe Flood Network, Tribe Flood Network 2000, and Stacheldraht CIAC-2319. California Univ. Livermore Radiation Lab. (2000)
5. Durcekova, V., Schwartz, L., Shahmehri, N.: Sophisticated denial of service attacks aimed at application layer. In: ELEKTRO, pp. 55–60. IEEE (2012)
6. Ficco, M., Rak, M.: Stealthy denial of service strategy in cloud computing. IEEE Trans. Cloud Comput. **3**(1), 80–94 (2015)
7. Girma, A., Garuba, M., Li, J.: Analysis of DDoS attacks and an introduction of a hybrid statistical model to detect DDoS attacks on cloud computing environment. In: 12th International Conference on Information Technology-New Generations (ITNG), pp. 212–217. IEEE (2015)

8. Gu, Z., Pei, K., Wang, Q.: LEAPS: detecting camouflaged attacks with statistical learning guided by program analysis. In: IEEE/IFIP International Conference on Dependable Systems and Networks, pp. 57–68. IEEE (2015)

9. Hameed S., Ali, U.: On the Efficacy of Live DDoS Detection with Hadoop. arXiv preprint arXiv:1506.08953 (2015)

10. Huang, J., Nicol, D.M., Campbell, R.H.: Denial-of-service threat to Hadoop/YARN clusters with multi-tenancy. In: 2014 IEEE International Congress on Big Data (BigData Congress), pp. 48–55. IEEE (2014)

11. Karthik, S., Shah, J.J.: Analysis of simulation of DDOS attack in cloud. In: 2014 International Conference on Information Communication and Embedded Systems (ICICES), pp. 1–5. IEEE (2014)

12. Khattak, R., Bano, S., Hussain, S.: DOFUR: DDoS forensics using MapReduce. In: Frontiers of Information Technology (FIT), pp. 117–120. IEEE (2011)

13. Kholidy, H., Baiardi, F.: CIDS: A framework for intrusion detection in cloud systems. In: Ninth International Conference on Information Technology: New Generations (ITNG), pp. 379–385. IEEE (2012)

14. Kholidy, H., Baiardi, F., Hariri, S.: DDSGA: a data-driven semi-global alignment approach for detecting masquerade attacks. IEEE Trans. Dependable Secure Comput. **12**(2), 164–178 (2015). IEEE

15. Kiciman, E., Fox, A.: Detecting application-level failures in component-based internet services. IEEE Trans. Neural Networks **16**(5), 1027–1041 (2005)

16. Koskinen, E., Jannotti, J.: Borderpatrol: isolating events for black-box tracing. ACM SIGOPS Operating Syst. Rev. **42**(4), 191–203 (2008). ACM

17. Lee, Y., Kang, W., Lee, Y.: A hadoop-based packet trace processing tool. In: Domingo-Pascual, J., Shavitt, Y., Uhlig, S. (eds.) TMA 2011. LNCS, vol. 6613, pp. 51–63. Springer, Heidelberg (2011). doi:10.1007/978-3-642-20305-3_5

18. Lee, Y., Lee, Y.: Detecting DDoS attacks with hadoop. In: ACM CoNEXT Student Workshop, pp. 1–2. ACM (2011)

19. Mizukoshi, M., Munetomo, M.: Distributed denial of services attack protection system with genetic algorithms on hadoop cluster computing framework. In: 2015 IEEE Congress on Evolutionary Computation (CEC), pp. 1575–1580. IEEE (2015)

20. O'Malley, O., Zhang K., Radia, S.: Hadoop security design. Yahoo! Technical report (2009)

21. Sabahi, F.: Cloud computing security threats and responses. In: IEEE 3rd International Conference on Communication Software and Networks (ICCSN), pp. 245–249. IEEE (2011)

22. Specht, S.M., Lee R.B.: Distributed denial of service: taxonomies of attacks, tools, and countermeasures. In: ISCA PDCS, pp. 543–550 (2004)

23. Ulusoy, H., Colombo, P., Ferrari, E.: GuardMR: fine-grained security policy enforcement for MapReduce systems. In: ACM Symposium on Information, Computer and Communications Security (ASIACCS), pp. 285–296. ACM, New York (2015)

24. Vavilapalli, V.K., Murthy, A.C., Douglas, C.: Apache hadoop YARN: yet another resource negotiator. In: Symposium on Cloud Computing, pp. 1–16. ACM (2013)

25. Wu, H., Tantawi, A.N., Yu, T.: A self-optimizing workload management solution for cloud applications. In: IEEE 20th International Conference on Web Services (ICWS), pp. 483–490. IEEE (2013)

Performance Comparison of Voice Encryption Algorithms Implemented on Blackfin Platform

Cristina-Loredana Duta[✉], Laura Gheorghe[✉], and Nicolae Tapus[✉]

Department of Computer Science and Engineering,
University Politehnica of Bucharest, Bucharest, Romania
cristina.duta.mapn@outlook.com,
{laura.gheorghe,nicolae.tapus}@cs.pub.ro

Abstract. Nowadays, secure speech communications have become a fundamental issue, due to the rapid development of digital communications and networking technologies. People want high security level during their communications, especially for military and business purpose. For instance, in order to operate properly and effective in a hostile environment is mandatory to have a secure military communication. The methods that are currently available for voice encryption include the use of cryptographic algorithms (which ensure secure data transmission and reception). However, taking into consideration the problem of the bandwidth of the communication channel (which appears frequently in military applications), it is important to identify encryption algorithms that ensure high throughput and low bit-rate speech compression methods. Various speech encryption methods have strict requirements such as power consumption, size, voltage supply, which are difficult to fulfil. A solution to meet these constraints is to perform optimization at all levels, starting from the algorithm design, continuing with the system and circuit structure and reaching also the design of the cell library. More exactly, these optimizations depend on the modification of the encryption algorithm selected for the applications (in order to reduce its computational complexity), the algorithm chosen, the arithmetic unit selected (fixed-point or floating-point), the mapping between the selected architecture and the cryptographic algorithm. This paper describes a comparison regarding the performance of various speech encryption algorithms implemented on Digital Signal Processor (DSP) platform. These algorithms are from different categories, such as: stream ciphers (Grain v1, Trivium, Mickey 2.0 and SOSEMANUK), block ciphers (Advanced Encryption Standard - AES and Data Encryption Standard - DES) and dedicated algorithms for voice encryption (Robust Secure Coder, scrambling encryption and encryption algorithm based on chaotic map and Blowfish). All the previously mentioned algorithms where implemented on Blackfin 537 (a fixed point DSP) and careful optimizations were performed to fulfil real time requirements. The goal of this paper was to evaluate all these algorithms to determine which one is the best suited for applications that require secure real time communications.

Keywords: Speech processing · Voice encryption · Digital Signal Processor · Grain V1 · Trivium · Mickey 2.0 · SOSEMANUK · AES · DES · Blackfin processor

© Springer International Publishing AG 2017
O. Camp et al. (Eds.): ICISSP 2016, CCIS 691, pp. 169–191, 2017.
DOI: 10.1007/978-3-319-54433-5_10

1 Introduction

Speech represents the fundamental form of communication between humans. There are two methods to represent the speech: through its message content (as information) and as an acoustic waveform (the signal which carries the message information).

In the last years, due to the advancements in communication technology and the increasing demand of speech based applications, security has become an important aspect. The purpose of secure communication is to overcome unwanted disclosure and unauthorized modifications while transmitting speech through insecure channels.

The redundancy of the language plays an important role in secure speech communication systems such that if the language is highly redundant, an intruder can decipher the information much easier. Traditional solutions to ensure communications confidentiality are based on scrambling techniques (which include simple permutations and affine transformations in frequency or time domain). Due to the fact that in the last decade, the computing power has quickly increased, these scrambling algorithms became vulnerable to attacks. In this context, many real-world cryptographic implementations shifted to integrating encryption with compression algorithms in order to reduce the size of the signal before encryption and to eliminate the redundancy.

In general, there are four main categories of speech encryption: frequency domain scrambling, time domain scrambling, amplitude scrambling and two-dimensional scrambling (combination of time-domain and frequency-domain scrambling).

Time domain scrambling represents a common technique to record the speech signals for some time and then divide them into small frames. Depending on a secret code, these frames can be sent in a different time order. The scrambling rate increases if the frames are small and the sampling of data is longer.

Frequency domain scrambling represents the inversion of the voice frequencies. More exactly, it converts high frequencies to low one and the other way around. This technique includes three categories: base-band inversion, variable-band scrambling and split-band inversion.

Amplitude domain scrambling implies the modification of the signal amplitude but this doesn't really change the signal. It is very hard to employ, therefore it is not practically used.

In the *transform domain*, there are many speech encryption methods. For instance, methods such as fast Fourier transform, discrete cosine transform and wavelet transform are widely used. Recently, some new voice encryption methods were developed based on chaotic maps and on circular transformations.

Speech encryption algorithms can also be classified into *digital encryption* and *analogue encryption* methods. *Analogue encryption* operates on the voice samples themselves. The main advantage of analogue encryption is the fact that no modem or voice compression method is required for transmission. Moreover, the quality of the voice which is recovered is independent of the language. This type of encryption is recommended to be used for the existing analogue channels such as telephone, satellite or mobile communication links.

Digital encryption involves, as a first step, the digitization of the input voice signal. Then, the digitized signal will be compressed to produce a bit stream with a suitable bit rate. The resulting bit stream will be encrypted and transmitted through insecure channels. This type of encryption ensures high voice quality, low distortion and is considered cryptanalytically stronger than analogue encryption. More specifically, except some advanced mathematical approaches, digital encryption can only be broken by using brute force attacks.

Regarding digital encryption techniques, there are several standards to choose from, such as Data Encryption Standard (DES), Advanced Encryption Standard (AES), Fast Data Encryption Algorithm (FEAL), International Data Encryption Algorithm (IDEA), Secure and Fast Encryption Routine (SAFER), Rivest's Code 5 (RC5) and Rivest's Code 6 (RC6). These algorithms usually have the same parameters, the key K (which ensures that the result of the encryption is unreadable) and the input block (which can be a digital bit stream or a block). Most of these standards can be used to ensure secure communications over insecure channels.

Complex digital speech encryption algorithms were developed due to the appearance of Very Large Scale Integration (VLSI) and DSP chips and are nowadays used in applications such as voice activated security, personal communication systems, secure voice mail and so on. A part of these applications require devices that have limited resources, which means that their implementation is dependent on constraints such as memory, size and power consumption. In this context, because of the advantages offered, DPSs represent the best solution for obtaining high performance speech encryption, under real time requirements. Moreover, hardware cryptographic algorithms are more physically secure, which makes it hard for an attacker to read information or to modify it.

The purpose of this paper is to optimize and to compare the performance of nine speech encryption algorithms which can be easily embedded in low power, portable systems and which can be used in real time. This paper focuses on the following speech encryption methods: four stream ciphers (Mickey 2.0, Grain v1, Trivium, SOSEMANUK), two block ciphers (AES and DES), a scrambling encryption algorithm, a Robust Secure Coder (RSC) algorithm and an encryption algorithm based on chaotic map and Blowfish algorithms. An important aspect presented in this paper is solving the problem of optimizing the implementations of previously mentioned voice encryption algorithms on DSP platforms. All the algorithms were ported onto a fixed point DSP and a stage by stage optimization was performed to meet the real time requirements. The goal was to determine which of the evaluated encryption algorithms is best suited for real time secure communications (in terms of performance).

This paper is organized as follows. The necessary background for our work is presented in Sect. 2. Related work is described in Sect. 3. Details regarding the architecture and implementation of voice encryption algorithms are presented in Sect. 4. The experimental results for the un-optimized code and for the optimized code of the speech encryption algorithms are described in Sect. 5. Conclusions are summarized in Sect. 6 together with our future work.

2   Background

This section includes a brief description of Mixed Excitation Linear Prediction (MELP), a speech coding algorithm, of stream ciphers such as Mickey v2, Trivium, Grain v1.0, SOSEMANUK, of block ciphers such as DES and AES, of recently developed voice encryption algorithms and the description of general aspects of DSP architectures.

2.1 Mixed Excitation Linear Prediction (MELP) Algorithm

Speech coding can be performed using voice coders (vocoders), which can be classified as follows. The waveform-following coders who are able to reproduce exactly the original speech signal if there aren't any quantization errors. The model-based coders do not try to keep the waveform of the original vocal signal, because they use the parametric representation of speech production which includes the encoding and transmission of the parameters, not the signal. The encoding stage is called analysis because through the analysis of the speech signal, the necessary parameters are extracted and the decoding stage is called synthesis.

Linear Predictive Coding (LPC) [1] is a compression method which models the process of speech production as a linear combination of past samples. These vocoders use white noise or a periodic pulse train as the excitation for a synthesis filter. Their main disadvantage is the fact that sometimes they sound buzzy or mechanical because of the inability to reproduce all kinds of voiced speech using a simple pulse train.

MELP [2, 3] vocoder is based on LPC model, but has some additional features such as: mixed-excitation, pulse dispersion, adaptive spectral enhancement and aperiodic pulses. The mixed-excitation has the effect to reduce the buzz, which is in general encountered in LPC vocoders. Aperiodic pulses are very useful for transitions between unvoiced and voiced segments of the signal. The advantage brought is the fact that the synthesizer can reproduce, without having tonal noises inserted, erratic glottal pulses. The pulse dispersion is usually implemented using a filter, which has the effect to disperse the excitation energy with a pitch period. This feature is very useful for synthetic speech, because the harsh quality of it is reduced. The filter for adaptive spectral enhancement provides a more natural quality to the outputted speech signal, by improving the match between natural and synthetic waveforms.

The block diagram of MELP encoder is presented in Fig. 1. MELP algorithm quantizes and transmits the following parameters: pitch, bandpass voicing strengths, two gain values, Fourier magnitudes, aperiodic flag and linear prediction coefficients. At the beginning of the encoding process the interferences are removed using a highpass filter with a cutoff frequency of 60 Hz. The integer pitch value is then calculated using the normalized autocorrelation method. The next step is to perform bandpass voicing analysis which extracts 5 bandpass voicing strengths. The aperiodic flag is determined by the voicing strength that has the lowest band. After this, a 10th order linear prediction analysis and an autocorrelation analysis are performed, which determine the linear prediction residual signal. After obtaining the final pitch, Gains and Fourier magnitudes are computed.

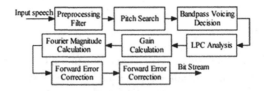

Fig. 1. Block diagram of MELP encoder.

Figure 2 shows the block diagram of MELP decoder. It is important to know that parameter decoding differs for unvoiced and voiced modes. In the first step, the pitch is decoded, which is then used to select the decoding mode that will be used further on. If there are quiet input signals, then both decoded gain parameters are attenuated. For each synthesized pitch period (voice signal), all MELP parameters are interpolated pitch-synchronously.

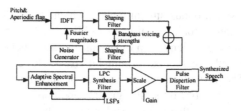

Fig. 2. Block diagram of MELP decoder.

2.2 Trivium Stream Cipher

Trivium stream cipher [4] has 80-bit initialization vector (IV) and a key of 80 bits and can generate a keystream up to 2^{64} bits. The structure of the cipher is illustrated in Fig. 3. The secret state of the algorithm has 288 bits, which includes three non-linear feedback shift registers of different lengths: 93, 84 and 111 bits. As the majority of stream ciphers, Trivium has two phases: the setup of key and IV phase and the keystream generation phase. The keystream generation operates in each clock cycle on three input bits and produces one output bit. The initialization includes 1152 steps of the clocking procedure. The algorithm is designed such that it allows improvement of the throughput using parallelization (64 iterations can be computed at once), without increasing the area necessary for implementation.

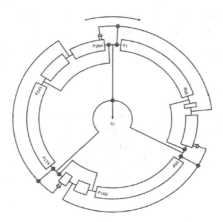

Fig. 3. Structure of Trivium stream cipher (Source: https://en.wikipedia.org/wiki/Trivium_(cipher)).

Even though many cryptanalysts studied the structure of Trivium so far, it hasn't been found an attack faster that exhaustive key search. However, variants of the algorithm with round-reduced key/IV setup have been successfully attacked, but these attacks cannot be extended to the full cipher.

2.3 Mickey 2.0 Stream Cipher

Mickey 2.0 [5] is a synchronous stream cipher, which stands for "Mutual Irregular Clocking KEYstream generator". The structure of Mickey 2.0 is presented in Fig. 4. The cipher works with an IV with length up to 80 bits and accepts keys of 80 bits length. Mickey produces the ciphertext by performing bitwise XOR between the plaintext and the keystream bits. The keystream sequence can be of maximum 240 bits. The state of the algorithm includes two 100-bit shift registers (one nonlinear and the other linear) which are clocked one by the other in an irregular mode. The designers have also created a version of the cipher (MICKEY1-28 2.0) which accepts an IV up to 128 bits and a 128-bit key. Regarding the implementation, the authors mention that they were able to generate, using a PC with 3.4 GHz Pentium 4 processor, 108 bits in approximately 3.81 s.

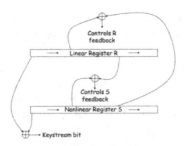

Fig. 4. Structure of Mickey 2.0 stream cipher (Source: http://www.ecrypt.eu.org/stream/e2-mickey.html).

Regarding the existing attacks, in 2008 [6] it was mentioned that the straightforward implementations of the cipher are susceptible to power and timing analysis attacks. Also, in 2013, a differential fault attack [7] was successfully conducted on MICKEY 2.0.

2.4 Grain V1 Stream Cipher

Grain stream cipher [8] uses an 80-bit key and a 64-bit IV. This initial version was revised because vulnerabilities were discovered in its structure and a new version Grain v1 was created which includes two stream ciphers: one for 128-bit keys (with 80-bit IV) and one for 80-bit keys (with 64-bit IV). These ciphers include a non-linear feedback register and a linear feedback register which are coupled using lightweight boolean functions.

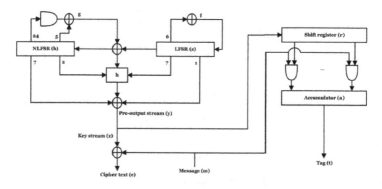

Fig. 5. Grain v128.a. (Source: https://en.wikipedia.org/wiki/File:Grain-128a.png).

The structure of Grain v128a is depicted in Fig. 5. Even though, the Grain family ciphers design includes an ingenious multiplication of throughput speed, this feature increases the occupied memory.

2.5 SOSEMANUK Stream Cipher

SOSEMANUK [9] is a synchronous stream cipher, very efficient when implemented in software. The cipher has an IV of 128 bits and works with a key with length between 128 and 256 bits. Regarding its design, it includes several principles from the block cipher Serpent and from the stream cipher SNOW 2.0. Compared with the last one mentioned, SOSEMANUK fixes some structural weaknesses and ensures better performance. The algorithm, depicted in Fig. 6, has two main components, a linear feedback register - LFSR (which operates on 32-bit words and has the length 10) and a finite state machine - FSM (which has two 32-bit memory registers). The cipher works as follows: at every step, the FSM receives an input from the LFSR and after updating the memory registers, it produces a 32-bit output. An output transformation (the same as in Serpent algorithm) is applied on every four consecutive output words from the FSM.

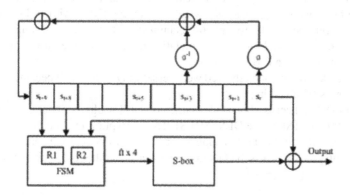

Fig. 6. Structure of SOSEMANUK stream cipher. (Source: http://article.sapub.org/10.5923.j.ac20120202.02.html).

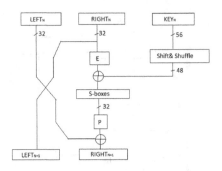

Fig. 7. Operations of a DES round.

Several attacks were performed on SOSEMANUK. For instance, a guess-and-determine attack was successfully conducted in 2006 [10], attack which included the recovery of all 384 bits of the internal state, after the initialization. In 2008, the authors of [11] were able to recover 384 bits of the internal state, by applying a linear masking method. The most recent attack on SOSEMANUK was presented in 2010 [12], called byte-oriented guess-and-determine attack.

2.6 Data Encryption Standard (DES) Block Cipher

DES was developed by the National Bureau of Standards (today called National Institute of Standards and Technology - NIST) with the help of the National Security Agent in 1970. DES is one of the best known block ciphers that became a US government standard for protecting sensitive commercial and unclassified data in the late '70 s. DES operates on blocks of 64 bits, using a secret key of 56 bits long. The other 8 bits may be used for error detection.

The operations included in a DES round are illustrated in Fig. 7. The message is divided into blocks and each block is encrypted in 16 stages (rounds). For each round, as input key, sixteen 48 bit keys are generated and 8 S-boxes are used. The block message is divided in two halves. The operations realized in a round are: expansion (of the 32 bit input to 48 bits, by copying some bits twice), key mixing (XOR with 48-bit round key), substitution (split the result into eight 6-bit chunks; pass each chunk through a different S-box so the output has 32 bits) and permutation (recomposes the information through a permutation given in a P-Box).

Many attacks and methods showed weaknesses of DES and so it became an insecure block cipher, as specified in [13, 14].

Due to these concerns about the security of DES a block cipher alternative was created in 1998, called Triple DES (3DES). The encryption method is very similar to the one of DES algorithm but it is applied three times to increase the encryption level. The disadvantage of 3DES is the fact that is slower than other block cipher algorithms.

2.7   Advanced Encryption Standard (AES) Block Cipher

In 2001, NIST selected AES as a replacement for DES. Rijndael algorithm was selected in 1997 after a competition to choose the best encryption standard. AES is a block cipher (blocks of 128 bits) with a variable key length of 128, 192, or 256 (default) bits. AES has been carefully tested for many security applications [15].

The design principle on which AES is based is known as substitution-permutation network. AES is a block cipher with 128-bit block size and with various key sizes: 128,192 and 256 bits. The operations are made on a matrix of 4 × 4 bytes called the *state*. The four functions processed during a round can be seen in Fig. 8 and they are: *SubBytes* (creates a nonlinear substitution for each byte in the state by using an S-Box), *ShiftRows* (represents a transposition operation because it rearranges the state bytes without changing their value), *MixColumns* (consists of multiplying each column of the state with a polynomial function), *AddRoundKey* (adds the round key, by doing XOR between each byte of the state and each byte of the round key).

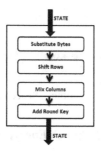

Fig. 8.   Operations of an AES round.

2.8   Scrambling Speech Encryption Algorithm

In [16], the authors use a scrambling technique for speech encryption. For this, they have developed a software program in assembly programming language for Digital Signal Processor ADSP 2181 (which is a 16-bit fixed point processor).

The algorithm works as follows. The first step is to acquire the voice signals, then to digitally code them and store the values in the memory of the processor (128 samples are stored). The scrambling of the speech signal is performed using Fast Fourier Transform (FFT) and Inverse Fast Fourier Transform (IFFT) techniques.

The next step is to perform decoding, in order to obtain the speech signal again, which will be transmitted to the receiver. After applying FFT, the signal is converted into spikes (in frequency domain). The signal spikes will be stored in the memory and based on circular buffers, their positions will be interchanged, ensuring in this manner the scrambling of the original signal (first 64 samples are displaced into next 64 samples position and vice versa). After scrambling, IFFT is applied to convert the signal from frequency domain, back into the time domain.

Fig. 9. Scrambling algorithm - Speech encryption process.

The last step is to convert the digital signal into analogue signal and to transmit it. Figure 9 illustrates the speech encryption process, where ADC represents the Analog-to-Digital Converter and DAC represents the Digital-to-Analog Converter.

The receiver performs the same steps previously described, obtaining at the end of the process the original speech signal. The original signal is obtained when the spikes (mentioned in the encryption process) are placed into their original positions, process which happens using the circular buffers. Figure 10 shows the speech decryption process.

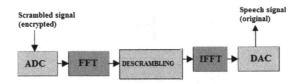

Fig. 10. Scrambling algorithm - Speech decryption process.

2.9   Robust Secure Coder (RSC) Speech Encryption Algorithm

In [17], the authors present their scheme for speech encryption, called RSC, which includes MELP compression algorithm, Triple Data Encryption Standard (3DES) encryption algorithm and a Forward Error Correction (FEC) algorithm. Figure 11 presents the speech encryption process. The original speech is passed through MELP encoder in frames of 22.5 ms. The frame is coded into 54 bits of compressed speech frame. Because MELP algorithm ensures FEC for unvoiced mode only, the designers of RSC use 10 parity bits to ensure error correction only for voiced mode. The 54 bits of speech previously compressed and the 10 bits of FEC are given as input for 3DES encryption process. The result is 64 bits of encrypted and compressed speech, which will be transmitted to the receiver.

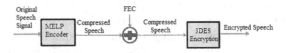

Fig. 11. RSC algorithm - Speech encryption process.

The decryption process is illustrated in Fig. 12 and is similar with the encryption process. The 64 bits of encrypted speech are given as input for 3DES decryption process, resulting 64 bits which will then enter in the FEC. 10 of 64 bits are used to correct errors and the rest of 54 bits are separated and given as input to MELP decoder. The output of the decoder is a synthesized speech frame of 22.5 ms.

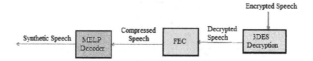

Fig. 12. RSC algorithm - Speech decryption process.

2.10   Chaotic Map and Blowfish Speech Encryption Algorithms

In [18], the authors describe a new solution to encrypt speech signal which includes chaotic encryption algorithm based on logistic map and Blowfish encryption algorithm. The advantage of using chaotic function is that it increases the security of the algorithm and the complexity of the encryption and decryption functions. The solution proposed by the authors' works as follows. For the encryption process, which is described in Fig. 13, as a first step, the raw speech signal is divided into frames, each frame containing 256 values.

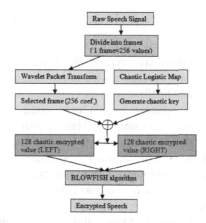

Fig. 13. Chaotic map and Blowfish algorithm - Speech encryption process.

Then, the speech frames chosen for encryption are decomposed using wavelet packet transform (WPT), to determine the decomposed frames coefficients of the level 2. At the end of this process, 256 coefficients are found for each selected frame. The next step is to use chaotic logistic map to generate a chaotic key which will be XORed with each frame value. The Blowfish algorithm provides two parts of 128 chaotic encrypted values which are merged to obtain an encrypted frame of 256 values.

The decryption process is illustrated in Fig. 14. In the first step, the encrypted speech signal is divided into frames (each containing 256 values) and each frame is split into left part (128 values) and right part (128 values). The two parts are given as input for Blowfish algorithm and then the decrypted frames are XORed with the chaotic key. At the end of the Blowfish decryption process, a frame of 256 values is obtained, which is passed through Inverse WPT (IWPT) restoring in this way the decrypted speech signal.

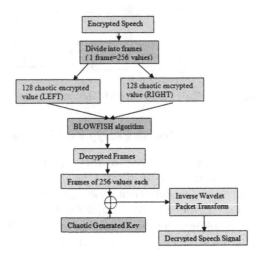

Fig. 14. Chaotic map and Blowfish algorithm - Speech decryption process.

2.11 DSP Architecture

In general, speech coding and speech encryption algorithms include intensive processing operations and for this reason it's recommended to implement them on dedicated DSPs which have instructions to handle these types of computations.

Several speech encryption applications are characterized by very tight requirements in size, voltage supply and power consumption. These requirements are difficult to fulfil, given the number of functions to be implemented and their complexity, together with the real time requirement and with the large dynamic range of existing input signals. In order to fulfil these constraints, thorough optimization should be performed at all levels, starting from algorithmic level, then at system and circuit architecture level, and also at layout and design of the cell library.

The most important components of this optimization are among others, the choice of the encryption algorithms, the modification of these algorithms such that computational complexity is reduced, the choice of a fixed-point arithmetic unit, the minimization of the number of bits required at every node of the algorithm, and a careful match between architecture and algorithms.

A simplified block diagram of embedded DSP architecture is shown in Fig. 15. This contains the processor core, the peripherals (serial peripheral interface - SPI, parallel peripheral interface - PPI, serial ports - SPORT, general purpose timers, universal asynchronous receiver transmitter - UART, general purpose I/O - GPIO, etc.), the memory (for stack space, for holding data and instructions, etc.) and others (event controller, Direct Memory Access - DMA controller, etc.). The DSP core includes register sets, Arithmetic Logic Unit (ALU), Data Address Generator (DAG) and sequencer.

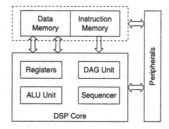

Fig. 15. A diagram of DSP architecture.

The most important aspect regarding the DSP is to decide between floating point and fixed point computational core. Floating-point processors offer very fast implementations, but these are not bit-exact. In this context, for real time implementations a specialized, fixed-point processor is the best solution. We have decided to implement the speech encryption algorithms using a fixed-point DSP, because we wanted to take advantage of the recent technological developments which enables DSP to provide implementations of very complex and sophisticated functions for analysis (encoding), synthesis (decoding) and encryption of speech signal.

For our project, we have chosen Blackfin ADSP-BF537 [19] processor core architecture, which combines: flexible single instruction multiple data capabilities for parallel computations, an orthogonal RISC-like microprocessor instruction set, zero-overhead loops, a dual-MAC (Multiply and Accumulate) signal processing engine, and multiple timed features into a single instruction set. Based on the literature reviews, these processors are the best solution for communication applications which have strict constraints regarding computational resources and power consumption (can be reduced to 0.8 V). Blackfin contains an internal Analog-to-Digital Converter and is much faster than microcontrollers. Also, we have chosen Blackfin due to its versatility in programming code. More exactly, we can write code in C/C++ and LabVIEW. Even before programming the processor, VisualDSP++ software can be used to simulate the behaviour of the DSP chip. Unfortunately, even with this specialized DSP, optimization techniques are still necessary in the implementation of stable speech encryption algorithms with real-time performances.

3   Related Work

To give a better perspective about the importance and utility of our project this section describes the results obtained by other researchers and other developed speech encryption algorithms.

Paper [20] presents the results obtained after comparing the optimized implementations of AES finalists on DPS. The evaluated algorithms were Mars, RC6, Rijndael, Serpent and Twofish and the implementations were done using TMS320C64x platform. The test scenarios included single-block mode and multi-block mode (two blocks at a time were encrypted) and the results were measured in: the number of cycles (necessary for the encryption process of each algorithm), the throughput (Mbit/sec) and memory usage. The Twofish encryption speed of 139.1 Mbit/sec and decryption of 148.8 Mbit/sec are by far the fastest throughputs that they have obtained.

In [21], the hardware performances of the eSTREAM competition finalists are presented. The framework designed by the authors takes into considerations the following evaluation elements: compactness, throughput, power consumption, simplicity and scalability. Their evaluation shows that the simplest algorithm is Mickey128, the most flexible one is Trivium and that Grain80 offers the best results for two sample applications of future wireless network and low-end of radio frequency identification tags/Wireless Sensor Network nodes.

In paper [22], the authors propose a speech encryption technique which uses low complexity perception based on partial schemes. The speech signal is compressed using ITU-T G.729 standard [23] and the result is divided into two classes: one is encrypted and the other is unprotected. Also, there are two level partial encryption techniques used, one low protection (for eavesdropping prevention) and one high-protection (for full encryption of the compressed bit stream).

In [24], a speech encryption method based on vector quantization (VQ) of LPC coefficients is presented. The secret key is generated using the indices of VQ corresponding to the neighbouring frames derived from the natural speech's characters. [25] presents an encryption algorithm based on time-trajectory model of the sinusoidal components corresponding to voiced speech signals. This method uses the amplitude and phase parameters of the discrete cosine functions which are applied for each voiced segment of the speech.

A method for speech encryption based on augmented identity matrix is presented in [26]. Enhanced encryption can be achieved by analyzing the redundancy parameters of the coded speech signal, with low computation complexity in real time applications. In [27], a voice encryption method called "DES with Random permutation and Inversion" is described, which solves the problem of penetrating the RPE-LTP vocoder by the encrypted voice. The solution proposed ensures secure communication in Global System for Mobile Communications (GSM) and a good compatibility to all GSM networks.

The authors of [28] describe a new speech encryption algorithm which integrates a personalized time domain scrambling scheme and is based on four level of hash based encryption. They encrypt the original signal four times using different algorithms (repositioning of bits, using twice random number generation and amplitude ascending ordering) at each level. Based on their experimental results, it can be seen that the proposed algorithm ensures a high level of security.

In [29] the authors illustrate how signal processing techniques can be used to design and implement cryptographic and security applications. Implementations on DSP processors of well-known hash functions, public-key algorithms are described in detail. Moreover, using the special features of DSP processor, they present a key derivation technique and other methods of pre-processing data which can be very useful in performing side-channel attacks.

In [30], the authors describe their implementations of AES, DES, SHA1, TDEA, and Elliptic Curve Digital Signature Algorithm (ECDSA) on an embedded system targeting the Blackfin DSP. The analyze their performance and they try to reduce the encryption/decryption time and to reduce the energy consumed, by taking advantage of several architectural features that are available on Blackfin platform. They were able to improve the execution time by a factor of 4 and to reduce the energy consumption with almost 90%.

Implementations of the five AES finalists and of public key cryptography on a DSP were discussed in [31] and in [32] respectively.

4   Implementation

In this section we present the details regarding real-time and offline implementations of nine speech encryption algorithms: Trivium, Mickey 2.0, Grain v1, SOSEMANUK, AES, DES, scrambling algorithm, RSC and algorithm based on chaotic map and Blowfish cipher.

A point of interest in this area is getting DSP microprocessors, embedded in a system which performs speech encryption and decryption. Implementation in C is structured and easy to follow and can be an important starting point for implementing these algorithms on various platforms.

The algorithms were implemented at the beginning in C language using Microsoft Visual Studio 2012, which makes the software processor independent and can be linked with any processor if the corresponding assembler is accessible. After we thoroughly analyzed their functionality, the code was transferred to the integrated development environment, called VisualDSP++, on a DSP platform. In the first stage, the algorithms were tested offline, using a single processor so that we could verify if the implementations remain functional even when their included in this new environment.

After we implemented the speech encryption algorithms on a DSP platform, we optimized the programs so that it allows real-time communication. This was done using two fixed point DSPs from Analog Devices, ADSP-BF537, as it can be seen in Fig. 16.

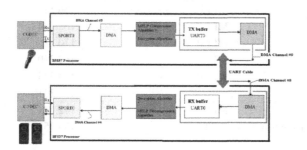

Fig. 16. Real-time communication on BF537 block diagram.

The communication between the DPSs is done using a serial transmission (through UART) and MELP algorithm was used to compress the speech signal. This block diagram is not available for the implementation of scrambling speech encryption algorithm (where the digital signal is given as input for the FFT function without compressing it) and for encryption algorithm based on chaotic map and Blowfish cipher (which uses WPT for compression).

Several optimizations were necessary to meet the real time requirement of completing all computation processes within frame duration (22.5 ms). The source code of speech encryption algorithms was thoroughly optimized at the C Level.

5   Optimization and Experimental Results

Since most embedded systems are real-time systems, code optimization in terms of execution speed is an important performance index which will result in lower power consumption. It is always easier to use a C compiler optimization. However, in cases where we have to save more MIPS or memory processing, assembly code optimization is the only way to achieve this level of performance. The development cost of writing 100% of the entire program in assembly language, far exceeds the performance gain.

A better approach is to start writing code in C, then create a detailed profile to identify time critical code sections and replace these code segments with code in assembly language. A common rule 80%–20% says that 80% of processing time is used for 20% of code. So if we can identify those 20% of the code and optimize it using assembly language, significant performance gains can be achieved. A method for identifying the region of interest is to use the statistical profiler (for EZ-KIT) or the linear profiler (for a simulator) that exist in the VisualDSP++. Running the applications in VisualDSP++ for the first time, generated the execution times (in milliseconds) seen in Table 1, for compressing and encrypting a single frame.

Table 1.   Execution time per frame before code optimization.

Speech encryption algorithm	Compression algorithm	Execution time/frame (in ms)
Trivium	MELP	168.312
Mickey v2.0	MELP	160.125
Grain v1-80 bit key	MELP	166.129
Grain v1-128 bit key	MELP	168.934
SOSEMANUK	MELP	170.226
AES-128	MELP	162.390
DES	MELP	158.344
Scrambling	–	162.331
RSC	MELP	172.624
Chaotic map & Blowfish	WPT	174.753

We started by applying different optimization techniques at C level (Table 2) then we applied different hardware optimizations which can be seen in Table 3. The execution time (given in milliseconds) decreased significantly for all encryption algorithms as it can be seen in Table 4. All performed computational processes lasted more than 170 ms before code optimization, result which is inacceptable, given the time available for a frame (22.5 ms). After the optimization, the execution time per frame was reduced to less than 21.5 ms for all implemented algorithms.

Table 2. C level optimizations.

Optimization technique
Enable: optimization for C code, automatic inlining, interprocedural optimization from VisualDSP++ options
Use pragma for optimizing loops
Use pragma for data alignment
Use pragma for different memory banks
Use pragma for no alias
Use volatile and static data types
Use arithmetic data types (int, short, char, unsigned int, unsigned char, unsigned short)
Using runtime C/C++ and DSP libraries
Use pragma to optimize for speed
Using intrinsic functions and inline assembly
Profile Guided Optimization (PGO)

Table 3. Hardware level optimizations.

Optimization technique
Special addressing modes – using different data sections (for add() function)
Using assembly code
Using hardware loops
Using parallel instructions
Using software pipeline

Table 4. Execution time per frame after C level and hardware level optimizations.

Speech encryption algorithm	Execution time/frame (in ms) C level	Execution time/frame (in ms) Hardware level
Trivium	71.034	15.884
Mickey v2.0	61.977	6.349
Grain v1 - 80 bit key	67.893	11.815
Grain v1 - 128 bit key	70.102	14.209
SOSEMANUK	73.448	19.091
AES-128	66.221	9.532
DES	60.172	8.113
Scrambling	65.340	10.053
RSC	74.298	18.644
Chaotic map & Blowfish	78.112	21.115

Intrinsic functions allow a more efficient use of the hardware resources of the Blackfin processor because they are predefined functions, "vendor-specific", which are treated specifically at compile time, are C-callable and they generate assembly language instructions that are designed to optimize code generated by the compiler or to achieve efficient access to system hardware. In addition, arithmetic intrinsic functions support saturation, which prevents overflow phenomenon. This is in contrast to the standard C program, which requires additional routines to check the overflow and set the arithmetic saturation.

VisualDSP++ supports *inline assembly* that lets a programmer insert small pieces of assembler code in the C program. However, inline assembly should be avoided when implicit built-in functions are available. The *inline* word is only useful for small and frequently used functions and offers the best result regarding speed execution with very little increase in code size. Inline code is often used instead of a subroutine because subroutines involve overhead. Although a subroutine is more efficient in terms of code size, the inline code offers better execution speed.

We have also performed optimization based on profiling results. *Profile Guided Optimization (PGO)* enables the compiler to use the data collected during program execution for an optimization analysis. Significant data sets are transmitted to the application to determine, in order, which code sections are executed most frequently, so that the compiler can perform a selective optimization. More specifically, PGO informs the compiler about the application that affects branch prediction, improves loops transformation and reduces code size. After using PGO, the processing time of the sample, for most of the algorithms, was reduced with approximately 66 ms.

As it can be seen in Table 4, the smallest execution time per frame (in ms) after the C level optimizations, is obtained for the implementations of DES and Mickey v2.0algorithms (approximately 61 ms). Also, Grain v1 (80-bit and 128-bit key) and the scrambling algorithm have small execution times, approximately 66 ms. Mickey v2.0 algorithm has the smallest execution time after the hardware level optimizations, only 6.439 ms, followed closely by DES and AES block ciphers (9.532 ms, respectively 8.113 ms). The highest execution time is obtained at software level and at hardware level by chaotic map and Blowfish algorithm (78 ms, respectively 21 ms).

Memory optimization techniques such as *caching* and *data placement* were also used to bring down the processing time. It was not possible to include the entire data inside the internal RAM of the DSP. For this reason, less frequently accessed data was kept in SDRAM which was comparatively slower. Frequently accessed functions were cached. A better optimization is achieved by writing the functions which are computationally intensive in assembly language. The result is a substantial reduction of the number of cycles needed for computation.

In Table 5, the CPU time for optimized and non-optimized speech encryption implementations is shown for each time consuming function.

For Trivium algorithm the most consuming function includes the multiplication of two Boolean functions using their algebraic normal form. Optimizing this function reduces the number of cycles with more than 2 Mcycles.

For Mickey v2.0 cipher there are two time consuming functions: register clocking and keystream derivation, which if optimized save approximately 1.5 Mcycles. The initialization phase is the most consuming for Grain v1 algorithm (80-bit key or 128-bit key). Optimizing this function, the number of cycles decreases with almost 2 Mcyles.

Table 5. CPU time for optimized and non-optimized algorithms implementations.

Algorithm	Time consuming functions	No optimization	With optimization
Trivium	Multiplying the algebraic normal form of two boolean functions	3.25 Mcycles	77 Kcycles
Mickey v2.0	Register clocking	2.0 Mcycles	55 Kcycles
	Keystream derivation		
Grain v1 - 80	Initialization phase	2.95 Mcycles	84 Kcycles
Grain v1 - 128	Initialization phase	3.20 Mcycles	98 Kcycles
SOSEMANUK	Initialization phase	3.85 Mcycles	130 Kcycles
AES-128	Key expansion	3.72 Mcycles	125 Kcycles
DES	Key expansion	4.1 Mcycles	145 Kcycles
Scrambling	FFT	2.80 Mcycles	96 Kcycles
	IFFT		
RSC	Forward Error Correction	3.55 Mcycles	120 Kcycles
Chaotic map & Blowfish	Chaotic key generation	4.2 Mcycles	155 Kcycles
	Subkey generation for Blowfish		

Similar with Grain algorithm, SOSEMANUK algorithm has the initialization phase as the most consuming function. After applying optimizations to it, the number of cycles decreased from 3.85 Mcycles to 130 Kcycles.

For DES and AES-128 encryption algorithms, the function which includes the key expansion is the one that consumes the most. Without the C level and hardware level optimizations, this function requires approximately 3.72 Mcycles, respectively 4.1 Mcycles. After the optimizations, the results have changed significantly to 125 Kcycles, respectively 145 Kcyles.

For the scrambling technique, the FFT and IFFT functions consume approximately 3 Mcycles. After the optimization, these functions require less than 1 Mcycle.

RSC algorithm has only one time consuming function, which is the Forward Error Correction. Its optimization is significant, from 3.55 Mcycles to 120 Kcycles. The cipher which uses chaotic map and Blowfish algorithm for voice encryption has two important functions: chaotic key generation and subkey generation for Blowfish. The reduction of clock cycles is high, from 4.2 Mcycles to 155 Kcycles.

Based on the results in Table 5, we can calculate the Clock Rate Reduction (CRR). This is defined as in Eq. (1), where X represents the number of clock cycles consumed by original code (before optimization) and Y is the number of clock cycles consumed by the optimized code. The CRR values for all implemented encryption algorithms can be seen in Table 6. As it can be observed, the best CRR was obtained for Trivium algorithm (41.21%), followed by Mickey v2.0 (35.36%). The smallest CRR was obtained for chaotic map and Blowfish algorithm, 26.09%.

Table 6. CRR value for all speech encryption algorithms.

Algorithm	CRR
Trivium	41.21%
Mickey v2.0	35.36%
Grain v1 - 80	34.11%
Grain v1 - 128	31.65%
SOSEMANUK	28.61%
AES-128	28.76%
DES	27.27%
Scrambling	28.16%
RSC	28.58%
Chaotic map & Blowfish	26.09%

$$CRR = \frac{(X - Y)}{Y} \times 100\% \qquad (1)$$

We have also performed subjective analysis for the offline and real-time implementation of the evaluated speech encryption algorithms and the results are shown in Fig. 17.

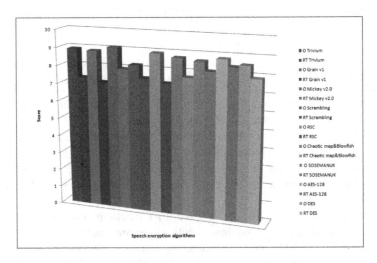

Fig. 17. Scores for offline and real-time implementations.

In subjective analysis, the encrypted speech signal is listened and the quality of it will be determined only based on the listener's opinion. Ten listeners have graded the nine algorithms. Each person has listened to 10 distinct audio files and then they gave grades on a scale of 0 to 10. As it can be seen from Fig. 17, the scores confirm the fact that offline speech encryption algorithms' implementations have better performances than the real-time implementations. "O" stands for offline implementation and "RT" stands for real-time implementation.

The best results in subjective analysis were for offline Mickey v2.0 algorithm (9.1), followed very closely by offline RSC (8.92) and by offline Trivium (8.91). The worst results were for real-time implementations, especially of algorithms such as Grain v1 (7.14), RSC (7.32) and Trivium (7.34).

In multimedia applications, *Mean Opinion Score (MOS)* gives a numerical indication of the perceived quality after compression-decompression of data or after transmission. MOS test for voice are specified by ITU-t recommendation P-800 [33]. A number of listeners rate the heard audio quality of test sentences read aloud by both male and female speakers over the communications medium being tested. The MOS is the arithmetic mean of all the individual scores, and can range from 1 (worst) to 5 (best).

Even with the previously mentioned results, the output speech signal of Mickey v2.0 algorithm was quite understandable, obtaining a MOS average score of **3.15** points (the algorithm was rated by 20 listeners). For Grain v1, AES and DES algorithms, the MOS score was approximately **2.60** points and for Mickey 2.0 it was **2.45**. The worst score was obtained by the encryption algorithm based on chaotic map and Blowfish cipher, approximately **2.1** points.

6   Conclusions

The purpose of this paper was to evaluate the performance of nine speech encryption techniques implemented on DSP platforms, in order to successfully identify which is best suited for secure real-time applications. The first step was to write the implementations of these algorithms in C and then to port the code on Blackfin ADSP-BF537.

In order to meet the real-time requirements, several optimizations had to be performed. Some of these are small function inline expansion, usage of the compiler tools, intrinsic functions, PGO, critical time functions written in assembly language and so on.

We were able to decrease the execution time per frame, for all the voice encryption algorithms, to less than 21.5 ms (which is the threshold for real-time implementations). Regarding the results, we can conclude that Mickey v2.0 stream cipher is best suited for real-time applications because it has the smallest number of cycles and the smallest execution time per frame. However, we can also use Grain v1 stream cipher, AES and DES block ciphers with confidence because their results are very close to the ones obtained for Mickey v2.0. Unfortunately, based on our results, it is not recommended to use the voice encryption algorithm based on chaotic map and Blowfish cipher, because it has the worst results and may not be reliable.

Based on the subjective analysis results, we can conclude that offline implementations of the algorithms provide better speech quality than real-time implementation. Even so, all the algorithms implemented for voice encryption have a good audio quality, which allows them to be implemented in real-time communication applications.

Our future work will involve implementing the algorithm selected for speech encryption on other DSP platforms. Moreover, we are going to develop applications for secure real-time communications and test these in practical environment.

Acknowledgements. The work has been funded by the Sectoral Operational Programme Human Resources Development 2007-2013 of the Ministry of European Funds through the Financial Agreement POSDRU/187/1.5/S/155536, by the Sectoral Operational Programme Human Resources Development 2007-2013 of the Ministry of European Funds through the Financial Agreement POSDRU/159/1.5/S/134398, and by the program Partnerships in priority areas – PN II carried out by MEN-UEFISCDI, project No. 47/2014.

References

1. Tremain, T.E.: The government standard linear predictive coding LPC-10. In: Speech Technology, pp. 40–49 (1982)
2. McCree, A., Kwan, T., George, E.B., Viswanathan, V.: A 2.4 kbit's MELP coder candidate for the new U.S. federal standard. In: IEEE International Conference Acoustics, Speech, and Signal Processing, vol. 1, pp. 200–203 (1996)
3. Supplee, L.M., Cohn, R.P., Collura, J.S., McCree, A.: MELP: the new federal standard at 2400bps. In: IEEE International Conference on Acoustics, Speech, and Signal Processing, vol. 2, pp. 1591–1594 (1997)
4. Canniere, C., Preneel, B.: Trivium specifications. In: eSTREAM, ECRYPT Stream Cipher Project (2006)
5. Babbage, S., Dodd, M.: The stream cipher MICKEY 2.0. In: eSTREAM, ECRYPT Stream Cipher Project (2006)
6. Gierlichs, B., Batina, L., Clavier, C., Eisenbarth, T., Gouget, A., Handschuh, H., Kasper, T., Lemke-Rust, K., Mangard, S., Moradi, A., Oswald, E.: Susceptibility of eSTREAM candidates towards side channel analysis. In: De Cannire, C., Dunkelman, O. (eds.) ECRYPT Workshop, SASC - The State of the Art of Stream Ciphers, Lausanne, CH, p. 28 (2008)
7. Banik S., Maitra S., Sarkar S.: Improved differential fault attack on MICKEY 2.0. In Cryptology ePrintAtchive, Report 2013/029 (2013)
8. Hell, M., Johansson, T., Meier, W.: Grain- a stream cipherfor constrained environments. Int. J. Wirel. Mob. Comput. **2**, 86–93 (2007)
9. Berbain, C., Billet, O., Canteaut, A., Courtois, N., Gilbert, H., Goubin, L., Gouget, A., Granboulan, L., Lauradoux, C., Minier, M., Pornin, T., Sibert, H.: SOSEMANUK, a fast software-oriented stream cipher. In eSTREAM, ECRYPT Stream Cipher Project (2006)
10. Tsunoo, Y., Saito, T., Shigeri, M., Suzaki, T., Ahmadi, H., Eghlidos, T., Khazaei, S.: Evaluation of SOSEMANUK with regard to guess-and-determine attacks. http://www.ecrypt.eu.org/stream/papersdir/2006/009.pdf
11. Lee, J.-K., Lee, D.H., Park, S.: Cryptanalysis of sosemanuk and SNOW 2.0 using linear masks. In: Pieprzyk, J. (ed.) ASIACRYPT 2008. LNCS, vol. 5350, pp. 524–538. Springer, Heidelberg (2008). doi:10.1007/978-3-540-89255-7_32
12. Feng, X., Liu, J., Zhou, Z., Wu, C., Feng, D.: A byte-based guess and determine attack on SOSEMANUK. In: Abe, M. (ed.) ASIACRYPT 2010. LNCS, vol. 6477, pp. 146–157. Springer, Heidelberg (2010). doi:10.1007/978-3-642-17373-8_9
13. Stallings, W.: Cryptography and Network Security, 4th edn., pp. 58–309. Prentice Hall, USA (2005)
14. Coppersmith, D.: The Data Encryption Standard (DES) and its strength against attacks. IBM J. Res. Dev. **38**, 243–250 (1994)
15. Daemen, J., Rijmen, V.: Rijndael: the advanced encryption standard. Dr. Dobb's J. **26**, 137–139 (2001)

16. Ravikrindi, R., Nalluri, S.: Digital Signal Processing, Speech encryption and decryption. https://www.scribd.com/doc/23336087/11-speech-encryption-and-decryption. Accessed April 2016
17. Babu, A.A., Yellasiri, R.: Symmetric encryption algorithm in speech coding for defence communications. J. Comput. Sci. Inform. Technol. **4**, 369–376 (2012)
18. Ulkareem, M., Abduljaleel, I.Q.: Speech encryption using chaotic map and blowfish algorithms. J. Basrah Res. **39**(2), 68–76 (2013)
19. ADSP-BF537 Blackfin Processor Hardware Reference manual, Revision 3.4 (2013)
20. Wollinger, T.J., Wang, M., Guajardo, J., Paar, C.: How well are high-end DSPs suited for the AES algorithms? In: Proceedings of the Third Advanced Encryption Standard Candidate Conference, pp. 94–105 (2000)
21. Good, T., Benaissa, M.: Hardware performance of eStream phase-III stream cipher candidates. In: State of the Art of Stream Ciphers (SASC), pp. 163–173 (2008)
22. Servetti, A., De Martin, J.C.: Perception-based partial encryption of compressed speech. IEEE Trans. Speech Audio Process. **10**, 637–643 (2002)
23. ITU-t recommendation g.729: coding of speech at 8 kbit/s using conjugate-structure algebraic-codeexcited-linear-prediction (cs-acelp) (1996)
24. Chen, N., Zhu, J.: Robust speech watermarking algorithm. Electron. Lett. **3**, 1393–1395 (2007)
25. Girin, L., Firouzmand, M., Marchand, S.: Perceptual long-term variable-rate sinusoidal modeling of speech‖. IEEE Trans. Audio Speech Lang. Process. **15**, 851–861 (2007)
26. Tingting, X., Zhen, Y.: Simple and effective speech steganography in G.723.1 low-rate codes. In: International Conference on Wireless Communications & Signal Processing, pp. 1–4 (2009)
27. Merit, K., Ouamri, A.: Securing speech in GSM networks using DES with random permutation and inversion algorithms. Int. J. Distrib. Parallel Syst. (IJDPS) **3**(4), 157–164 (2012)
28. Kaur, H., Sekhon, G.S.: A four level speech signal encryption algorithm. Int. J. Comput. Sci. Commun. (IJCSC) **3**(1), 151–153 (2012)
29. Knezevi, M., Batina, L., Mulder, E., Fan, J., Gierlichs, B., Lee, Y.K., Maes, R., Verbauwhede, I.: Signal processing for cryptography and security applications. In: Bhattacharyya, S.S., et al. (eds.) Handbook of Signal Processing Systems, pp. 223–241. Springer, New York (2013)
30. Bassalee, W., Kaeli, D.: Resource-conscious optimization of cryptographic algorithms on an embedded architecture. http://www.ece.neu.edu/groups/nucar/publications/ODSPES08bassalee.pdf
31. Wollinger, T.J., Wang, M., Guajardo, J., Paar, C.: How well are high-end dsps suited for the aes algorithms? aes algorithms on the tms320c6x dsp. In: AES Candidate Conference, pp. 94–105 (2000)
32. Itoh K., Takenaka M., Torii N., Temma S., Kurihara Y.: Fast implementation of public-key cryptography on a dsp tms320c6201. In: CHES 99: Proceedings of the First International Workshop on Cryptographic Hardware and Embedded Systems, pp. 61–72 (1999)
33. ITU-T Recommendation P.800 Methods for subjective determination of transmission quality. http://www.itu.int/ITU-T/recommendations/rec.aspx?rec=3638

An Efficient Approach to Anonymous Distribution of ITS Messages in Geographic Areas via LTE and IRS Networks

Carsten Büttner[1]([⊠]) and Sorin A. Huss[2]

[1] Adam Opel AG, Advanced Technology, Rüsselsheim am Main, Germany
carsten.buettner@opel.com
[2] Integrated Circuits and Systems Lab, Technische Universität Darmstadt,
Darmstadt, Germany
huss@iss.tu-darmstadt.de

Abstract. A common use case for Intelligent Transportation Systems (ITS) is the distribution of information to all ITS Vehicle Stations (IVSs) located in a geographic area. In this work we present a novel approach which allows an ITS Central Station, located in the Internet, to efficiently distribute information to all IVSs exploiting a specific application and located in a certain geographic area. It supports different communication technologies like LTE and Dedicated Short Range Communication (DSRC). In addition, it distributes the information only in the affected area. Furthermore, the proposed scheme preserves the privacy of the IVSs by not storing the visited locations anywhere. To demonstrate its feasibility we created a prototype implementation for DSRC on hardware and evaluated it in real-world scenarios. In addition, we compare this approach to two state-of-the-art schemes for distributing information to receivers in a geographic area. The comparison includes how the schemes affect the privacy of the IVSs, their scaling property for a large number of IVSs, how complex they are, and their compliance to the requirements necessary for ITS applications.

Keywords: Geocast · Intelligent Transportation Systems · DSRC · LTE · Anonymity · Location privacy

1 Introduction

Applications in Intelligent Transportation Systems (ITS) such as information or warning on weather hazards, wrong way drivers, traffic jams, or road works ahead require that the corresponding messages are distributed in a specific geographic region, called *dissemination area*. A mechanism that spreads messages in a certain geographic region is called *geocast* [15].

If an ITS Vehicle Station (IVS) acts as the origin of such a message, it is typically already located within the dissemination area, because generated messages are based on locally detected or triggered events. Therefore, it simply

© Springer International Publishing AG 2017
O. Camp et al. (Eds.): ICISSP 2016, CCIS 691, pp. 192–214, 2017.
DOI: 10.1007/978-3-319-54433-5_11

distributes the message to all IVSs in communication range which are part of the Vehicular Ad-hoc NETwork (VANET) directly exploiting Dedicated Short Range Communication (DSRC). The receivers continue to forwards the message in the dissemination area by means of suitable routing algorithms [14].

Besides of an IVS, an ITS Central Station (ICS) may also be the origin of such messages. An ICS can be in this case, for example, a Traffic Center or a Service Center operated by an Original Equipment Manufacturer (OEM). It may also have access to a meteorological service or to a database of up-to-date road works information to generate the messages. Typically, an ICS is stationary and accesses the ITS network via the Internet, i.e., it is not integrated into geographic wireless routing mechanisms. Therefore, the messages have to be transported to an edge of the geographic wireless routing network in the target region first. The final transmission medium can be part of any wireless communication technology, most probably mobile networks or DSRC. The IVSs located in the area can then further spread these messages.

There exist further requirements for a geocast such as receiver subset selection, data encryption, dynamic overlapping dissemination areas, and message validity periods. Various ITS applications are addressing a subset of the local IVSs only, for example paid application subscriptions or all IVSs of a vehicle brand. Hence, application data delivery must be restrictable to an IVS target group. Messages of some applications may further be of a commercial value and therefore require an appropriate protection. Given that an IVS does not have a high computational power onboard, it makes sense that only the desired IVSs receive and process these messages. The dissemination area of the messages may also be dynamic. An ICS could, for example, warn about distinct weather hazards present in various areas at the same time. The dissemination area may in addition change over time. Another special requirement of messages sent by ITS applications is that they may feature a strict validity period, in which they should be sent to each IVS entering the dissemination area too.

Long Term Evolution (LTE) is the current high speed communication standard for mobile networks. Several LTE-based ITS geocast approaches have meanwhile been proposed. However, none of them satisfies the requirements of the outlined ITS applications because they either do not scale with the number of recipients or they are not able to automatically distribute messages to IVSs entering the dissemination area. Furthermore, the procedure becomes rather complicated when different messages have to be distributed in various frequently changing geographic areas at the same time. In addition, none of them considers the privacy of the IVSs accordingly. When exploiting DSRC, ITS Roadside Stations (IRSs) within the dissemination area are in principle able to distribute the messages to relevant IVSs. However, DSRC currently does not support an addressing of a group of IVSs as the only receiver of a message. Therefore, the current mechanisms for mobile networks and DSRC are not suitable to distribute ITS messages to a group of IVSs in a given geographic area.

One has to consider the fact that the messages need to be distributed by different means because it will be rather common that there will be IVSs only equipped with either a mobile networks connection or DSRC. Furthermore, none of the communication technologies is perfectly suited to the envisaged application. The coverage of DSRC is limited because networks of IRSs are unlikely to be deployed comprehensively. However, they will be most likely deployed at dangerous locations. In contrast, mobile Networks are widely available and provide a nearly complete coverage, but there is a fee to transmit data over the network. DSRC does not charge a transmission fee, only the costs for setup and operation. Therefore, a new mechanism is necessary to distribute messages of ITS applications efficiently in a certain geographical area, preferable via different communication technologies like mobile networks and DSRC.

These are the main reasons why we propose an Anonymous Geocast scheme for ITS Applications (AGfIA), which enables an ICS to forward an ITS message to all IVSs subscribed to its application and located in or entering a certain area. It can handle the distribution of different messages at various, even overlapping, areas at the same time. The proposed scheme works for a versatile distribution via both technologies, i.e., mobile networks and DSRC. Moreover, it protects the privacy of the IVSs, whereas no central entity is able to track the exploited applications of an IVS. This is achieved by minimizing the information on current application subscriptions of an IVS being stored within the network.

This work is a more elaborated and extended version of a previously published paper [7]. Besides numerous improvements we provide more details about the created prototype implementation, a deeper discussion of the evaluation of ITS requirements, and additional comparison tables in the evaluation section. Furthermore, the scheme detailed in this work has been filed as a patent [6].

The rest of the paper is structured as follows. In Sect. 2 we discuss the requirements of ITS applications regarding a geocast. The related work on geocasts for ITS applications via mobile networks is reviewed in Sect. 3. We then propose the fundamental AGfIA approach in Sect. 4. Subsequently, we compare it with the state of the art and present our real-world evaluation in Sect. 5. Finally, we conclude in Sect. 6.

2   Requirements

Different kinds of ITS applications require a geocast mechanism to distribute messages. To support a wide variety of such applications, a geocast mechanism must fulfill various requirements. In the sequel we discuss these requirements in detail.

Multiple Applications. A geocast mechanism in general introduces overhead. In order to minimize it, such mechanism should be generic enough to be exploited by quite different applications. This way, applications do not have to maintain a geocast themselves. The overhead is bundled to a single mechanism and thus minimized.

Receiver Groups. Usually an IVS does not employ all available applications. Each IVS does just subscribe to the applications it is interested in. In order to transmit the messages only to the subscribers of an application, a geocast mechanism should support the addressing of a subset of all IVSs present in a given area.

Content Type. ITS messages are small and thus need to be handled differently compared to large data streams. Therefore, a geocast mechanism does not need to support the transmission of a huge amount of data but it should be optimized for small messages. This simplifies flow management and buffer design of involved entities and reduces the system complexity.

Dissemination Area. Each ITS message distributed via geocast has a dedicated dissemination area. Some applications, like a weather hazard warning, might intend to distribute messages in a large area like a whole state, while others, like a particulate matter emission or road works warning, target only a town or just a road section. The dissemination area may also change over time. An application might further distribute different messages to various areas at the same time. In addition, these areas may overlap. Therefore, it should be possible to specify both the dissemination area and the granularity for each message.

Validity Period. Distributed messages may have a validity period of several minutes for, e.g., traffic jam ahead warnings, of hours for, e.g., weather hazard warnings, or of even days for, e.g., road works warnings. During this validity period the ITS message should be transmitted to each IVS entering the dissemination area. Accordingly, a geocast mechanism needs to support the transmission of messages to all IVSs entering the dissemination area.

Scalability. An ITS application may be exercised by quite many IVSs. Consequently, a geocast mechanism should be able to scale for a large number of receivers.

End-to-End Delay. Some ITS applications like a wrong way driver warning require a real-time delivery of the messages in the dissemination area. Therefore, a geocast mechanism should have an as small as possible end-to-end delay.

Efficient Transmission. In order to avoid unnecessary load within the communication network at hand, ITS messages should be transmitted in an efficient way. This covers mechanism and message overhead as well as message duplication.

3   Related Work

In [13] the authors propose a Grid-Based Geocasting Scheme (GBGS) for ITS applications. They divide the surface of the world into rectangles in order to define possible dissemination areas. The size of each rectangle is adjusted according to the number of IVSs within. When more IVSs than a threshold value are present in a rectangle, it is subdivided into two rectangles of equal size. If the number of IVSs in two neighboring rectangles drops below another threshold value then they are merged. Each IVS is aware of the rectangle it is currently in. Every time an IVS leaves a rectangle, its current position is transmitted to a so-called Geo Messaging Server (GMS). On reception, the GMS determines the new rectangle the IVS is located in and sends it back to the IVS as illustrated in Fig. 1. Therefore, the GMS is all the time aware of the position of all IVSs. An ICS aiming to send a message to each IVS in a geographic area needs to query the GMS for all IVSs in the dissemination area first. The server then determines and returns all IVSs located in the corresponding rectangles. The disadvantage of this scheme is clearly the central GMS, which is aware of the coarse position of all IVSs and is therefore able to track them and thus may infringe their privacy. Furthermore, the scheme does not scale because each message has to be distributed to each IVS via a single unicast message. In addition, this scheme does not support the addressing of a group of IVSs in the first place. However, this feature was later on added as part of the CONVERGE project [9]. In the evaluation section we compare this scheme to our AGfIA approach.

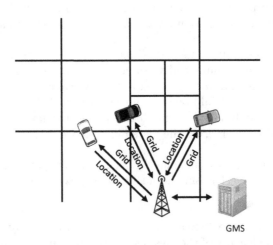

Fig. 1. Working of the grid-based geocasting scheme.

In LTE the Multimedia Broadcast Multicast Service (MBMS) [1] can be exploited to distribute data from a content provider to a group of recipients in predefined broadcasting areas by means of multicast. In order to apply MBMS, each application has to register an MBMS User Service at the Mobile Network Operator (MNO) first. An IVS aiming to exploit several applications has to register for each application separately. MBMS was developed to download a huge amount of data or to stream audio or video data from a radio or TV station to many recipients. For this reason it is based on multicast in order to save bandwidth. Therefore, this scheme is not well-suited to distribute the rather small ITS messages. In order to support the distribution of different messages in various broadcasting areas, one MBMS session has to be initiated for each broadcasting area, but this introduces a high complexity. Furthermore, it is not possible to have overlapping broadcasting areas. In addition, messages are not repeated automatically in order to inform IVSs entering the broadcasting area. Consequently, the messages have to be sent periodically from the content provider to the MNO, which spreads them in the broadcasting area. Obviously, this method is not very efficient. We compare this scheme with AGfIA in Sect. 5.

The authors of [8] analyze the LTE unicast and MBMS transmission modes for safety-related ITS applications. They further study the configuration of MBMS for safety-related ITS applications. Their proposed configuration consists of a central entity which receives all messages. It is accessible by all MNOs and distributes the messages via all mobile networks covering the dissemination area. The authors also state that a new data delivery method for MBMS is necessary to fulfill the requirements of ITS messages. They conclude that MBMS is more efficient in terms of resource consumption when compared to unicast messages. However, this seams obvious, because less messages have to be transmitted in multicast compared to unicast. Furthermore, they do not consider multiple ITS applications with different subscriber groups.

The transmission of ITS messages via LTE and MBMS has been studied in [3,12,16] but none of these works provides a solution which fulfills all requirements of ITS applications.

Three methods of cellular geocast which form the current state of the art were studied in [13]. In the first method a central server, aiming at the distribution of a geocast message, sends an inquiry to all clients requesting their location. From the response, the server selects the relevant clients and sends the message to them. This method clearly does not scale for a large amount of clients and features a considerable delay in message delivery. The second method requires all clients to send periodical position updates to a central server which stores them in a database. When a message shall be sent to all clients in a geographic region, the central entity queries its database and sends the message to the relevant clients. This method does not suffer from the additional delay of the first method. However, it introduces some blur on the position data, because some clients might have moved away since the last position update. In the third method the clients autonomously update their current location at the central entity when they moved a certain distance. This improves the accuracy of the positions in comparison to the second method. Nonetheless, it still has scalability problems as the first two methods. Last but not least, all these methods do not protect the location privacy of the IVSs.

4   Anonymous Geocast

ITS applications like a weather hazard warning require a geocast to distribute relevant messages to all IVSs located in a specific geographic area. As communication technologies to perform the geocast we consider LTE for mobile networks and IRS Networks for DSRC. In LTE the clients are connected to evolved

NodeBs (eNodeBs) which are linked to the core network of the MNO. We assume a Mobile Network Central Station (MN CS) as part of the core network to handle all incoming ITS geocast messages. An IRS Network consists of one or multiple ITS Roadside Stations, which are connected to one IRS Central Station (IRS CS). This central station handles like the MN CS for mobile networks all incoming ITS geocast messages. In case that the network consists of only one IRS, the IRS CS may also be part of this IRS. IVSs communicate with the IRS Network if they are in its communication range. Both, the Mobile Network Central Station and the IRS Central Station, are connected to the Internet.

AGfIA can be exploited for mobile networks like UMTS and LTE as well as for IRS Networks. The mechanisms to register for ITS geocast messages as well as the way how the messages are distributed are described for LTE and IRS Networks in the sequel. Furthermore, a suitable message format for both communication technologies, a possible usage-based billing mechanism, and an example are detailed. We show, that our novel mechanism firstly satisfies all outlined ITS requirements and secondly protects the privacy of each IVS.

4.1   IVS Registration

To initiate the geocast mechanism, each IVS has to register at the central station of the network operator first. This registration is independent from the exploited ITS applications. For the two network types different mechanisms need to be applied. They are detailed as follows.

LTE. Registering for geocast messages in LTE is similar to joining an MBMS User Service. There devices join MBMS User Services in order to receive messages belonging to this applications. In comparison to MBMS not only one application utilizes this User Service. Instead, all ITS applications are handled by the same MBMS User Service. Therefore, each IVS has to join only one User Service, independent of the number and types of ITS applications it runs. This protects the privacy of the IVSs because the MNO does not learn the applications an IVS exploits. Therefore, the subscribed IVSs of an application remain anonymous to the MNO.

Furthermore, we assume a continuous MBMS service to minimize the time overhead for setting up an MBMS session. A time sequence diagram detailing the registration scheme is depicted in the upper part of Fig. 2.

IRS. For IRS Networks no registration is necessary because the ad-hoc characteristic of the network does not need any registration. As a consequence, without a registration the operator of an IRS Network is not able to track the IVSs subscribed to a certain ITS application. Therefore, the receiving IVSs stay anonymous.

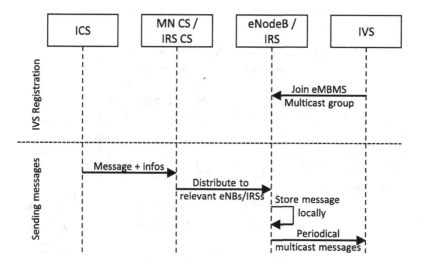

Fig. 2. Time sequence diagram.

4.2 Sending Messages

Whenever an ITS Central Station aims at distributing a message in a geographic area, it has to lookup the present mobile and IRS Networks in the area first. To achieve this, we assume the ICS has a coverage map of all mobile and IRS Networks it has a contract with. After all relevant networks have been identified, the ICS passes the message containing the dissemination area, a distribution frequency, an expiry time, and an Application ID (AID) to the central station of each network. The dissemination area defines the region in which the message shall be spread. To distribute the message also to IVSs entering the dissemination area, it is repeated at the given distribution frequency until the expiry time. The AID uniquely identifies the ITS application responsible for the message. Therefore, it is necessary for an IVS in order to determine if the particular message is relevant or not. The message distribution by the different network types as discussed in the sequel is illustrated in Fig. 3 and the corresponding sequence diagram is presented in the lower part of Fig. 2.

LTE. In order to handle ITS geocast messages in LTE a Mobile Network Central Station is necessary. It consists of a database, containing the position, communication range, and address of each eNodeB within the network. Each time an ICS aims at distributing an ITS message in a certain area, it passes the messages to the MN CS. There the relevant eNodeBs to distribute the message are identified first. Then, the geocast message is forwarded to these eNodeBs by means of Xcast [5]. Upon reception the eNodeB stores the message locally. All locally stored messages are sent at the given frequency to all IVSs in the communication range belonging to the ITS MBMS User Service until they expire.

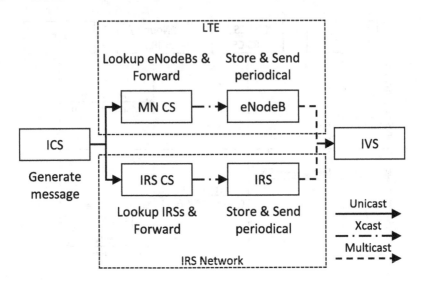

Fig. 3. Message distribution in AGfIA.

This mechanism protects the privacy of the IVSs since each IVS member of the ITS MBMS User Service for ITS applications receives the message. Therefore, the MNO is not able to determine which IVS processes the messages and consequently can not identify the applications exploited by an IVS. Furthermore, the IVS does not periodically send its position to a new central entity. This prevents tracking attempts.

IRS. For AGfIA on top of DSRC, the geocast messages are passed from the ICS to the IRS Central Station. The IRS CS has access, like the Mobile Network Central Station in LTE, to a database containing position, communication range, and address of each of its IRSs in order to select the relevant ones for distribution. After selection, the messages are forwarded like in LTE via Xcast to these IRSs. There the message is stored locally and sent periodically according to the given frequency to all IVSs in communication range until it expires.

Considering that the IRS does not get any feedback which IVS in communication range processes the received message, no entity is able to determine the applications exploited by a certain IVS. Therefore, the distribution of geocast messages over IRS Networks protects the privacy of the IVSs too.

4.3   Message Format

An important property of the message format elaborated in this work is that it can be applied for both communication technologies. Therefore, it becomes quite simple for the ITS Central Station and ITS Vehicle Station to handle messages. The ICS needs to create only one message and can provide it to all networks. The IVS may parse the message in the same way, independent of the applied

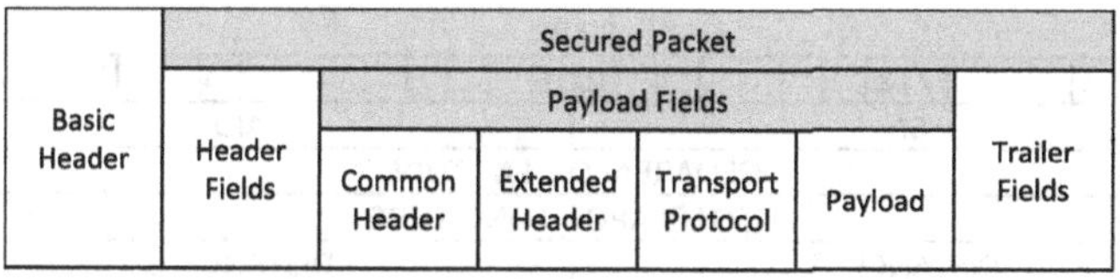

Basic Header	Secured Packet					
	Header Fields	Payload Fields				Trailer Fields
		Common Header	Extended Header	Transport Protocol	Payload	

Fig. 4. GeoNetworking packet structure.

communication technology. Furthermore, an IVS may simply forward a message received by LTE to other IVSs via DSRC without the need to convert it.

We aim at the GeoNetworking message format as standardized in [10]. It consists, as illustrated in Fig. 4, of a *Basic Header* and a *Secured Packet*. The *Secured Package* comprises of *Header Fields*, *Payload Fields*, and *Trailer Fields*, whereas the *Payload Fields* cover a *Common Header*, an *Extended Header*, the *Transport Protocol*, and the *Payload*. The *Basic Header* specifies basic information like the version and remaining hop limit of the package. The *Header Fields* contain security related information like the creation time and the certificate of the sender. The *Common Header* consists of immutable information like the maximum hop limit, length of the payload and the applied traffic class. The *Extended Header* defines the routing of the message. The currently most important standardized mechanisms are the Geographically-Scoped Unicast (GUC) and Geographically-Scoped Broadcast (GBC). As *Transport Protocol* it is currently possible to exploit the Basic Transport Protocol (BTP-A) [11] or IPv6. The *Payload* section contains the actual paylad of the GeoNetworking message. The *Trailer Fields* contain the digital signature of the GeoNetworking message.

This format was developed to exchange messages by means of DSRC between IVSs or between IVSs and IRSs. Therefore, it is well-suited for a geocast over an IRS Network. We now discuss how it can be also utilized for a geocast over LTE. GeoNetworking supports unicast and broadcast messages. For the outlined scenario it is necessary to support the addressing of a group of IVSs too. Hence, we provided support for multicast messaging by adapting the Geographically-Scoped Broadcast header.

Besides of the adapted header aimed to support multicast, we apply the message format as denoted in [10] and exploit the Basic Transport Protocol (BTP-A) [11] as transport protocol.

The detailed format of the header supporting multicast is illustrated in Fig. 5. The changes compared to the original GBC header are as follows. We first removed the location of the source because it is an ICS whose location is not relevant for the receiving or forwarding IVSs. Additionally, we utilize the reserved octets to encode the Application ID (*AID*) into the message and add fields to embed the frequency (*FREQUENCY*) and expiryTime (*EXPIRY_TIME*) of the message. The multicast routing is added by encoding the AID into the message. Therefore, an IVS which does not support the corresponding application can drop the message without further processing. The frequency indicates how often the message shall be distributed to the IVSs in communication range by either

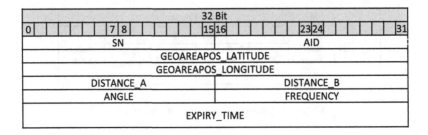

Fig. 5. Detailed message format of the geographically scoped multicast.

an IVS, IRS, or eNodeB. The message is valid until the point in time encoded in expiryTime. After this point in time, all entities will drop and no longer distribute the message. All other fields are applied as in the original GBC/GAC message. The sequence number (SN) indicates the index of the sent packet and is utilized to detect duplicate GN packets. The remaining fields are applied to describe the geometric shape of the dissemination area as defined in [10].

This message format can be applied for both LTE and IRS Networks to deliver geocast messages to a group of IVSs. When distributed over mobile networks, the GeoNetworking message is the payload of the IP connection. For DSRC the GeoNetworking message is also used within the Network and Transportation Layer, respectively, to deliver the message. In both cases the receiving IVS parses the GeoNetworking message by its G5 stack and checks if the message is relevant. Different relevance checks like validating the region and comparing the included AID to its supported AIDs are done. Figure 6 illustrates the location of the GeoNetworking message in the OSI layers for LTE and DSRC, respectively. Furthermore, if an IVS receives a GeoNetworking message via LTE, it is able to redistribute it via DSRC without any modification.

Payload	GeoNet. Message	GeoNet. Message
Network / Transport Layer		PDCP
Link Layer	LLC	RLC
	MAC	MAC
Physical Layer	PHY	PHY
	DSRC	LTE

Fig. 6. Comparison of the GeoNetworking message location within the DSRC and LTE layers.

4.4 Overhead

When messages are transmitted in a wireless way, all entities in communication range receive the message. Messages are dropped at the network layer when MBMS is applied and the receiver is not part of the corresponding MBMS User Service. In the proposed scheme, each IVS will receive the messages of all ITS applications, independent if it is subscribed to the application or not. This introduces a certain overhead because all received messages need to be forwarded to the DSRC stack. There the messages are dropped if they are not relevant. Whenever messages are received via DSRC, all incoming messages are checked for relevance at network level. This analysis includes an inspection of the messages geographic region. Therefore, this check needs to be extended in order to drop messages from not supported applications at network layer.

Subsequently, there is no overhead introduced when messages are received via DSRC. For LTE each message needs to be forwarded to the DSRC stack. However, these messages are only distributed a few times per minute and have a size of less than 3000 bytes. Furthermore, it is not expected that several dozens of messages are valid in the same region at the same time. Therefore, AGfIA clearly does not introduce a significant overhead.

4.5 Billing

For economical reasons it must be possible to bill the network usage of geocast messages. In the outlined scheme an ICS may pay a basic amount for service provision by the operators. Furthermore, the ICS might be billed by the number of messages it sends, depending on the size of the dissemination area, sending frequency, and validity period of the messages.

Therefore, a function to calculate the costs for the message distribution might look like Eq. 1. It adds the costs of all messages to the basic amount for serice provisioning.

$$costs_{total} = costs_{provisioning} + \sum costs_{message} \tag{1}$$

The costs for each single messages can be calculated as written in Eq. 2. To the basic fee for message transmission the number of times it was repeated multipiled by the size of the area it was distributed is added.

$$costs_{message} = basicMessageFee + numberOfRepetitions * areaSize \tag{2}$$

To get the number of messages distributed the MNO can multiply the frequency of the message transmission with the validity period as shown in Eq. 3.

$$numberOfMessages = frequency * validityPeriod \tag{3}$$

Subsequently, the network operators do not need any information about the IVS exploiting the messages or even the number of receivers of a message. Accordingly, it is not necessary for the network operators to track the IVSs by exploiting a certain ITS application for billing. Therefore, this scheme protects the privacy of the ITS Vehicle Stations.

4.6   Example

We illustrate the advantages of the described geocast scheme by means of the example illustrated in Fig. 7. The figure shows the two hazards $Hazard_1$ and $Hazard_2$ like an icy road and ongoing roadworks. The rectangles depict the dissemination areas of possible warning messages. Furthermore, the eNodeBs and IRSs covering the area are depicted together with their communication range. When exploiting the proposed scheme, only the eNodeBs and IRSs covering the respective dissemination area by their communication range distribute the message to the IVSs.

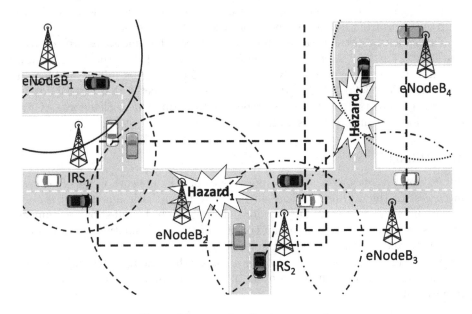

Fig. 7. Message distribution example.

In the example IRS_1, IRS_2, and $eNodeB_2$ cover the dissemination area of $Hazard_1$, while IRS_2, $eNodeB_3$, and $eNodeB_4$ cover the area of $Hazard_2$. Since IRS_2 and $eNodeB_3$ are covering both areas, they distribute both messages. The other IRSs and eNodeBs covering only one of the areas distribute just this message. Consequently, the eNodeBs and IRSs not covering any dissemination area do not forward any message. Therefore, the messages are only disseminated by the relevant eNodeBs and IRSs. Moreover, only the ITS Vehicle Stations depicted in black exploit the application warning of $Hazard_1$, while the white ones utilize the application that distributes information about $Hazard_2$. The gray ones illustrate IVSs exploiting both applications. Only the IVSs applying the corresponding application display a warning to the driver, all other IVSs discard the message. The selection of the relevant IVSs is done without having any knowledge on which IVS exploits any specific ITS application at the network level, nor knowing which IVSs are located within the dissemination area. Therefore, the privacy of each IVS present in the dissemination area is well preserved.

5   Evaluation

For evaluation purposes we compare the privacy, complexity, and scalability figures as well as supported network types and the fulfilled ITS requirements of the proposed scheme to the grid based geocasting scheme and MBMS. In addition, we implemented AGfIA for IRS Networks and evaluated its properties on top of real-world vehicles.

5.1   Privacy

In order to compare the privacy of the different schemes, we analyze which entities are getting positions updates from the IVSs and therefore are in principle able to track them. Furthermore, we analyze if it is possible to identify the applications utilized either by a certain IVS or by all ITS Vehicle Stations subscribed to a specific application. The results of the evaluation is shown in Table 1 and discussed in the sequel.

Table 1. Privacy evaluation of the geocast schemes MBMS, GBGS, and AGfIA.

	MBMS	GBGS	AGfIA
Position updates	MNO	MNO and GMS	MNO
Utilized applications of IVS	Yes	Yes	No
Subscribed IVSs of application	Yes	Yes	No

In each scheme the MNO is able to track the IVSs. To enable a steady connection for clients, the MNO must perform mobility management. This covers packet rerouting and handover management between cells. Therefore, the MNO must know the location of each IVS. However, schemes like Privacy Augmented LTE as proposed in [2] are aimed to prevent tracking by the MNO.

For the grid based geocasting scheme the central GMS is, in addition to the MNO, aware of the positions of each IVS. This is a major privacy drawback compared to the other two schemes. In case that AGfIA is applied for distribution over IRS Networks, a tracking of the IVSs is technically impossible.

An attacker may aim at identifying all IVSs subscribed to a certain application or at all applications exploited by an IVS. Both GBGS and MBMS both maintain a central subscriber database. For MBMS the MNO hast knowledge on which IVS is subscribed to a specific service. When exploiting GBGS the GMS is thus aware of the applications an IVS utilizes. Therefore, an attacker with access to these databases is able to yield the sought information.

In contrast, AGfIA does not maintain such a database. The relationship between IVSs and applications is not stored anywhere. Therefore, it is not possible to identify the IVSs subscribed to a certain application or to all subscriptions of an IVS. The MNO is only able to determine all IVSs exploiting ITS applications. However, this is not a privacy threat at all since the MNO knows anyway from its contracts which entities are IVSs.

5.2   Complexity

To assess the complexity of the schemes we compared the procedures for application registration, geocasting a message in an additional area, utilizing an additional network to distribute the messages, and updating the position information of the IVS within the network. The results of the complexity evaluation are shown in Table 2.

Table 2. Complexity evaluation.

	MBMS	GBGS	AGfIA
Registration	Per application	Per application	Once
New area	Additional session	Receiver lookup	eNodeB lookup
Additional network	1 additional message	Nothing	1 additional message
New position	Nothing	1 message to central entity	Nothing

In case that an ITS Vehicle Station aims to register or unregister for an application, it has to send an additional notification message to a central entity for MBMS and GBGS. There, the relation between the IVS and application is either created or deleted. This is not necessary in AGfIA, because each IVS registers itself only once for all desired ITS applications and not for each application separately.

Each time an ICS intends on broadcasting a message in a new area, which happens quite often for ITS applications, an additional session has to be created if MBMS is applied. For GBGS all IVSs in the new area have to be selected at the GMS, which may result in a considerable effort. For AGfIA only a lookup for all relevant eNodeBs and IRSs in the new area has to be made. Therefore, AGfIA has a considerable lower complexity than both MBMS and GBGS when messages shall be distributed in a new area.

When the message shall be distributed via an additional network, one extra message has to be sent to this network in case of MBMS or AGfIA. For GBGS nothing has to be done, because each message is sent to each IVS individually, independent of the network it is registered at.

For MBMS and GBGS the IVS does not need to do anything when it changes the eNodeB. Every position update is handled automatically by the mobile network. When GBGS is applied, the IVS has in addition to regularly report its position to the central GMS.

5.3   Scalability

An ITS geocast message might be sent to a large number of receivers. Therefore, it is important that the applied geocasting scheme does scale with respect to the number of receivers. We compared the outlined scheme with MBMS and the GBGS regarding the number of messages the ICS needs to send to the network operator, the amount of messages within the network of the network operator, the number of messages received by the IRS or eNodeB, and the messages sent from the network to the IVSs. The results of the scalability evaluation are shown in Table 3, whereas U stands for unicast, M for multicast, and X for Xcast messages, respectively.

Table 3. Scalability evaluation.

	MBMS	GBGS	AGfIA
ICS to network	1 per message (U)	1 per message and receiver (U)	1 per hazard (U)
Within network	1 per router (M)	1 per receiver (U)	1 per router (X)
To IRSs/eNodeBs	1 per eNodeB (M)	1 per receiver (U)	1 per eNodeB/IRS (X)
To IVSs	1 per eNodeB (M)	1 per receiver (U)	1 per eNodeB/IRS (M)

For MBMS, the ICS has to pass one message to the network each time a message shall be sent to the IVSs. For the grid based geocasting scheme one message needs to be sent to the network for each IVS at each point in time a hazard message needs to be distributed. When AGfIA is applied, only one message for each hazard needs to be sent to the network no matter of how often it has to be forwarded to the IVSs. Therefore, AGfIA scales better than the other schemes mentioned, whereas MBMS performs better than GBGS in terms of scalability.

For the distribution of the messages within the network, MBMS applies multicast, whereas almost one message is processed by each router. In contrast, one message per receiver is sent in case of GBGS. AGfIA does use Xcast to distribute the messages within the network and needs accordingly almost one message per router. However, the applied Xcast features a larger message header compared to multicast. Therefore, both MBMS and AGfIA scale much better than GBGS within the distributing network.

One message is forwarded to the eNodeB or IRS, respectively, in case of MBMS and AGfIA. When GBGS is applied, one message per receiver is sent to the eNodeBs and IRSs of the network, which results in considerably more messages compared to the other schemes.

The messages are distributed by means of multicast from the eNodeBs and IRSs of the network to the IVSs if MBMS or AGfIA is applied. For the GBGS scheme the messages are distributed by means of unicast to each receiver, which requires more messages compared to multicast.

This evaluation shows clearly that MBMS and AGfIA do scale better than the GBGS with respect to the number of receivers. In these schemes the number of messages does not depend on the number of receivers, but only on the size of the geographic area and on the numbers of eNodeBs and IRSs located within. For AGfIA a larger message header is applied within the network to enable Xcast in comparison to MBMS. However, AGfIA requires only one message per hazard from the ICS to the MNO. For MBMS the message has to be sent periodically to the MNO, which has to redistribute it in its network in order to reach IVSs entering the area.

5.4 Supported Networks

If a scheme is able to support different kinds of networks, it may have a better coverage and therefore it may reach more ITS Vehicle Stations in the dissemination area. Furthermore, an ICS might have a better choice of networks to utilize for message distribution. Our analysis shows that MBMS can be applied to LTE networks only, because there is no support for DSRC communication. GBGS can be utilized for transmissions over LTE and IRS Networks if the IVS and IRS Network do support IPv6 over GeoNetworking. In contrast, AGfIA enables the transmission over both LTE and IRS Networks without the limitation on IPv6 support in DSRC. A summary of this comparison is given in Table 4.

Table 4. Supported networks of the geocast schemes.

	MBMS	GBGS	AGfIA
Mobile networks	Yes	Yes	Yes
IRS networks	No	GN6 only	Yes

5.5 Requirements

We evaluated which of the previously outlined requirements for ITS applications are fulfilled by the different schemes and discuss the results in the sequel. A summary is presented in Table 5.

Multiple Applications. All three schemes support multiple applications. For MBMS there is a bigger effort necessary to support additional applications because a new MBMS user service has to be created first. When employing the other two schemes no such costly operation at the infrastructure side is necessary.

Receiver Groups. Different receiver groups are supported by all these schemes. In case of MBMS and GBGS all interested IVSs must explicitly subscribe in order to be part of the group. For AGfIA no such action is required by an IVS in order to join a group.

Table 5. Comparison of requirement fulfillment.

	MBMS	GBGS	AGfIA
Multiple applications	o	+	+
Receiver groups	o	o	+
Content type	o	+	+
Dissemination area	−	o	+
Validity period	o	o	+
Scalability	+	−	+
End-to-End delay	+	o	+
Efficient transmission	+	−	+

Content Type. GBGS and AGfIA are well suited to transmit ITS messages. MBMS was designed for long-tailed traffic, e.g. multimedia streams. This causes substantial overhead in the ITS scenario featuring short messages. However, a delivery method for short ITS messages may be defined to improve things.

Dissemination Area. For GBGS the dissemination area can be specified for each message. However, the actual distribution area depends on the size of the grids. Accordingly, the area might be much greater than specified. When applying MBMS it is not possible to define the dissemination area in the same granularity. The areas are limited to predefined service areas. Furthermore, it does not support overlapping service areas for the same application. Therefore, messages with overlapping dissemination areas have to be distributed in all service areas covering the dissemination area. In contrast, AGfIA allows to specify the dissemination area for each message separately.

Validity Period. AGfIA repeats the ITS messages in the dissemination area at a given frequency until they expire. Therefore, IVSs arriving in the area also receive older, but still relevant messages. When applying MBMS and GBGS the messages are not repeated in the first place. However, an ICS might either send a message in the desired distribution frequency to the MNO or query the GMS. Then, new arriving IVSs would get the message too. Nonetheless, this introduces unnecessary overhead. To reduce the overhead for the GBGS the ICS can cache the IVSs located in the dissemination area and send the message only to the new IVSs returned by the GMS.

Scalability. As outlined in the previous section, MBMS and AGfIA do scale better than the GBGS.

End-to-End Delay. The end-to-end delay of the distributed messages is smaller for AGfIA and MBMS than for GBGS. In the first two schemes the messages are directly forwarded to the network operators, which distribute the messages to the IVSs. When employing GBGS the geo messaging server introduces an additional delay by identifying the relevant IVSs. Furthermore, one unicast message has to be generated and transmitted for each IVS.

Efficient Transmission. The message transmission scheme applied by GBGS is not very efficient because messages are transported by means of unicast, which introduces more load within the communication networks than Xcast or multicast as applied by MBMS and AGfIA.

5.6   Experimental Evaluation

For the real-world evaluation we implemented software modules to integrate the proposed scheme into IRS Networks consisting of one IRS and of several IVSs equipped with DSRC communication. We evaluated the software prototype in several scenarios.

Implementation. The implementation consists of two Java programs running on the IRS and each IVS, respectively, and was done as part of the work documented in [4]. Both programs utilize a GeoNetworking stack written in Java. The program running at the IRS gets as input the distribution information from an ICS. As its output it distributes the message via DSRC to the IVSs in communication range.

The GUI running on the IRS displays a list of messages to distribute. It is possible to specify the name, area, AID, repetition interval, expiry time, and payload of a messages. Furthermore, it contains a map which shows the targeted dissemination area. For debugging purposes the GUI also displays a log containing all sent messages.

As input, the program running on the IVS takes the AIDs of the running ITS applications, the current position of the IVS, and the received messages. On reception, it parses the messages and checks their relevance. There are three criteria which must be satisfied to consider a message to be relevant: Firstly, the ITS Vehicle Station has to be located inside the relevance area. Secondly, it must support the AID. Thirdly, the message at hand must not be expired. The relevance area is encoded into the message and denotes the actual warning region of the event. In general, this area is smaller than the dissemination area. For debugging purposes, the GUI also displays a log with all received messages and a map containing the IVSs current position and all received messages. The messages are coloured in order to visualise their state. Whenever a message has an AID supported by the IVS and the IVS is located within the relevance area of the message, it is highlighted in green. If the AID is not supported, but the IVS is in its relevance area, it is displayed in yellow. If the receiver is outside of the relevance area of the message, it has a white background. All expired messages are depicted in grey.

Measurement Setup. The evaluation setup consist of two IRS Networks featuring one IRS each. The IRS also runs the IRS CS. Each IVS and IRS consists of an Application Unit (AU) and a Communication Unit (CCU): the AU runs the application software, whereas the CCU is responsible for the transmission of the DSRC messages. Both units are connected via Ethernet.

Results. Within the outlined setup we evaluated several basic and realistic scenarios. The principles of the basic scenarios are depicted in Fig. 8. *Scenario A* consists of a message from *Application 1*, which is outside of the vehicles route, whereas in *Scenario B* the message from *Application 2* is on the route of the vehicle. *Scenario C* contains messages from different applications, where as not all are on the envisaged route of the vehicle. The reception and processing of multiple overlapping messages from different applications are addressed in *Scenario D*.

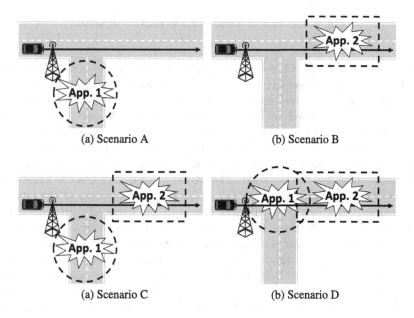

(a) Scenario A   (b) Scenario B

(a) Scenario C   (b) Scenario D

Fig. 8. Basic evaluation scenarios.

We ran several different tests on these basic scenarios. We varied the AIDs an IVS supports from those applications not applied in the scenario up to all AIDs of the message. To evaluate the message validity check we ran tests with valid messages, expired messages, and messages that will be valid in the future. The evaluation of the different scenarios and configurations showed that the IVSs running the particular application consider a message as relevant only in case that they are within the relevance area of the message and the message is still valid.

As an example for a realistic and complex evaluation, a scenario around Rüsselsheim, Germany is depicted in Fig. 9. This scenario features two IRS

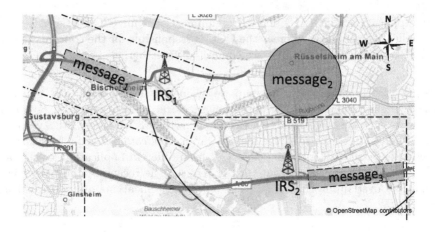

Fig. 9. Example of a real-world evaluation scenario.

Networks, $IRS1$ and $IRS2$, respectively, and a possible route of an IVS is drawn in red aiming from Rüsselsheim city towards a motorway.

In this scenario three messages denoted as $message_1$, $message_2$, and $message_3$ are distributed to the IVSs, each with a different Application ID. The relevance area of the messages is indicated by the filled shape surrounding the message name. The larger enclosing shape indicates the dissemination area of the messages. $message_1$ may be, for example, an icy road warning. Therefore, its shape is enclosing the icy road. The dissemination area has the same shape but covers a much larger area. $message_2$ located in the center of the city may be a notification about road closures due to a big event. To inform all IVSs reaching the center, the dissemination area covers the whole city. The third message warns about a traffic jam eastbound on the highway located south to the city. Therefore, the dissemination area is only extended towards west, where the IVSs reach the traffic jam. Because of the large dissemination area of the second message, it is in reach of both IRSs and is therefore distributed by all of them. Only IRS_1 is located within the dissemination area of the icy roads warning. Therefore, only this IRS is distributing the message. For the traffic jam ahead warning only IRS_2 is located within the dissemination area and distributes the message.

This scenario clearly demonstrates one of the main advantages of AGfIA: Only the IRSs and eNodeBs located within the dissemination area of a certain message distribute this message. In contrast, even IRSs or eNodeBs in overlapping areas distribute all relevant messages. In addition, only the ITS Vehicle Stations exploiting the corresponding application process the message. All other IVSs drop the messages at network layer. To sum up, we demonstrated that AGfIA works well on both real devices and in a complex traffic scenario.

6 Conclusion

A common use case in ITS applications is the distribution of information to all or to a subset of IVSs present in a defined geographic area. We conceived, implemented, and evaluated an geocasting scheme which supports such a distribution while preserving the privacy of the IVSs. Furthermore, this scheme can be exploited for various underlying communication technologies. In order to do so we modified the standard message format in ITS to directly support the addressing of a receiver group. We detailed the registration of IVSs for geocast messages and the distribution of these messages for LTE and IRS Networks. Furthermore, we discussed how billing can be realized in such a context.

In comparison to other geocast schemes, the presented AGfIA approach protects the privacy of the IVSs. An attacker is not able to discover the applications exploited by an IVS or to identify IVSs subscribed to a certain application. Furthermore, this scheme does not rely on a central entity, which may track the location of the IVSs. AGfIA also reduces the system complexity compared to other known geocast schemes. By exploiting AGfIA it is simple to register for ITS applications, to distribute a message in a new area, or to disseminate the message via a new network. Furthermore, no additional effort is necessary, if the location of an IVS changes. AGfIA scales in addition for a large number of receivers or for huge dissemination areas. Moreover, messages can be distributed by means of different communication technologies like LTE or DSRC. Its major advantage is that it fulfills substantial requirements of ITS geocast applications.

To show its suitability, we created a prototype implementation of this scheme. We ran this implementation on an experimental set up IRS Networks. In addition, we took test vehicles equipped with DSRC communication technologies to thoroughly evaluate the prototype implementation. We therefore demonstrated, that the developed scheme works as designed and can directly be deployed to real vehicles.

Acknowledgement. This work was funded within the project CONVERGE by the German Federal Ministries of Education and Research as well as Economic Affairs and Energy.

References

1. 3GPP TS 23.246: 3rd Generation Partnership Project; Technical Specification Group Services and System Aspects; Multimedia Broadcast/Multicast Service (MBMS); Architecture and functional description (Release 12) (2013)
2. Angermeier, D., Kiening, A., Stumpf, F.: PAL - privacy augmented LTE: a privacy-preserving scheme for vehicular LTE communication. In: Proceeding of the 10th ACM International Workshop on Vehicular Inter-networking, Systems, and Applications. VANET (2013)
3. Araniti, G., Campolo, C., Condoluci, M., Iera, A., Molinaro, A.: LTE for vehicular networking: a survey. IEEE Commun. Mag. **51**, 148–157 (2013)
4. Bartels, F.: Senden und Empfangen von C2X-GeoMulticast-Nachrichten. Technical report, RheinMain University of Applied Sciences (2015)

5. Boivie, R., Feldman, N., Imai, Y., Livens, W., Ooms, D.: Explicit Multicast (Xcast) Concepts and Options. RFC 5058 (2007)
6. Büttner, C., Huss, S.A.: Verfahren zum Verbreiten einer Nachricht. Patent application, DE 102015009599.4 (2015)
7. Büttner, C., Huss, S.A.: An anonymous geocast scheme for ITS applications. In: Proceedings of the 2nd International Conference on Information Systems Security and Privacy (2016)
8. Calabuig, J., Monserrat, J., Gozalvez, D., Klemp, O.: Safety on the roads: LTE alternatives for sending ITS messages. IEEE Veh. Technol. Mag. **9**(4), 61–70 (2014)
9. CONVERGE: Architecture of the Car2X Systems Network. Deliverable D4.3 (2015)
10. ETSI EN 302 636-4-1: Intelligent Transport Systems (ITS); Vehicular Communications; GeoNetworking; Part 4: Geographical addressing and forwarding for point-to-point and point-to-multipoint communications; Sub-part 1: Media-Independent Functionality (2014)
11. ETSI EN 302 636-5-1: Intelligent Transport Systems (ITS); Vehicular Communications; GeoNetworking; Part 5: Transport Protocols; Sub-part 1: Basic Transport Protocol Functionality (2014)
12. ETSI TR 102 962: Intelligent Transport Systems (ITS); Framework for Public Mobile Networks in Cooperative ITS (C-ITS) (2012)
13. Jodlauk, G., Rembarz, R., Xu, Z.: An optimized grid-based geocasting method for cellular mobile networks. In: Proceedings of the 18th ITS World Congress (2011)
14. Maihofer, C.: A survey of geocast routing protocols. IEEE Commun. Surv. Tutorials **6**(2), 32–42 (2004)
15. Navas, J.C., Imielinski, T.: GeoCast - gographic addressing and routing. In: Proceedings of the 3rd Annual ACM/IEEE International Conference on Mobile Computing and Networking. MobiCom (1997)
16. Valerio, D., Ricciato, F., Belanovic, P., Zemen, T.: UMTS on the road: broadcasting intelligent road safety information via MBMS. In: Proceeding of the IEEE Vehicular Technology Conference. VTC Spring (2008)

Author Index

Printed in the United States
By Bookmasters